A
TWELVEMONTH
AND A DAY

Christopher Rush

The twelvemonth and a day being up,
The dead began to speak:
'O who sits weeping on my grave
And will not let me sleep?'

ABERDEEN UNIVERSITY PRESS

First published 1985
Aberdeen University Press
A member of the Pergamon Group

© Christopher Rush 1985
This edition 1986

The publisher acknowledges subsidy from the
Scottish Arts Council towards the publication
of this volume

British Library Cataloguing in Publication Data
Rush, Christopher
  A Twelvemonth and a day.
  I. Title
  823'.914[F]   PR6068.U7/
  ISBN 0 08 032428 2
  ISBN 0 08 032469 X

PRINTED IN GREAT BRITAIN
THE UNIVERSITY PRESS
ABERDEEN

A
TWELVEMONTH
AND A DAY

PREFACE

In writing A Twelvemonth and a Day I have drawn freely on autobiography, family tradition and social documentary in order to produce an evocation of a place and an era (the East Neuk of Fife, particularly the St Monans of the 1920s and 1930s, the last great days of the Scottish herring fishing and the steam drifters), a lament for their passing, and, more positively, a celebration of their vanished values. Perhaps not entirely vanished—for the book is also about growing up; and all of us have been children, and there must be very few of us who have not felt the mystery and the magic of ships and the sea. Or who have not partaken of the formative influences of family and community, church and school, storytelling and games, sex and death.

My grateful thanks are due to my patient wife and children; to Peter Smith and Eugene D'Espremenil of Cellardyke, who gave me more than I can repay; to all the folk and family of St Monans who made me what I am; and to Harry Quinn, who first suggested to me that I should expand the Introduction to my first book, *Peace Comes Dropping Slow*, into a book in itself. That brief article was a splinter from the old mosaic: what follows is my attempt to rebuild the entire stained-glass window. Look into it, reader, and grant me absolution.

Christopher Rush
Edinburgh
January 1985

For all the old folk—
and for the young, who never knew them.
And for all fishermen whose last haul has been made...

JANUARY

To start with I was nothing more than a wafer-thin cry, a winter wailing that went up through the thick green panes of our skylight windows at number sixteen East Shore Street, where it mingled with the smoke from all the other village chimneys. My first noises drifted out over the clusters of red pan-tiled roofs, and was lost among seagulls and steeples and the huge fluffed-up clouds which the fishermen called Babylonians.

It was the time of the winter herring.

The sea was busy with boats, their white nets winnowing the waters of the Firth of Forth, searching for the shoals that silvered the linings of our pockets, keeping my family alive. Now here I was, with my gannet's mouth ragged and raw, tearing another hole in those pockets.

But at first I knew nothing of all this. I was a white wordless little world, dumb as a snowflake, many of which were falling around me now; unable to speak a single syllable to the earth on which I had been so suddenly dropped, a silent crystal. Too easily forgotten about, I decided, among the harsh high hunger-claims sent out by the shuttling seabirds as they knitted the sky a white shawl for winter. But though I could not talk I could screech and skirl, and so I opened up again that bellowing red wound in my face, which the milk of human kindness closed at once. Satisfied, I returned to my sleeping, the strangest I had slept for months, and repeated this process of bawling and bullying my way to milky slumbers several scores of times before it occurred to me to bestow the least part of my attention upon the world that was now mine and mine alone.

I think water was the first thing I was ever conscious of—the sound of the living sea. This was to be my first and final language, my alpha and omega, my beginning and my end. Before my mother was the sea, my alma mater who taught me the irrelevance of talk, then as now—and yet spoke; and spoke; and spoke, to my unspeaking. Mother stood on the edge of the world and threw me my umbilical, my lifeline. She drew me painfully out of the twisting tangles of the water, with white shiftings of seabirds and snowflakes like cells in the sky. So I crawled along my lineage, out of the deep drowned memories of men, made fast to their bones. And I arrived on the wave-swept rocky shores of January: a mortal mooring, the frail end of a long line, the sunken sea-dreams of my folk locked hard in my head.

The harbour crooked its arm around me.

St Monans.

Mare vivimus, we live by the sea.

It could not have been anywhere else. It had to be St Monans. That was where I was landed in time. St Monans was my salt-splashed cradle with its fringe of gold. And even now it is that same cradle that rocks me nightly towards my grave.

I lay back then in the slow dawns and darknesses of my pillow, waiting for understanding to break, and I listened to the language of the sea as it roared past our windows like an angry express train my eye could never catch. The sun slipped into Aquarius, the water-bearer. The tides turned my ears to coral shells; spiralling through the whorls of my brain as it grew and knew, they made my sleeping rich and my waking strange. That was life—a breaker-beaten bank and shoal, beset by a running sea that sang the song of eternity.

At my baptism there was ice in the font. Alec Fergusson, the old beadle, had placed the water there the night before, so that when the Reverend Kinnear went to perform the sacrament he was prevented by a frozen silver shield which his fingers could not penetrate. But his arm was strong to smite, as all the Sunday schoolers knew, and his fist great as his faith. He brought his huge clenched knuckles down into the stone font with force enough, my mother said, to kill a whale. The shield splintered but yielded no water. There was none to be had in the church either at that time, and Mr Kinnear stood breaking the third commandment between his teeth and muttering his determination to break others. So the old beadle ran down the outer steps of the kirk, to where a bursting sea was spraying the tombstones of my ancestors. He brought back a glimmer of cold brine in a brass collection plate. That was how it happened that the waters of the firth, which had been wetting the bones of my forefathers for uncountable tides, were used that morning to baptize me—in the name of the Eternal Father (strong to save) and of his Son and of the Holy Ghost.

One day without warning the sea was breaking on my forehead like white thunder.

I was set down from the safety of my mother's breast onto a shore that was full of sound and fury. The firth, which had first touched me out of a sedate circle of holy brass, was flinging itself at me now with wild wet flicking fingers that blinded and stung. Bright screams were tearing the sky apart. I felt the hard heaviness of the bouldery beach, heard the soggy scrape of shingle as the sea gargled. Too indignant to protest for the moment, I reached down and took up a handful of this alien dimension. I sat up again, opening up my pink starfish hand for inspection. A sudden universe of golden grains swirled before my amazed eyes and disappeared. Once more I grabbed at the world and let go—and watched several thousands of worlds tumbling through incredible inches of space from the hand of me, the sower. To my astonishment I realized that I was a god. I cast another cosmos to the wind and blinked grittily. My eyes told my fingers with blinding revelation that godhead would have its aches and agues too. I lifted up my head to the hills of my mother's breast, from whence came my milk, and in bitter rage that I had been cast away upon a stage of fools, I wept until I was lifted.

The next persuasion that I was far from ague-proof came to me in my pram. The road down to the harbour was a winding brae with our house on one side. Down we came in winter—my first memory of being taken out at night. Was I one, perhaps, or even two? I was sitting up in my carriage, with my mother's pale face hanging in heaven, and her smile was a warm lamp lighting up the darkness. But there were other lights scattered about her head, like the slow spray of the winter firth frozen across the sky. And the words were coming out of my mother's mouth.

I can hear them now.

> *Twinkle, twinkle, little star,*
> *How I wonder what you are.*

She blew on the rhyme with her hot frosty breath. Sparks floated across the darkness to me and I reached out for them. The sounds were living cinders lighted on my lips as she blew me her kiss. I reached out again for the embers of the tune and my hand came into contact with the sharp prickles of the cold stone wall. Millions of frost-diamonds glittered and winked in that wall. They scored my flesh beautifully, a perfect cut. A soft crimson glove ran over my hand like velvet, ruby rings enriched my fingers, and the deep red wine stained my lips as I tasted and saw—that I was king of the salt sea that ran in my veins. It was then that I saw the moon in the sky for the first time—a wild bride who had flung aside a veil of stars—and a terrible

3

beauty was born. Inside the house a moment later I looked round an adult circle of concern, a ring of goggling lips and eyes, questioning my divinity. When I saw their faces I bawled. But here at least was intimation that the world had grandeur in it, that pain was golden. Even as I write about it now, several decades on, I wish I could recapture that first blood which made the writing so inevitable.

Another pram memory recreates for me a January journey—a journey for snowdrops. Balcaskie Wood was a gothic cathedral, vaulted over by the interlocking boughs of ashes, elms and oaks. Birches and beeches too laid their leaves in drifting generations along the gusty green aisles, the dim transepts of the trees. The nave of this great wood was a spacious footpath, soft with its own prayermat of moss, deep-piled a mile or more from the gate. So many dead had trodden out their printless footsteps here that silence hung over it like a hallowed arch. It was known locally as The Bishop's Walk.

Balcaskie was a mile inland, and when my pram set out the wintered sun was low in the west, an angry orange flare, raging the last inches of its dreary descent, so far and near from spring. For as the day lengthens the cold strengthens, a voice whispered to my baby brain, a voice from beneath the horizon. Through the white gate of the year we went, and into the wood, where the sun never shone except in broken shafts, and only the glossy dark flames of the evergreens rose in their own incense to the sky: the burnished ivy bushes, the sharp crackle of the Christmas trees, the porcupine spruce, the long needle-slender billowing of the pine. And on a single ash-grey trunk glowed Balcaskie's only sun—a vast splash of lichen. A golden fire, smouldering and pulsating with the year, but never setting in all the years I could remember.

Then it was dark and a chilly lamp was lighting up a gathering of voices like deep bells all about me. I was lifted from my pram and placed on my brand new feet at the perilous edge of a frozen sea, a green bank topped with foaming white droplets.

Snowdrops. I sucked up their scent and my head was flooded with fragrant foam. Through the ecstasy of my drowning there came a girl wearing a green cloak. She bent down, holding out for me a bunch of flowers—little green knights with the holy white helmets. I reached out, accepting them from her, my spirit sealed in a slumber that there were still no words to break; for the locks of language had not yet been placed on my lips and the prison-house of speaking was still to close. That green-caped young girl is now a white-haired lady, and even as I begin to rage against the fading of my light, her glad young smile lights up my remembering. I was aglow only with the knowledge of

4

snowdrops, a knowledge into which no cancerous worm had yet bitten the bitter recognition that I should surely die.

Perhaps that knowledge came to me in the dimmest possible way with the passing of Epp.

Epp was our landlady at East Shore Street, for the house was not our own. She was Queen Victoria at number sixteen, well into her eighties when I knew her and dead before I was three. Thrones will perish, kingdoms rise and wane, and queens may never redden from their dust. But I shall never forget old Epp.

It was Epp who began my literary education. Throned on her massive moss-green velvet armchair, all curves and buttons, she sat there in a black waterfall of lace, her skirts spilling across the floor, and thundered at me: 'The Charge of the Light Brigade'. I stood no higher than her dark silken knee, a tiny little man. Stormed at by the shot and steady shell of her wrathful cannonades, I would watch with horror the trembling of her dreadful dewlaps when her frail white fists descended on the sides of her chair, beating out the rhythms of the verse. She held the windowed sky in her spectacles and her head was lost in the clouds of her snowy white hair.

She was always erect.

'Be a brave wee man,' she said to me when I cut my thumb and cried, 'or you'll never be a sailor like your father, or a soldier like my bonny sons.'

I roared at her in mortal anguish.

'I don't want to be a soldier or a sailor! I want to be a fisherman!'

'A fisherman!' she scoffed. 'You might as well be a tinker!'

'And you'll never get a wife either if you greet like that,' she admonished me. 'None but the brave deserves the fair!'

> *None but the Brave,*
> *None but the Brave,*
> *None but the Brave deserves the Fair.*

I wept all the louder.

When I was bad and uncontrollable, and all the men in the house at sea, I was taken to Epp.

'Oh you scoundrel!' she scolded. 'You bad wild boy!'

Then she would tell me that the horned and hoofed devil had flown over the rooftops on black, scaly pinions of soot, that he was sitting on our chimney right this minute, listening to me, and would be down the lum at my next word. His mouth was full of sinners and that was why I couldn't hear him mumbling, but at the next swallow there would be room in his jaws for one more gobbet of begrimed humanity, and that would be me. Didn't I hear the soot falling? Open-mouthed, I looked from her to the lurid red glow within the black grate of her fireside. Sinister scrabblings came from the awful tall blackness of the chimney, which led up to the universe, the unknown corners of God's coal-cellar. Quaking, I turned my eyes back to my torturer, her pale old face laved in flames. She spitted me on her tongue.

'You will go to hell,' she leered. 'You will be crying for a single drop of water to cool your parched mouth. Your throat will be like the desert. But Satan will just laugh at you before he crunches you up. And not one drop of water will you get! Oh yes, my bonny man, you'll get something to cry for in hell!'

When I ran to her, screaming, she never softened.

'Go away, you bad lad! You're like every other boy that was born, picked up from the Bass Rock you were, that's where your father got you, didn't you know? Why didn't he go to the May Island, the silly kipper that he was, and bring us all back a nice wee lass instead of you, you nasty brat!'

Epp assured me that boys came from the Bass and girls from the May. Where had my father's ship gone wrong? What hand at the helm had blundered? Ah well, it had been wartime, and many errors had been made. I was one of them.

'Ours not to reason why,' she proclaimed.

And then she was off again at her poetry and her preaching. When she came out of it she told me that since I was a boy I had better make the best of it and behave as well as I could. But like all boys I was born to be bad. There's your bairn, God had said, make a kirk or a mill of him for all I care. And like Pontius Pilate he went and washed his hands.

Poor Epp.

Her two sons had run away from home and had died in scarlet in the war against the Zulus, leaving her naked in her age. If she never stopped blaming them through these tireless tirades of hers against the whole masculine world, perhaps it was that she kept up a kind of praise and lamentation in her wild volleys of heroic poetry, dedicated to their reproach and their renown. At any rate she was a stern Eve. She had known a sharper sting than the serpent's tooth. And the apple of life had turned to ashes in her mouth. So she bit back with venom.

But she unbent for the ceremony of the pan drop.

I was summoned to the hearth.

JANUARY

Taking a pan drop from a glass jar, the holy grail of her dresser, she would place it on the fender and pulverise it with the poker. She turned the fire-iron the wrong way in her hand. Its head was a burnished bronze mushroom. With this she would execute the frivolous indulgence that was the sweet, and I always feared for the precious pieces. It was placed on the whorled corner of that fender and broken between bronze and brass, smashed like a criminal on the wheel—rendered innocuous for the tender tongue of the anxiously waiting youngling. Epp waited there to the end, watching me haughtily as I sucked away the last white crumbs. She stood straight as the poker, still gripped in her white hairless knuckles, and with which she looked as ready to crack my skull as please my palate. My eyes turned again to the glass container. Still it hovers before me, shining like some mystic churchyard urn through the mists, never quite touching the surface of that dark dim piece of furniture which endless recollections have left but half defined.

'Away you go now, you young rascal, that's all there is.'

She lifted the poker and shook her free fist at me. I ran from the room. I was horrified of her in those moods.

But she was my first queen and I her quaking subject. Her sceptre was the gleaming poker, her court the flickering hearth with its high-backed buttoned throne. The pan drops were the favours she dispensed. And how could she or I know then, in that dark backward and abyss of years, that I should pay tribute to her in the only coins I have ever had to spend—memory's mintage of hard-won words? Why is it, Epp, that the old lady and the little boy have to meet again after all these years, and go on meeting until the last day's tribute has been paid?

Is it because of what happened one winter's night that still grips me like guilt, like some dreadful disease? For I can remember such a night when the grownups faced one another across a bare table, all of them as dumb as stones for sheer poverty, the fishing that year having proved a failure. I was up whining for food, but there was none to be had, nor a toy in the house between ceilings and floor. I roamed about the distempered walls following my gaunt hungry shadow beneath the gasmantles, glancing narrowly at the grown ones as they sat there in that grim-faced gathering that both angered and upset me. So it was I who heard the small silver chiming at the dark brown door—so small a sound I saw that the others had not even taken their faces out of their fists. Blotting myself against the wall I moved silently to the door. I stared down in wonderment at two shining circles on the floor, two bright winter moons that lit up the linoleum.

7

Two half crowns.

Down to the edge of our door, where the gray daggers of the winter winds struck her between the ribs, my great queen had knelt in the lonely darkness of her empty hall. She had laid her old bones down there unseen and had pushed back our rent money that we could not afford to pay. Through the door it had come again, from the probing tips of her white ringless fingers. Epp who never said a word, though everyone knew of that tender mercy which became her in the end better than her reign of terror.

But she breathed her last, old Epp, before she could receive the thanks of her meanest vassal. Such is the breath of old queens—brief in the bitter mornings of little boys.

When there had been no pan drop for a day or two, I pestered my mother to know where Epp had gone to. She tried to soothe me with an old rhyme, which I can still remember because it was repeated to me with such sadness.

> *God saw that she was weary,*
> *And the hill was hard to climb,*
> *So He closed her weary eyelids,*
> *And whispered, 'Rest be thine'.*

But the words drew mysterious veils over something which I gathered to be awful and ultimate. I pursued my quest relentlessly for the vanished Epp, drawing whispered riddles and quiet murmurings out of the mouths of everyone in the house. Old George, my great-grandfather, said that she was now a pilgrim before God, my grandmother told me that she had gone to a better land, and grandfather that she was being made ready for the kirkyard. Many were the sacred seals and stoppers that they used rather than show me a mystery. Asleep in Jesus, gone to glory, singing hymns at heaven's gate—Epp haunted me from a thousand hiding places.

At last somebody said that she was dead.

Dead. I repeated the word over and over to myself. It had a heavy sound, that word. Why did they say it so quietly, and why was everyone still so unable to explain how it was that I would never see Epp again, to reveal the curious circumstances of her departure? Dead, dead, dead. What does being dead mean? I expect my upturned face and earnest questionings must have preyed on their nerves.

So they took me into death's physical presence.

I can vividly recall the total blackness of the room where she was laid out. It was the dead vast and middle of the night.

JANUARY

We entered the room of death.

The enveloping silence hung like a tapestry. I stumbled into its heavy invisible folds. The tightly hushed whispers still deafen me, years later, like a black beating sea. A match was struck. There was no electricity in that house of gasmantles where at that moment there was no shilling to read the meter. A flaring yellow nova burst the silence of the universe in which I cringed, frightened now. Criss-cross patterning of the trestle on which lay a big dark shape. Arms lifting me up. Darkness again and another match struck. Then there she was, old Epp, my queen, clothed in whiteness to the wrists, the first time I had ever seen her out of black, or her stern eyes so softly closed. And finally, in the plunging confusion of more darkness and exploding matches, a heavy lid closing with a thud, the dark inscrutable workmanship of shining oak, the brass mirror of the polished name-plate—Elspeth Marr, her name, her years. Where's Epp? That's where she is now—in there.

The rest was silence.

With Epp gone I ran wild for a few days before I forgot her, if I can ever forget that old queen of the night. From then on some other threat of punishment had to be found to hold over my wicked head and restrain me from mischief.

That ultimate threat turned out to be the Marship.

The Marship was a floating borstal, a gray hulk to which bad boys were sent instead of going to jail. I never saw the Marship but I was told whenever it happened to be in the harbour, which was whenever I happened to be bad, and the night was dark, and the curtains were drawn. It was then that I hovered anxiously between the devil on the chimney and the Marship on the deep blue sea.

On the Marship boys were made to scrub the decks all day long. That was all they ever did—scrubbed until their kneecaps wore whitely through the red rags of their skins, like the elbows of the old women, and their hands were sodden lumps of carbolic soap, scarlet from the constant immersions from dawn to dusk. They had to use freezing water, and if there was a single speck of dirt left on deck by any boy, that boy was tied to the mast and flogged. Buckets stood ready to catch the blood as it leaped from the cat-o'-nine-tails which they used for the flogging. The Marship boys lived on hard tack, with maggots for meat. They slept with rats in their bunks, but when they had been especially bad they were put in the bilge and the wobble-eyed crabs came and linked claws round their necks, fringed their raw

9

wrists and picked off their toes one by one if they dared to move a muscle.

It was the thought of those living necklaces and bracelets that convinced me. And I knew just what it would be like to have no toes. An old man called Tom Tarvit used to hobble up to the house to see my great-grandfather. He was an ex-whaler and had lost all ten toes in the Antarctic. He came in on two sticks, bent in half, his red eyes leering out of the rat's hair that grew on his face.

'You'll be like Tom Tarvit,' they used to say to me. 'Not a toe to your foot and not a tooth to your head.'

Once only I was picked up, slung over a shoulder, and told I was being taken to the Marship. My response was instantaneous. I went rigid and stopped breathing. The frightened adult put me down and shouted for help. The whole family beat me in turn until I was as black as I was blue, but they could get no more breath out of me than out of an iron bar. They stuck their fingers down my throat, they tore my hair, they held me upside down and rained blows on my back. Somebody even shouted at me that I'd be taken to the Marship if I didn't come out of it! It was an ingenious but futile suggestion. My face must have been like a bursting purple plum when old Leebie drove her largest darning needle into my behind. This blood-letting let air into me at once and I lived to recall something of the horror of that moment. The puncture in my rear had to be repaired, but at last I managed to sit at peace.

From then on I committed only minor crimes.

I dry-shaved myself with grandfather's open razor and wore the red results for months afterwards. I gulped down a bottle of Indian ink and thought it not at all unpleasant. I put back a large quantity of my uncle Alec's home-brewed beer, considering it passable ale at the time and afterwards revolting. I swigged off the rum which my father had left in a brown bottle in the medicine-chest in the bathroom, just before he went back into the navy. I thought myself a proper sailor as I reeled downstairs, half clutching half demolishing the banisters. My two young aunts shrieked at the tops of their voices, the air silvery with their laughter; my grandmother raised her eyes to the skies, proclaiming the Apocalypse; uncle Billy began singing a song about fifteen men on a dead man's chest. I never thought of it as a sea-chest. I saw fifteen rum-raddled sailors, each with a foot set in triumph on a dead old pirate, his chest cracking like a crab's shell as they caroused fiercely over his corpse. I felt as drunk as all fifteen men put together, and ready to take on the whole family, all nine of them.

But there were no punishments that I can recall following these misdeeds. Were they afraid that I might throw another Marship fit? Perhaps the effects on myself of actions such as these were considered punishment enough. This might well have been the case with my next escapade. I developed a desperate desire to leave the house without the hand of a grown-up. The danger lay in the nearness of the harbour to the house and the fascination water has for all children.

It did not take too long for me to break loose. But as soon as I had achieved my first escape I made a straight line, not for the harbour, which was quite literally on our doorstep, but for the open-air swimming pool, a half mile east of the village. No-one stopped me as I made my way, magically in my invisible coat, past swaying forests of masts, the smoky smells of the fish-curing sheds, and the high sylvan din of the boatbuilder's yard; here the scents and sounds of sea and forest met each other in a strange mingling, and the men laboured minutely within the giant curving rib-hulls of the boats like Jonahs in the bellies of great wooden whales.

Leaving behind me then the last black-painted house, I walked the crumbling concrete edge of the village pond, over which the salt sea poured itself twice a day. Down towards the shallow end a bare plank acted as a bridge for the bathers. I trotted to the middle of this red-painted gangway, hunkered down, and peered into the infinite pale depths of three feet of water. What a calm cold world of weeds was waving at me from out of this magic mirror, so green and clear! I bent down and dipped my head deep into the mirror and through to the other side, into eternity. I could hear all the oceans of the world roaring in my ears like armies on the march. The pinkish pearls were pebbled with tiny bubbles of silver. I lifted my dripping head, waiting for the water to clear again. A god's face was peering at me through the swaying curtains of water. My red hands turned deathly white as I slipped them through those cool silk curtains. The god came up to laugh at me, closer. Closer.

Did I fall in or did I just let myself go? There is no recalling. But once in the water I can remember making no effort at all to leave it. Lying on the cool bed of the bottom, curtained by weeds, looking up at the world through this transfiguring element—there was something actually enjoyable about it. I just lay there and started to drown, in the pleasantest way imaginable, though nothing told me that I was in fact drowning. With remarkable clarity I can see the bending frightened face of the girl who came down to the water's edge to pull me out in time. She lifted me again into the world of air, and it was only then that I burst into a blizzard of tears and vomiting torrents of water. In a nearby house I was smothered in a gray army

11

blanket with scarlet stitching and given brandy mingled with warm water. Then my mother arrived on the scene trundling my old pram, in which I was wheeled home in disgrace. It was after many more escapades that I finally arrived at what was considered to be the age of safety, and was allowed to go out to the shops.

Battling to the baker's then through heavy seas of wind that pitched me from side to side of the street and did with me what they would. Clutching the coppers tightly in my pink freezing fist, I pushed open our front door, only to be knocked flying by the wild weight of the heavy wood as it came at me like a cannon on the recoil, rattling the whole house on its foundations. My mother held it open for me, and I edged my way through the blue murder-hole of the screaming slit and found myself in the grip of my first north-easter.

It ripped off my cap, sending it to a specky distance halfway across the harbour, to be intercepted by a disappointed gull. It tore at my hair, tugging at the roots, shredding it to spikes, forcing the tears from my screwed-up eyes. It punched me full in the face, bullied the legs from me, knocked me flat on my nose, spun me like a top, lifted me up by the seat of my pants, catapulted me to the corner of our street. I tried to turn up the narrow wynd but the wind shot down there like an invisible battering ram and thudded me against the harbour wall, panting for breath. When I wanted to walk it made me run, if I ran with it, it drove me back, I stood still and it rocketed between my legs, sending me sprawling splay-footed into the gutter.

At last I came somehow to the foot of the broad wynd and began to ascend. Far up there, at the top of the hill, the houses were puffing like steam drifters, chugging a passage through the storm. The crews were safe inside, munching their morning rolls, mothers and fathers, little children, living a life of cabined ease. Only I was out and about this morning, riding the winds of dawn, battling like a beserk cork in this wild open sea, and still not a roll for breakfast in our house. I had to reach the baker's or we would perish one and all. But the winds made it impossible. There was only one thing to be done. I spread my arms wide, turned myself into a gull, and flew straight up the brae, landing in a perfect pouncing dive right at Mrs Guthrie's shop door. Why is it that I have never been able to perform that feat again, except in dreams? Once only I took the wings of the morning, on that one morning that never came to noon. And I did it in the very teeth of the north-east gale.

JANUARY

But they never understood the dangers I had passed, the men in the bake-house that day, safe in their solid world of dough that rose no further than their oven doors. It was a dim windless world, the bakehouse, in which flour and icing lay in silent scatterings of make-believe snow, and where no north-easters blew. They stood white-elbowed among the slow storm-swellings of yeast, their faces as red and contented as their fires. They were surrounded by ranks upon ranks of baking: drumrolls and rows of baps, bread in battalions; crusty loaves, half loaves, brown loaves, white loaves, plain loaves, pan loaves, bran loaves, seed loaves—wild aromas that would bring a dead man back to life, making his tongue sing in his skull, and knock a living man stone dead for hunger and frustration.

'My mother's rolls, please.'

Mrs Guthrie picked a baker's dozen from the last piping tray, handing them to me with an expert swirl of the paper poke.

'Run all the way home now,' she said.

But she took a cream cookie, as she always did, from a very small tray of cakes. She put it in a separate bag and passed it over the counter to me with a wide pearl-strung smile.

'That's for you.'

I stood before her, open-mouthed with gratitude and worship—Mrs Guthrie now my queen, the apple-cheeked baker's wife with the flashing teeth, apples in her face and apples in her pink brocaded bosom, as she rested her breasts on the high counter and placed her broad bare arms across the wood, bending to say goodbye. Flour on her wedding-ring touching my face; flour sprinkling her butterfly spectacles, snow-blinding her flashing eyes till I wondered how she could see; flour in her hair, lending it its only whiteness at that time, raven-haired Mrs Guthrie, queen of the apple-tarts, now queen of my heart, Mrs Guthrie, now white bones in the green mound of the kirkyard hill, still smiling beneath the white unbroken bread of the January snow.

Or I was sent for the messages to Agnes Meldrum's shop and house, by the east pier. Agnes served between endless cups of tea while her mother, who had lasted a century by the time I was born, sat unblinking in a basket chair, her hands knotted round the head of her stick, never speaking a word. She greeted no-one out of the far corners of her hundred years. Agnes herself was in her seventies. Her counter was her dresser with the mirror removed. In its dark walnut drawers she kept her unmentionables, as she called them—her own personal bits and pieces of linen, along with whatever other spinsterish secrets could not be sold over the counter to a mere boy.

'Don't you go near that drawer,' she was forever warning the boys who came into her shop. 'Them's my unmentionables.'

But all the goods that could be named were laid out with neat precision upon the oaken shelves that lined the walls of the house from ceiling to floor. Agnes's father had been a master-mariner, and a most extraordinary one, with a taste for literature. He had gathered together books from all over the globe: a library which might have graced a medieval monastery or a Renaissance university, and to which the ministers and dominies of the last decades of the nineteenth century must have come like bees to exotic flowers, the desert blossoming like the rose.

Captain Meldrum perished in China seas in his early fifties and his library suffered an even more terrible fate. Agnes and her mother had no liking for books and no understanding whatsoever of their value. The shelves were stripped bare, the books bundled off to the cellars, where they lay for years in tea-chests, to be forgotten about by the few souls in the community who might have had an interest in letting them see the light of day again. There were no egg boxes in those days, and for years afterwards customers with a taste for eggs and academic literature might have found themselves eating interesting breakfasts. Agnes used the contents of her father's books as paper packing. Systematically she tore away their pages, crumpling them into balls and using them to separate the eggs, which were themselves individually wrapped in classical leaves before being popped into the ordinary paper pokes that would not have been proof against message boys.

An entire library was shredded in this way over a period of many years, in the course of which a dozen eggs could have improved a man's mind enormously, and an egg a day for three or four years produced a Master of Arts. But no-one knew that the mice were nibbling at the roots of the tree of wisdom; and now, where leather-bound, gilt-spined editions of Shakespeare and Milton had stood like palms in the wilderness, packets of Chivers' jellies and jars of humbugs offered themselves like manna to the hungry boy.

Agnes went round the shelves with the line: a tin of Lyle's Golden Syrup; a tin of Fowler's treacle; a half pound of margarine; a half a dozen eggs; a tea loaf; a packet of Rinso; a bar of Sunlight; a packet of Woodbine; and a quarter of black striped balls.

'That'll be nine shillings and elevenpence, and no doubt you'll be getting the penny for going. Do you want to spend it here?'

JANUARY

'The boat's not in yet, my mother said to say.'

'I'll put it on the slate. Your grandfather can pay me when he goes to the lines.'

'My mother says he doesn't go to the lines until the spring.'

'There will be no herring in the firth this winter,' said the old Mrs Meldrum suddenly, staring sightlessly over the head of her stick into seas of space a hundred years away.

I looked into the far fathoms of her eyes. She repeated her prophecy as I reached the door. Her voice came out of an empty eggshell, tiny and cracked and dry as if the ghost of a bird had spoken. Agnes looked from her mother to me.

'If she breaks her silence it's only to speak the God's truth.'

I opened the door and the whisper from the shell followed me into the bitter wind.

'There will be no herring in the firth this winter, you mark my words.'

The prophecy was fulfilled.

The winter fishing began on the second day of January and lasted until the end of March. The days were gone that my grandfather talked about, when the winter mizzen masts and sails were stepped and rigged—though still the change was made in the nets from black to white at the start of the year, and the new nets set down on board, white for winter. The fleet left the harbour every day and night, drifting up and down the firth in the hope of herring. From east to west, from north to south, from Fifeness to Elieness, from close inshore to as far as the May Island, and across to the Fidra, the Bass and Berwick Law, they shot their nets over and over, hauling them in heavy with living silver, or, as my grandfather used to say, as empty as Kilrenny Kirk.

This particular January was a disaster.

'It's like hauling in the middle of the first week that ever was,' said grandfather, 'before God made the fishes.'

His voice was low and level, uncanny, like a flat calm on the water.

'There's not a fish in the sea,' he said. 'Not in the whole creation. Now I know what it was like in the beginning.'

So he came in for sheer poverty that year, and told me instead about his first night at sea, when he was a boy, not much older than me.

Years later now, when I shut my eyes in winter, I can hear the story and see its teller, sitting on a bench by the white bowling-green.

15

Another old man was with us there, an older man than my grandfather. Gloved and scarved, capped and overcoated, he was little more than a shrunken voice, trembling on the edge of the bitter wind that blew that day.

'It's a cold wind,' he said, 'a cold cold wind.'

'It is that,' said grandfather, 'but it's turned westerly at long last.'

The old reedy voice became thinner still.

'Ah,' he said, 'it's farther west than that. It's farther west than westerly, let me tell you.'

Grandfather smiled.

'How far west can the wind get?' he asked.

The old head shook, its eye sharing the secret with the invisible eye of the wind.

'Aye sir, it's a far west wind, farther west than westerly by far.'

Grandfather never replied.

But I hear him speaking.

It was on a boat called the *Regina* that I first went to sea—a sixty foot boat made of Scottish larch, with a keel of American elm. 1071 KY, that was her number. Old Jock Dees was the skipper, Adam his son, Alan Keay his son-in-law, Ecks Ritchie, Rob Ritchie, and my father. That was the crew for my first time at the winter herring.

It was the second day of the year.

My father wrapped me in a huge jacket and I stood on the fo'c'sle trap. Cold! I have never felt cold like it, a westerly half-gale it was. And there was no appearance in the Mill Bay off Kilrenny, or off the Coves at Caiplie, or even at Crail, when we had all the lights in a line in the small hours of the morning. But off Kilminnin farm we saw five gannets that took a sudden dive, like a white hand plunging into the water.

'That's the hand of God,' said my father, and I thought of the dove that descended on the head of the Son of Man.

'Let's follow that hand then,' Adam said.

So we shot the anchored nets and left them there.

Head on then, it was, coming home in the dark, with all the harbour lights lighted and the white spray flying in our faces. Lumps of it struck me right between the eyes like ice, the white whips lashing my cheek until it quivered. I wouldn't sit down though, and my father put his arm around me.

JANUARY

Some of the men wondered what the morning would bring forth, when we sailed back to the nets. Would we be able to haul them for the weather?

Jock Dees, the skipper, was in no doubt.

'It'll be a fine morning the morn's morning,' he said, 'for the wind's far west now.'

We got three cran that morning, the first catch of the season, and me ten years old. Twenty-three shillings apiece these crans were sold at. Each man got ten shillings and the boat got five. The skipper should have had two shares but he only took one. He gave me the shilling that was left over, for my first time at sea. A mere pittance for a night and a morning of cold and sleeplessness and hunger. But I never spent it yet.

I still have that coin of grandfather's that he could never bring himself to break, with the head of Queen Victoria, and the date, 1875, I who pay more in taxes each month than my grandfather ever earned in his whole life. And at the turn of the year now, as I sit in rooms of amber before an embering fire, and I hear the wind receding from west-south-west to north-west, I take out the shilling and stare at it, and these old scenes and stories come echoing back again into my mind. And the faintest feeling of guiltiness stirs inside of me as I remember one more saying. It was first said to me by a scolding aunt when I came home far too late one night, in the small hours of the morning. Not from catching herring like my grandfather—they were both gone by then—but from a youthful party.

This is what she said :

'A far west wind, like all good young men, goes soon to its bed at even.'

But he could never sit down for long during the day, my grandfather. When he tired of mending the nets in the garret, he gathered whelks when he could not fish, refusing to take me with him because of the cold.

'The whelks is a miserable wet job in January,' he said. 'A depressing month for melancholy folk, and bad enough for me.'

'But,' he said, 'January is wondrous good, to lop trees or fell wood.'

And he took me by the hand, slung his axe and sack across his shoulder, and started off with me for Balcaskie.

There was a thin wind.

17

Fieldfares fluffed their feathers in the leafless hedges, ignoring the handfuls of withered black berries that shivered there uselessly—old widows in the winter wind. Not a hip or haw was to be seen. But the robins were lighting their fires in the bare hawthorn bushes, and the whins were sending out yellow sparks from the hills.

We waited until Peter Hughes, the farmer, had gone over the road past Balcaskie. He was carting dung to his fields. Lumps of it lay among the frosted grasses, where the herring gulls and blackheads were stabbing at them alongside jackdaws and rooks.

'Poor wee beggers,' said grandfather, 'they should be out there looking for herring, instead of doddering about up here with these ploughmen's pets.'

He looked over his shoulder at the darkening fields.

'And so should we.'

He leaned over the fence, pulled off his cap, and set it back on his head in exactly the same position.

'When you see these birds looking for a beetle in a bit of cow-dung, you know there's not a herring to be had in the whole firth.'

Peter Hughes passed us again with his rich brown load, his horse breathing like a steam engine. His sheep were shivering over their frozen turnips. The cattle stood, a black huddle, around the drinking trough.

'Let's give the poor beasts a drink.'

Grandfather broke the seal of ice with his axe, throwing out the tinkling shards. He watched with satisfaction as the pink tongues shot into the water like hot melting pokers.

'A man like that,' he said, 'who can't even see to it that beasts can get their drink. Don't expect now that he would let you break a single stick in his wood. Or as much as cross his field to break anyone else's.'

We went over the fence.

'Do you want to taste the sun?'

He snapped off the withered skull of a cow-parsnip and put one of the seeds into my mouth.

'What do you taste?'

'Earth,' I said, spitting.

'That's the sun in the earth,' he said, 'suns of spring, summer and autumn. And that seed has held it locked up all through the winter.'

In the wood we found a fallen tree. Grandfather hacked and sweated while I poked about among the litter of dead leaves. I found a bunch of snails fastened together in the frost, sealed up in sleep and slime for the winter.

'Don't separate them, they'll be warmer together.'

JANUARY

I tried to stick back the one I had separated from the cluster. Grandfather bent down beside me.

'All God's creatures were made with sense in their heads,' he said. You won't find any worms down there right now. They've delved down deep, and all the moles have gone down after them.'

His old eye spotted something among the leaves and branches.

'Acorns,' he said. 'Still lying there nice and dry from the autumn. Let's gather a few.'

He came out of the wood like January itself, my grandfather, white-haired bright and bearded, blowing on his fingers, his bag of logs on his back.

By this time the heavy sky had fallen like lead on the hilltop, but he hurried me up there with him to cut a branch of whins, to put in water for my grandmother when I got back. We could see the wild glare from Jamieson's forge long before we reached the village, a blood-red frown on the water, like a ghostly moonrise mocking the sun that had just gone down in the west.

We put the whins into a jam-jar and set it on the sideboard. Their yellow lamps were still dimmed as yet by the dark-green shades, but in a day or two they would be lighting up the corner, making the whole room bright.

'If I had hives now,' said grandfather, 'I could get you the sweetest honey that there is from these flowers, and the finest coloured honey too that the bees make from the golden gorse.'

Then he remembered his acorns.

He brought them out of his baggy blue pocket and laid them on the grate. One by one he crushed them with the end of the poker, as old Epp had once crushed the pan drops. The blackened kettle was on the boil. He poured a scalding of water over the crushed acorns, into his half-pint china mug with the faded blue tea-clipper on the front. Then he threw in a screw of sugar.

'There,' he said, 'that will do me better than coffee any day, since there's no tea in the house.'

He put the steaming brew to my lips. I shook my head, watching him in wonder as he sipped his own special brand of Balcaskie coffee, as he called it. It wasn't until I was nearly left school that I tasted a more palatable coffee substitute, 'Camp Coffee' from Agnes Meldrum's shop. It looked like thin brown sauce in a sauce-shaped bottle. But grandfather would never drink it.

A strange man, my grandfather.

No, not strange at all. He was very ordinary. That was the strange thing.

19

A TWELVEMONTH AND A DAY

Later I lay back in my gray blankets in the long night, listening wide-eyed to the loud hallooing of the owls as they tore their prey with rough strife and devoured their mating-time in the wild Balcaskie woods. And from farther west and up country I could hear the weird and wilder cries of the geese in their midnight arrivals at Kilconquhar loch, where they drowned the witches long ago, and yesterday.

I opened my eyes wide as the windows in my sudden terror.

Not far from where I was sleeping lay the dead of the village, frozen like fish in a black fathom of earth. Could they hear this terrible tingling cold, these cries, these terrible thoughts of mine?

And old Epp was lying up there with them.

One day we would all be dead.

I closed my eyes tight in my terror, shutting out the stars.

These are the brightest bits in the start of the mosaic, brightest in the blackest month of the year. Bright with remembering.

And so many are the pieces which have been taken apart by time.

Then freeze, freeze, O bitter sky. You will never bite so keenly as the sting of unremembered friends.

Bright splinters of people still sticking in our hearts.

FEBRUARY

Some time after Epp died we moved to a house on the braehead, further back from the harbour, but with a high windiness which allowed us a gull's eye view of the village and the whole of the firth. A clutter of red rooftops jostled daftly down to the shore from our windows, their chimneys sparkling in the sun; puffing through the winter storms. The firth flashed its fire at us. Or we watched its grey glimmerings moving all the way from Earlsferry on the west side, up past Pittenweem and Anstruther on the east. The village steeples linked land and sky and sea, fish and fishermen and fishers-of-men; and to the south and east the big blue folds of firth and firmament were pinned together by the three seamarks of my maiden voyage— the May Island, the Bass Rock, and Berwick Law on the other side of the world.

The house itself was one of the left-over wonders of the ancient world. The old bit of the house was separated from the new bit by the transe, a narrow funnel two feet wide, which led to the yard, and through which the north-east wind whistled like an arrow, giving an instant cold in the eye to anyone who went down that way on windy days, to be struck like Harold at Hastings. If it was blowing a full gale from the sea you would be lucky to escape with nothing worse than flayed ribs and blurred vision for a week.

On the east side of the transe was the new house. It was no newer than the old part, but we called it that just because it was properly lived in, the other building being scarcely used at all, except for one room which was used by my great-grandfather.

The door of the new house opened immediately on to 'The Room', which was my grandmother's holy-of-holies—cold and clean as a new gutting knife and joyless as an unbaited hook. Only at funerals was I allowed into this special room, which no-one else apart from my grandmother particularly wanted to go into anyway, except perhaps old Leebie, who sometimes sat there in the cold, revolving many memories. The doctor was taken into it when he came, and the minister and the undertaker; once a man in grey, who my mother said was a lawyer—and all people who seemed to carry death and

21

depression in their soft white hands and faces, their terrible black bags. They sat there among the polished oak and cold brass, rehearsing for their coffins. Staring at them from dresser, sideboard and mantelpiece were my rusted brown ancestors in their framed photographs, grimly assuring the younger world that life was a deadly business. As I peered through the keyhole of The Room on these state occasions, the black-clothed visitors seemed to stiffen and grow tarnished and brown, merging with the gowned ghosts, the faded frock-coated phantoms in their frames; disappearing into the dimension of the dead, where they really belonged.

One only among these photographs used to fascinate me—a young bride, sad and slender as a white willow, almost weeping, it seemed to me, on her wedding day. Her husband had such gigantic whiskers— how could they possibly kiss, I asked myself? He carried the commandments in his eye and a bible in one hand, his other hand grasped his wife's with an inflexible caress, and with her free fingers she held a single brown rose to her bosom—so unlike Mrs Guthrie, with her floury fingers and the apples in her dress. An invisible sea was breaking on her beautiful brow.

I touched her with my nose, wiping the breath from the flower, the rose that was red on her wedding night. If only she could have known the ecstasy I might have given her, had I sailed ever backwards through the frames of generations on my grandfather's boat, saving her from life with that dreadful beard, that bible. Three words of a text were visible behind them in the photograph. 'Thou shalt not . . . '

'Come out of that room this minute, you young rascal!'

She was always there whenever I went back for her, always awaiting the rescue that could never be, forever young and yet to be enjoyed, her petals not yet fallen though the photograph was faded. And that stern sea beating on her brow.

But I passed her by behind the closed door nearly every day, going straight through to the kitchen where we all lived, eating and drinking, singing and sighing, telling stories and falling asleep and falling out, year by yesteryear.

Yet it was not a kitchen really. It was the heart of a ship, with its dark driftered beams brushing my grandfather's head, its sun-slanting, small-paned windows that let in the light and beat off the rains, and its winter-thick walls in which we were cribbed and cabined from the winds of the firth. Long long since, in the long agos before the flood, some bewintered boat had been caught up by the biggest wave in the world, right up onto this braehead. The sails had been ripped away, the masts toppled over, the hull splintered and stove in. But the mariners, unwilling to abandon their craft so utterly to the ploys of wind and weather, had built this house around the knotted heart of the ship, hearts of oak that they were. Then the jolly tars had sailed back again, into the iron age of the sea and before, before the bronze age, before the stone age, right back into the age when ships were made of wood and men were made of steel.

And we had inherited their house.

The heart of the kitchen was the hearth. Its big black-leaded grate was our ship's boiler, for this was the time of the steam drifter. So the fire was never allowed to die, summer or winter, rain or sun, it simply rose and fell like a red sea, like a tide that turned at dawn, reached its full flood at evening time, and ebbed away in the night. The first sounds would be my grandmother's worrying it into life, raking out the white dust of yesterdays; giving up her precious morning breath to blow the cold embers back into being. She made the doors of the grate to shine with Zebrite, she polished its knobs and rails with Brasso, she kept the blackened kettle on the boil, as if her own short breathings depended on the rhythms of the fireside, pulsing through winter. When everyone was at home there were ten of us sitting round that hearth, myself and nine adults, ten pairs of eyes drawn to the heart of the house, listening to its red beatings against the white beatings of winter, watching it sink like the long slow summer suns.

Everything in the kitchen had its appointed place, and from its low black beams hung the humble constellations of my childhood—the bunches of dried herbs and ling, the various mugs, pitchers and ladles, the pots and pans, the toasting-fork, the brass tankard, the potato masher, small hand lines of brown twine rolled around bits of kindling,—and the various odds and ends of clothing that were put off and on at the last minute by the adults in their comings and goings; my grandfather's cap on a hook nearest the door.

Between the kitchen and The Room a polished staircase of solid wood wound its dim way steeply upwards to the bedrooms, where the big ones of the family, all beards and bosoms, slept out those few desperately short hours of their lives when they were not working or wanting, or putting food into their busy mouths that murmured endlessly in front of the fire.

It was the back of the house which faced the sea. It had a paved yard with a coal-cellar, the barking boiler and a gear-loft built over the wash-house. And it was the wash-house which was the scene of the most furious activity in the life of the family. When my mother lit the fire beneath the washing boiler, I could not be got out of the way. I loved it when the water in the copper began to boil and bubble, and the whites were thrown in—the flannel shirts and vests, the long johns for men on stilts, and nightgowns for spare sails; shifts and sea-boot stockings, sheets and slips and pillowslips, and here and there the strange small underthings worn by my two young aunts, bringing the scents of India to mingle with the saltiness and sweat of the living firth, the frills of foreign lands to the shores of Fife. And there we all stood, knee-deep in our own dirty washing, drowning beneath the warm waves of bleach winnowed by sunlight on the walls.

I liked it even better when the huge washings of heavy woollens and beddings took place. At the end of the long herring seasons, every woman in the house, young and old, seemed to be washing every day for a fortnight. Set upon set of working clothes piled up in the yard— thick brown kersey trousers and oiled-wool jerseys; barked jumpers and reefer coats; all the boat's bedclothes, in which grandfather and his sons had slept hard in their bunks in the nights broken by sea and herring. They came into the yard and emptied their clothes-pokes upside down on the stones, drawing the tie-ropes through the brass eyelets, shaking the bags upside down until everything that had suffered the direst cruelty of the sea, from crown to toe, from woollen hats to pepper-and-salt socks and in between, came tumbling out silently in a sudden solid bundle to be dumped straight into the dolly barrel.

This is what the women used for the really heavy washes. Into the great tub they were thrown, and my mother, my aunts and my great-aunt, the four of them, stood round the tub in a striving circle, armed with their dolly sticks. They were like massive wooden mashers for giant potatoes. With handles the size of walking-sticks and three times as thick, their great club heads could have split the skull of an armed knight. In the hands of the women they swayed like Norwegian pines, and as they thudded them up and down in the barrel, beating the brine out of the blankets, the body-sweat from the clothes, the women were women no longer, but white Lapland witches, singing and thumping in a circle of suds, scarlet-armed, their red faces like rising moons above a foaming sea.

'I'm forever blowing bubbles,' shrieked my auntie Jenny, foam on her cheek and in her hair—foam flying from her as she floated round the yard in a wild fairy dance.

> *I'm forever blowing bubbles,*
> *Pretty bubbles in the air.*
> *They fly so high, nearly reach the sky,*
> *Then like a dream they fade and die.*

FEBRUARY

Fortune's always hiding,
I've looked everywhere,
O I'm forever blowing bubbles,
Pretty bubbles in the air.

My grandmother stood watching them out of the gray prison of her asthma. This was no work to which she could put her frail hand. But her three daughters heaved and sweated in the glory of their youth, their dresses drenched and clinging to their bosoms, hair flying in the bright winds, bubbles blown from their red lips like spume from two goddesses of the waves. My mother wielded the scrubbing brush on the aluminium board, larding the dirtier linens with monster bars of yellow soap. And the great-aunt worked the mangle, rinsing and wringing with arms made of anchor-rope—she was tough and long and slippery as an old conger-eel, was old Leebie.

'All hands on deck!' she would shout on wash days, and the yard would at once become the busy deck of our boat, warm and wet and wild with female life. Soon the pinned-up sheets would be walloping in the big-bellied wind, transporting us like sails over the roofs of all the other houses, into the far-flung foam of the clouds.

But it was the garret that was my favourite part of the ship.

It was where I slept after I had been banished from my mother's bed, and where I passed most of my time in the house on my own when it was too cold and wet to go out, or when the sun steeped it in quiet dreams. In the garret there were over seventy nets belonging to my grandfather's boat. He used to say that if he shot his whole fleet of nets together he would have fifty million meshes waiting in the water for the fish to swim into them and drown.

'And if I had a herring come into every mesh,' he said, 'how rich a man do you think I'd be?'

I shook my head.

'Rich enough to retire?' I asked.

'What would I have to live for without the herring to fish?' said grandfather. 'It's what I was born for.'

All his gear was stowed in the garret.

Coils of net-ropes and messenger ropes beneath the benches; green glass floats and canvas buoys hung from the rafters; herring baskets and barrels stacked in piles; sculls, lobster creels, partan creels, lanterns, dead-eyes and grappling irons. There were all kinds of lines too—the small lines and great lines with their huge hooks that went down hundreds of fathoms, and the sprools and jigs that sank into the sea unbaited but came up jerking with fish. Boxes of pirns, corks,

25

mending needles ; bottles of oil, tins of alum and cutch—and a great kist crammed with old seaclothes. Oilskins hung from hooks round the walls—the yellow shades of ancient fishermen, vanished heads haunting the empty sou'westers, great thigh-length leather boots standing strangely upright, hardly lacking, it seemed, the sealegs which had steadied them so staunchly on slippery decks of long ago. Across the rafters lay giant cod, every drop of juice squeezed from them by the June suns of the season past.

On summer days, when the high heat came in through the skylight, I lay back on the piles of half-mended herring nets and half closed my eyes. The spirits of the sea were everywhere, and the strange wraiths of the deep, lingering in the lobster-creels, flitting between the cotton meshes, the wickerwork through which the sunlight waved and winked like the sea itself, coiling into nostril and brain, salting the brain with the scents of ocean. The hooks that had hung deep down in the water, so many fathoms out of sight—what invisible stories flickered on them now, brought up from the seabed to be taken off and heard? When it rained I put on the giant oilskins, opened the skylight, stuck out my head from the wheelhouse roof, and steered the ship right into the blur that lay beyond the harbour; till down in the galley the cook called me to come below decks and take my tea. And by night on my bed the rafters moved and shivered in black waves, the dried cod came to supple life, swam in white shoals through my sleep, and the yellow oilskins were the drowned fisherfolk of the family past, floating in the night sea of my dreams like golden ghosts.

We were a motley crew.

My grandfather was the skipper of the boat that was our house, and the house followed the fortunes of his steam drifter, the *Maggie Main*, as it breasted the seasons in search of the herring, the mainstay of our lives. Nights of hard hauling streaked my grandfather's arms, the blue veins standing out like knotted string, and lay in the tiredness of his eyes. But days he tossed back like spray from his head. The years broke over him as though he would never be done.

How can I describe him? Lock him in a frame of words.

He looked like a Spaniard, my grandfather, the midnight blue of his hair streaked with white foam. His skin was burnished by the burning suns of the high seas, the Bay of Biscay breaking in his eyes. They were eyes that held the lure and lore of the long horizons. The sea sounded in his mouth, in the tall lunge of his walk. Or it lay flat calm as he sat at peace, taking his sore sleep, upright in his chair. The big bones of his chest and shoulders showed up through the tightness of his navy-blue guernsey. Shrunk in the washes of all seasons that ever were, its sleeves came up over his knobbly wrists, and his elbows shone through. Two mother-of-pearl buttons fastened his jersey at the side of the neck, where he wore always his loose-knotted kerchief, dark blue with white spots. The trousers were two dark waterfalls plunging to his stocking soles. In winter he stuck his huge feet on the fender and puffed dreamily at his rolled cigarettes, his feet steaming away furiously. I touched them and they burnt my fingers. But he never noticed. His eyes were lost in the red embers of that deep remembering that was always his.

Or he strode out like a Viking in his thigh-length leather boots that took him across the seven seas in one of his giant strides. He spread the black honeycomb of his nets wide on the waters, filled them with the salt sweetness of the sea, lifted them dripping with moonlight and fish. He came back smelling of tar and tangle, saltness and the sun. Seawinds and woodbine and bottled beer. Then he lay down in his box bed, and the tides turned him in his sleep, the sea rolling his cigarettes for him as he dreamed and dozed.

Sleep on now, grandfather, and take your rest.

It was grandfather who took me on my first teetering walks as a toddler. He bestrode the burn, like the Mississippi in its foaming winter spate. I gazed, horrified, through the huge arch of his legs, his outstretched hands reaching in rainy July to the other side, for the ears of winter barley which had listened loud and long to the rattling waters in times of snow and thaw. He rubbed the grain between his brown millstone palms, gently blew away the chaff, and urged me to eat. We walked on then by the clamouring water, chewing in silence, the freshness of the earth in our mouths. I asked grandfather whether the farmer would be angry if he knew we were eating his barley.

'The disciples ate corn on a Sunday from the hand of our Lord himself,' he told me. 'That's a higher hand than belongs to any farmer.'

There were times he took me on his shoulders, down into the belly of his boat, where the dead fish lay in stilled shining legions, open-mouthed with the sheer horror of the world of air. I winced at these wild silent protests of theirs, emanating from a thousand accusing, astonished eyes. The dead in the kirkyard swam at me again in a dense shoal. How awful to be a fish, or to be where old Epp was now— to be underneath the floor of the world, beneath the waterline, to be in the black wave of earth or sea, where the blind worm and the slippery eel never saw the sun. I shuddered and followed grandfather down to the little cabin.

It was full of men.

Heavy and bulky like woolly bears, they sat round the tiny table in a red-faced circle, sipping scalding tea through their whiskers and their laughter. Half a dozen half-pint mugs clattered on the wooden board, slammed down by scarred, knotted knuckles. Grandfather took me over to his bunk and showed me where he slept. A space too small for a man like him—a space between dark wooden boards, with blankets stitched together as though they were a shroud. So this was where he slept while his vessel drifted—in this narrow underwater coffin. I saw Epp in her box again. But as I looked again at the bunk, I noticed the small strands of shag scattered about the pillow. My grandfather would lie smoking his cigarettes in death, rolling and puffing at his ease while the old earth itself rolled like a ship and sped on into time through the dark blue seas of space. And when the good old ship, the earth, anchored at heaven's gate, grandfather would sit up, and nip out his cigarette, sticking it behind his ear. He would throw out a mooring line, stretch his legs, take two mother-of-pearl buttons from the pearly gates to replace the ones he'd lost from his guernsey last winter. Then he'd walk in and ask God for a light.

But I remember him best sitting in his fireside chair, stretched out the whole of his loose-limbed length, his head tilted back at an angle, eyes in the embers, feet on the fender, his pepper-and-salt stockings a raggedness of holes and darns. Telling me stories of sea and sail, and of his own childhood. Of how when he was a boy, he had a tame seagull—a gold cutsie he called it, a kittiewake which he had taken from the nest when it was young, feeding it on fish-scraps and crabs until it grew. After he'd let it go, it kept coming back to perch on his chimney pot every morning and wake everyone up, to see him on his way to school, landing on his shoulder to be fed.

And I saw my grandfather, a golden youth upon a golden shore, hallooing to the heavens as a flock of seabirds winged their way across the clouds. In answer to his godlike summons a flash of golden wings burst from the flock, defying instinct and the laws of life, and came swooping down to light upon his outstretched hand.

I longed then for a kittiewake to answer to my call. But they could be obtained only from the May island, and I had to make do with a sulky jackdaw with clipped wings. Apart from gobbling crusts it did nothing, according to my great-grandfather, but sit there in its splendid black silence, brooding miserably upon the sins of the world.

Even when he liberated it from its rabbit-hutch on the clothes-pole, it refused to accept its feeedom, but remained with us to become a source of nuisance, and eventually of outrage. Mr Guthrie, the baker, delivered rolls by horse and cart in the early morning, to those who could afford the extra delivery charge of one penny. We did not have them delivered ourselves, but many of our neighbours did. Guthrie's horse plodded up and down the streets never stopping, while the baker's boy ran up and down the various pathways and stairs throwing the bags onto the doorsteps. This provided my jackdaw with an easy breakfast. As it could not fly, it took to early morning forays on foot into our neighbours' territories, and always it came back with half a dozen rolls inside it, sitting in its hutch with half-closed eyes for the rest of the day. We had to pay for the rolls. Then its appetite improved; it took to eating them by the baker's dozen. This was too much. One of the rare occasions on which my great-grandfather left the house was when he walked more than a mile up the burn to the Burn Woods, the jackdaw under his arm. He left it there surrounded by tall towers of nettles and the endless green garrisons of thistles that flourished up there—left it to work for its living at last, so he said.

Great-grandfather, my grandfather's father, kept to one room in the old part of the house, on the other side of the transe, separated from us by a streaming river of wind. There he lived on among broken creels and coils of rotten rope, deep into his eighties and the black silences of his bible. He was a bible-boatman, old Geordie, who had given up the fishing in his youth to go to the whaling, and was now voyaging to eternity and its tideless seas—a journey going every day, as he liked to put it. The scriptures were his charts of navigation, the star of Bethlehem his guiding light, a broken Christ his figurehead. The hand on the helm was steady as the rock of ages. His eyes never looked back a single day. He rarely remembered things, as my grandfather did, seldom referred to the past, unless it was the biblical past.

And he never changed his gear. Every day, just as if he were going to sea, he put on his old pilot-rig of navy blue—his coarse trousers, waistcoat and reefer coat; his polished black shoes on his feet that so seldom left the house, and his cheese-cutter cap squarely on his head, though he hardly needed to care for rain, wind or sun. For he sat on his old sea-chest throughout most of the day, at a low table facing the sea, his back to the door. His arms were spread out stiffly on either side of the great open bible into which he stared for hours upon hours, the pearls of understanding growing in the oyster-beds of his old deep-sea brain, his lips clammed shut behind the spiky silvery beard.

But though he was an iceberg of a man, nine-tenths of him sunk beneath the waves of the present, yet the tip of his nose stayed alert and electric to whatever was going on around him. So on my to-ings and fro-ings in and about the old house, he would suddenly spring open if he detected my near presence, which he never failed to do.

'Is that you, laddie?'

I stood still as a pebble among the heaps of old nets, creels and baskets that littered the room next door to his. I listened to the salt smells drifting like tuneful ghosts from one to the other, pretending I was a fish, hovering among all those meshes, too cunning to be caught.

'Come on up now, I can hear you breathing.'

I went slowly up the bare wooden steps.

'What is it, Gramps?'

I went over and stood by his side, taking my place among the smells of mothballs and nearly ninety years, more than seventy of them spent at sea. He rose and went to the grate, where a black pot of broth was simmering. He dipped in the ladle twice, filling the deep dish to the brim with the rich steaming soup. He jabbed a large spoon into the bowl and it stood there like a sword.

'Eat,' he commanded.

'I've had my dinner, Gramps.'

'Eat them up,' said the stern voice, 'they're good for you.'

Soup was always plural. I ate as I was ordered, while he watched every mouthful with a kind of grim satisfaction. Then he pushed the plate to the side, lifted me onto his knee without tenderness, and began his sermon.

Jonah and the Whale,

'Do you know what size a whale is, lad?' he asked me when he had finished reading.

I shook my head.

'As big as this room?'

'Bigger,' he said.

'As big as the whole house?'

'Bigger.'

I shut my eyes tight and tried to see leviathan.

'Go into Miller's boatyard,' the voice commanded, 'and stand right underneath one of these great big boats they're building there now. Look up at it from where you're standing. That will give you some idea of the size of a whale.'

30

FEBRUARY

I saw again the men in the boatyard—labouring minutely like worms in the great curving coffins that they built around themselves day by day, little morsels of humanity weirdly working away within those dead wooden whales which a slow creation was bringing strangely into life.

Old George's voice brought me out of the mouth of the whale. His eyes wandered to the windows, touched the blue horizon. His voice shook as it remembered.

'A whale can make the sea boil like that broth over there. A whale can lift a ship on its shoulder, crack it open like an egg with a toss of its head. It can deliver it to the deeps with a single whack of its terrible tail. That's just one of the things a whale can do.'

And what a whale did to a man was even worse. To be swallowed like Jonah was a frightful fate. Imagine going through those curtain-like teeth, and them swishing shut behind you—into the awful theatre of your own death with all the lights out and your last act played out in darkness. Consider that terrible darkness, deepening, ever deepening, as the great fish plunged downwards to the bottom of the sounding sea, and you inside its belly, like being in an express train in a never-ending tunnel. And you rolled and slithered in despair at the stench of carcasses caught in those walls of flesh, some of them even attacking you in the terrors of their last agony.

> *Stone walls do not a prison make,*
> *Nor iron bars a cage.*

Ah, but for one imprisoned in these overwhelming ribs, these mountains of blubber, there would be no hermitage of quiet mind, no dignity in the dreadful last hours between him and judgement. God would see to that—God who put him to his living grave.

'For it was disobedience to God's will that put Jonah in the way of the whale,' the old man stormed at me. 'And that should teach you to obey, and to love the Lord with all thy might, and with all thy heart, and with all thy soul.'

But it had not always been that way with old George, my mother told me. He had turned to God in his age. As a young man he had lived wild and wicked at the whaling. She told me the stories that she had taken out of the mouth of my grandfather, and she pressed them to my lips like secrets with her bedtime kisses, warning me not to let my great-grandfather be aware that I knew anything of his wild days without the Lord.

The story I remember best of all was about one of his drinking

31

episodes. In a public house in Stromness, just back from the Arctic whaling, he placed bets with an Icelander and a Dane that he could outdrink them both. Mug after mug of frothing ale they lined up on the bar in rows. They drank them down doggedly, desperate men that they were, glaring at one another dead in the eyes, searching for the bolting blue madness of despair. None of them was going to give way. At last young George made his move.

'I'm tired of playing boys' games,' he announced. 'To the cellars.'

They bought a barrel of ale each, turned on the taps, and lay down on the floor, each one gaping-mouthed to catch the flow of beer. The streams of gold were slow but steady. Their eyes grew larger and their fists clenched, their nostrils dilating. Their feet went rigid. Only their throats worked convulsively.

The Icelander was first to go.

He suddenly rolled over on to his side and began to be sick. The other two opponents never heeded his retchings. They lay side by side—apart, yet locked in terrible struggle, each determined to prove himself the drinker rather than the drunkard. The changing bets flew round the closing circle of men, the odds altering according to the slightest flicker of expression in the eyes of the prostrate giants. Sovereigns, crowns and krona jostled in sweating palms, and the heads of kings and queens of the northern hemisphere were set at odds.

It was over without warning.

The Dane's stomach ruptured suddenly and he died where he lay, in a terrible torrent of blood and beer. The young George calmly stood up, all eyes fixed on him like fires, and with his head a red, expanding balloon, he walked back to his ship. He had drunk enough, he said, to float it all the way back to Baffin Bay.

'He was a knocker-out,' my mother said simply. 'Every man was afraid of him. He just laid them all low.'

My bible-punching great-grandfather—a knocker-out of men. I closed my eyes tightly, trying to fuse the sedate, stern-jawed old scripturalist and the ale-swilling giant of the Davis Straits.

Once only the savage and the saint flashed together in the one picture, which burned itself into my recollection. That was the day the Jehovah's Witness came to the door. It was a Sunday and everyone was at home when the knock came. On the doorstep stood a man grinning widely behind a pair of glittering glasses. He had thin limp hair and red cheeks.

'Do you want to buy a copy of "Watchtower"?' he asked.

'No thanks,' my grandfather said, shutting the door.

'If you'd be good enough to ask me in I'd be glad to explain to you what it's all about.'

Grandfather opened the door before he had quite closed it, letting in the last two words.

'I think you'd better see my father,' he said.

He turned to me, his eyes twinkling.

'On you go lad, take the man over to the old house, will you?'

I led him up the old wooden steps while he patted my head, knocking with his leather-gloved hand on the blistered door. Behind it sat old George in his Sunday silence, steeped in the scriptures to the very lips—the only parts of him that moved, whispering the words to the sea-fronted windows, pondering the prophets, nodding all to himself. There was no answer to the first knock, so the man with the glasses knocked louder a second time. I turned the handle and went in.

The old one half turned in his chair and saw the man standing behind me. His eyes were chips of ice. His jagged beard froze.

'What do you want?' he asked quietly.

'I wondered if you'd like to buy a copy of "Watchtower", sir.'

Old George moved faster than I had ever seen him move before. He sprang at the man like a silver lion, seizing him by the lapels of his raincoat, drawing him up close to his bristly jaws so that their eyebrows nearly touched.

'How much?' he spat.

'Sixpence.'

The man's voice shook with fear.

'Sixpence!' roared the old man. 'You want me to give you sixpence, do you, for your own perverted little brand of the bible?'

The man's arms dropped limply to his sides and all his pamphlets tumbled in a holy river, littering the steps all the way down. My great-grandfather had him by the throat.

'Have you ever read the bible?' he sneered.

'Yes, yes, of course, many times.'

'What are the first words of Isaiah Chapter 55?'

'I don't know, sir.'

'Think!' demanded George, leering fiercely.

'I can't remember.'

'You can't remember!' the old man roared, eyes and teeth flashing, beard bristling with rage.

'Well I'll remember for you!'

He jabbed the sky with his forefinger, his arm straight as a steeple.

'Ho! everyone that thirsteth, come ye to the waters, and he that hath no money, come ye, buy, and eat!'

He let his victim go but remained with his arm aloft, a magnificent ruin, dwarfing the other man like a church, his finger still stabbing the air like a spire.

'How can you have the bold neck to ask money for preaching the scriptures when the scriptures themselves expressly forbid it?'

He breathed heavily through his nostrils. The man in the raincoat twitched his mouth into a quick smile.

'Isaiah didn't have any overheads,' he said.

The desperate joke failed.

George spun the man round, gripped him by his starched collar and the seat of his trousers, and trundled him down the steps, flinging him out into the street. Every member of the family was standing there awaiting the expected exit, huge grins on their faces—all except my grandmother, who was hiding inside the house for the sheer shame and disgrace of it, she said. George looked at them all laughing, but the anger never left his mouth. He harried the fleeing figure with his righteous rage.

'And if you ever dare to darken my door again I'll break your bloody neck!'

The seller of pamphlets hurried even faster on his way.

'Just think yourself lucky this was a Sunday! If it hadn't been the Lord's day I'd have thrown you off the pier!'

And he stormed back up the steps to his room without a single word to any of us.

Such was my great-grandfather.

When he threw the Jehovah's Witness out of the house he had nearly ninety years sitting on his back.

Cold porridge he was, old George, the fires of his youth burnt out of him long ago, his mouth full of ashes—except for that one time I saw the live coals flaming on his lips. So when it was coddling and comforting I wanted, I went to my grandmother. Out of her gray frailty she doled out kindness and warmth from kitchen and fireside, her two appointed places. She served us as if she had nothing else to do. Weak in wind and limb, she loved and protected us with the heart of a lion.

Asthma was her curse. It kept her shackled to the house all day long and all her days. It was a chain that you could hear rattling inside her, a chain forged from gray gaspings and breathlessness and wild wheezing cries. It kept her in her chair for hours at a time some days, with head bowed, her hand over her eyes, shoulders shaking, the drowning going on in her mouth as she battled for air like a spent fish.

When she was a girl of twenty her father died at sea on the way home from Yarmouth. There was no telegram to warn the family that the skipper lay dead in his boat. When she heard it was coming in, she ran down to the harbour early in the morning, waiting on the pier to welcome him, and the presents he always brought. But it was a body draped in oilskins that was brought ashore and given to her. She fled home with her grief from the sea, shut herself in the cellar, and threw herself face down on an old mattress which had lain there for years. She cried herself to sleep on that damp dismal bed, soaking it with her tears. Exhausted, she lay there till night. They couldn't rouse her, make her answer the door. Fever blazed through her for a week afterwards, and for a month or more she could scarcely walk about the house. Her constitution was ruined, a prey to asthma ever since, so the doctor said. When I was born she was barely fifty. Now I realise that she always looked eighty.

But a lifetime of illness did not harden her to the aches and ailments of other folk. She felt for them all the more sweetly. She was an expert on all the old homely cures that could never be bought from the chemist's shop. For her own asthmatic coughing bouts she used a remedy which made me gasp my lungs out to be granted just a single gulp: honey and vinegar simmered together with bruised sugar candy, and oil of sweet almonds and lemon-juice stirred in. Nectar this was, that snatched me from the imagined brink of my grave a hundred times that I can remember. These and many more medicines she soothed me with when I felt like being ill. She held my head when I banged it hard against the sides of the whirling world; she cleaned my cuts and wiped my nose; she warmed my bed with the big stone hot water bottle, always wrapping it round twice with a towel so that it would not burn my toes. And when I came in dirty, she stripped me and plunged me into the big bubbling kitchen sink, beating the blackness out of me with bars of carbolic, rubbing me down in front of the fire until I was pink and tingling and resurrected.

Still when I think of her, she is the provider, flooding the kitchen with waves of rich aromas from her plain and wholesome fare. Kail and potatoes were the staple diet, with the mutton removed from the soup to serve as the second course along with the mash. Or she turned the tatties into a meal in themselves by beating them in with turnips and onions and lashings of pepper, whipping them into an explosive mixture which she called clapshot. Or she used dripping and a little sausage meat instead, and the tatties were turned into stovies. The simple wooden chapper and spurtle were the tools that worked the magic, and the results were served up on the faded azure background of willow-patterned bowls and plates and dishes—mild-mouthed monks and love-lipped ladies, serene and sedate by their blue-leafed pools and bowered bridges, bowing to their pig-tailed lords; fanning themselves from the heat of our scalding hot meals, faded lords and ladies; faded but never fading throughout the twelve eternal years of my childhood.

Bannocks and baps and loaves of crusty bread came out of the side-ovens, heated by the fire—she baked for us when we could not afford to buy from Mrs Guthrie. But more than anything I recall how she worked her way through endless quantities of fish. The king of fish, the humble herring, became in her hands the fish for a king. She boiled them, fried them in oatmeal, roasted them on the brander, dished them up as kippers, as bufters, as bloaters, shredded them into hairy potatoes; producing variety out of monotony. Herrings and haddocks and cod she fed us on—and shoals of flatfish to be picked to the bone.

They were brought to the house in bunches of six or twelve, knotted together, the twine threaded through their tough, gaping mouths. Dangling like bells from my grandfather's crooked finger, jangling inside my head out of their silvery silence, their tails sweeping the pathway as he strode through the door, slapping them heavily into the sink. Grandmother wrenched off their heads, she from whose gentle heart pity ran so soon. She threw them through the open window to the hysterical gulls and the sniffing cats. She cut off their tails and slit open their bellies with her terrible flashing knife. The dark red slivers fell out, desecrated, like wounds on display. She ripped off the scaly sheen of their skins just as my auntie Jenny peeled off her nylons without thought. She stripped them quietly of death's last dignities, dumb brutes of the sea, boning them till they were nothing more than flabby slabs of fresh white meat—the quicksilver of the sea brought down to earth so that we might eat. *Mare vivimus.* We live by the sea.

So she stood there at her kitchen sink long hours at a time, stood there while the tides came and went, her menfolk going out and coming home, the years passing as she grew older without ageing. Sometimes she paused, the knife slippery in her still hand, fighting away her asthma. I looked at her in wonder—the bowed, beaten back, bent with the stripes of pointless suffering, the mouth opening and shutting in the same silent agony as the fish she waited patiently to dress for death's dismemberment. She laid her hands on my shoulders for a few minutes at a time, and we stood together in silence, each of us incapable of finding words.

Then she carried on patiently. She taught me how to gut and fillet. She showed me St Peter's thumb-mark on the side of the haddock— and now, alas, in this age of frozen food in plastic packets, my fish-fingers have become indeed all thumbs.

But it is the crabs that remain—crawling horribly into the present. The big partan crabs were brought into the house looking like fallen knights, their armour-gauntleted claws folded quietly on their bellies as if they were dead and laid to rest. But when they were picked up they sprang to attention, opening their claws wide and waiting for the attack, to clutch and pierce and tear. Grandmother had no fear of them and laughed at the panic that sent me to the other side of the kitchen. She dropped them into the pot on the grate, holding them round the back, where the blind, waving pincers could not grip her. Horrified, I watched the water begin to boil, and the crabs crimsoning in the agonies of death, the claws now gripping grimly onto the rim of the pot as they tried to vault their way to escape, to joust with me on the kitchen floor.

It was then that I screamed.

'Gran, they're getting out!'

It was probably for my benefit that she put on the heavy iron lid, with a stone placed on top to prevent this armed escape and a scarlet revenge. But still they come scrabbling out of the pot and into my dreams, those crabs that dined on sailors, all bubbling and bulging and red with rage and terror. Could a merciful stiletto not have been inserted between the joints of these armoured plates, to reach the vital parts and deliver a quick kill? Or to still the beating of that brutal brain. I imagined grandmother's knitting needle used in the manner of a misericorde on a medieval field. But she who was so pitiful told me that they must be boiled alive. And so, having failed to secure mercy for them, I dreamt again of those demon faces that would be visiting the sins of the grandmothers upon the children down the generations; starting in sleep with myself, with punishing infestations of eyes that wobbled wickedly on stalks, and claws that tore me to gobbets where I lay. For a time they made night hideous.

Between them my grandparents had produced five children who had survived. My mother, Christina, was the eldest. She had two sisters, Jenny and Georgina, and two brothers, Alexander and Billy.

They filled the house with sound and fury, these aunts and uncles of mine. They seemed to have stopped on the road of life all together at one point, and gone into the golden garden of their teens and early twenties. From there they danced and sang to the older wayfarers who were further along the dustier road than they, calling to the youngster who never saw them change from one end of the year to the next, and from year to year, until the youngster himself had vanished into mere recollection, and so had they—leaving the garden empty and gray as February.

Auntie Jenny was the wildest one—a whirlwind of inescapable affection. She had inherited grandfather's dark colouring, with her nightfall shock of hair, her big brown eyes, her brow of Egypt. Like a black tornado she swept through the house leaving no-one or nothing standing where it had been before she cleaned it, embraced it, kissed it, threw it aside or out of the house, or tore it to tatters in the very tempest and torrent of her passion. Being the youngest and the smallest human entity about the place, I was the most vulnerable target for her attacks. She lifted me like the wind, singing and howling as she clasped me, kicking madly, to her bright bosom, restless as the sea, and aimed at me her red, wounding lipsticky kisses.

'Let me be! let me be!' I yelled.

She rocked me fiercely on the deeps of her blind undirected longings.

Ae fond kiss and then we sever,
Ae fareweel, alas, forever.

Then she was out of the door and pedalling her four furious miles to Cellardyke, where she worked in the oilskins factory. And singing all the way she went, to the clouds in their flying, the sun on the sea.

It was odd that she got on so easily with Georgina, who was in all ways her opposite. Georgina's fair hair hung round her head like morning, and her blue eyes were bright as dew. She was Mary to her sister's Martha, was Georgina. She was the quiet waters by which I wandered and pondered, often stopping to study her as she cupped her chin in her hands, fixed her far eyes on an unknown strand, and withdrew softly into the glowing core of her secret inner life. No tear-floods, no sigh-tempests for whatever lovers never crossed the seas to win or leave her. She melted into herself and made no noise, Georgina, who stood like February between winter and spring, a landscape locked up and silent, waiting for the sun to free her and fill her full of life.

She was not always at home. When she was with us she worked as a fisher-lass with Burgon the merchant. But for part of the year she followed the southward path of the herring as they shifted from Shetland down to East Anglia like a shining harvest, Georgina walking in their wake like Ruth, gleaning her meagre living from the silver stalks of the sea. She came home from her travels with the sands of foreign shores on her shoes, her hair coarse with the salt sprays of the eastern coastline. Her knuckles were rubbed raw to the bone when she returned, ugly purple cuts on her pale fingers. I kissed them for her and she smiled.

But she brought home with her sometimes sheets of music that were different from the old Scots songs which were the only pieces to be found in the house at that time. Then she went into The Room, where she sat by herself and played over her new found treasures. I watched her white fingers run over the old brown piano keys, and I saw the thunderous wounds from the gutting troughs grow silent, miraculously healed by the sheer power and beauty of the melodies which her hands played. She accompanied herself in a slow sad voice, not turning round when I went in, but smiling to me with the lilt of her head.

> *The poor soul sat sighing by a sycamore tree,*
> *Sing all a green willow;*
> *Her hand on her bosom, her head on her knee,*
> *Sing willow, willow, willow;*
> *The fresh streams ran by her and murmured her moans;*
> *Sing willow, willow, willow;*
> *Her salt tears fell from her and softened the stones.*

'Sing me another one, Georgina. Sing me another one of those, please, another one.'

I kissed away the hurts from the gentle hands and they did my bidding.

'Another one,' she said, closing her eyes and smiling to herself. 'All right, another one.'

She waited and a long time seemed to pass. Then she opened her eyes again, sighed, and sang.

> *How should I your true love know*
> *From another one?*
> *By his cockle hat and staff,*
> *And his sandal shoon.*
>
> *He is dead and gone, lady,*
> *He is dead and gone,*
> *At his head a grass-green turf;*
> *At his heels a stone.*

39

The walls of The Room fell away and Georgina and I were the only ones left in all the world. We sat together under a single tree, spread out in a green cornfield that extended out of time. I was her dying lover, for whom she mourned alone. I kissed her on the cheek and she bent her head, brushing my face with her hair, while the music came up out of the ground, filling the sky.

> *White his shroud as the mountain snow,*
> *Larded all with sweet flowers;*
> *Which bewept to the grave did not go*
> *With true-love showers.*

The song went through my groin like a sword. What was it that it was telling me? It spoke of ladies dead and lovely knights, and beauty making beautiful old rhyme; it spoke of old unhappy far-off things and battles long ago; it aroused in me something wafer-thin, tenuous as a wailing ghost, the mere memory of a memory, something I had forgotten but never truly known or understood. And in this first faint and far remembering of mine, Georgina was no longer a girl, no aunt of twenty she, but a quivering harp from which the winds plucked their sweet savage tunes of life and death.

They were broken up, those tunes, when the 'boys' came bursting into the house, bearing breezes from the sea.

'What are you playing that dirt for, Georgie?' they called in passing. 'Come and make us a cup of tea.'

Alec and Billy were in their late teens. They were the male counterparts of the girls in their looks—dark and fair. Alec was the dark one, his beetle-black hair brilliant with brylcreem, the hair on his huge chest running over his shoulders, onto the nape of his neck and all the way down his spine. He loped about the house constantly looking for lost shirts and jumpers, always naked to the waist, a good-looking gorilla with a genial grin. He read books about explorers and talked of going to Australia. Billy was fair-faced, like my mother to look at, with red hair. But it was he who had my grandfather's deep abiding passion for the sea. It always seemed to me that he smelled of the sea much more than his brother, as if the vapours of the element clung to the sympathetic soul. Billy never brylcreemed his hair, never hurried to get out of his fisherman's gear when he came into the house. He padded around the whole time in his thick white sea-stockings, exuding the scents of the old fishing ways like a poem he never recited but carried in his head, and which made his eyes shine softly. But like the girls they were planets whose orbits intersected with mine only at brief points in my first years; they swum suddenly into my ken, then they were off for days or nights at a time.

My mother was the most sedate and sensible of our gathering. She too, though, was out of the house for most of the day. She worked the switchboard at the post office down at the harbour, taking the telegrams from the boats when they wired home from their away ports. She heard their messages, transmitted their calls, sent out the information. She was both mouth and ear of all the local news and fishing gossip, listening closely to the heartbeat of the village against the wider commercial rhythms of life, the dates and sizes of catches, and all the prices that the fish were bringing in from Lowestoft to Wick. She had an astonishing capacity for storing all this information away in her head. She could quote you chapter and verse, pounds and pence, the day and the hour of what was said, by whom, to whom, about whom. But being by nature kind and gentle, my mother, she turned over only figures and facts that could not hurt a soul.

'Bertie Stewart's had a good shot of cod behind the May this morning.'

'The *Shepherd Lad* has landed ninety-six cran at Peterhead.'

'Burgon's put the lobsters down to ninepence a pound.'

When I lay in bed with mother, talking to her in the close, comfortable darkness, she told me all about the boats and the men who sailed in them, how they toiled hard and lost their lives and feared God.

It was then that I would ask her about my father.

'Oh, he's still in the navy,' she always said.

'What's the navy?'

'Oh, that's lots and lots of ships. You could take your grandfather's boat, and you could just push it through one of the portholes of your father's ship. They could float it in their bathtub.'

'What's his ship called?'

'Ah well now, he sails on different ships.'

'Is he the captain?'

'Och, Lord no, boy. He's just an able-bodied seaman. At least he was.'

'What do you mean he was? Doesn't he catch fish any more?'

'He didn't go out to catch fish, wee lad. He sailed under the white ensign. On ships of war.'

'What's war?'

'That's what happens when very wicked countries send their

41

soldiers and their sailors and their airmen to lose their lives attacking ours. A great many folk have been killed. It just ended the year after you were born, the war.'

'Why didn't we get killed?'

'We were lucky.'

'What's lucky?'

'Shh. Go to sleep.'

'When will my father come home?'

'Some day.'

'When?'

'Some day soon, we'll all be seeing him, in God's own time.'

'But when?'

'Wheesht, go to sleep now.'

And in my dreams my father telegraphed the post office that he was coming home. His ship came swaying drunkenly over the morning horizon, sending the low sun spinning into space. It sliced the May Island in two and sank the Bass Rock, which went growling to the bottom of the sea. Then it crashed through our small harbour and kept on coming, right up the brae, battle-scarred and glorious, until the point of its prow splintered our window panes, and there was my father straddling the bowsprit with bell-bottomed trousers and waving madly to me from on high as I lay back on my bed in amazement.

'Get up, you lazybones. Up with you now!'

It was Leebie poking me in my dreaming ribs. Leebie was an ancient female who lived with us. She was part of the family tree, but from which branch I could never understand. She was a great-aunt, that much was sure, though exactly whose great-aunt was far from clear to me, and I suspect none of the adults really knew themselves. Leebie Marr she was sometimes called, but always to me she was just Leebie, a faded old signpost standing on the very edge of the family circle, outside of which were the faces of the strangers.

Leebie's undoubted great age was a deceptive quantity because the longer she lived the further she seemed to grow away from senility. Her lifeline had run parallel to the grave for a time, and now it began to incline just a little away. She was long and slender as a whip—supple, quick, leathery, and with a crack in her voice and hand. Through her thin, shining, bunched white hair her lumpy skull was a polished nut. Her bare arms were tough as congers, fingers nippy and nimble as spider crabs. She worked craftily at her sewing machine, the black polished shoes tip-tapping on the treadles. The ancient knees and shanks shuttled and sped like pistons in the dark corner where she worked. She did all our sewing. When buttons came off they were shot back on with a few quick flicks of her flashing fingers, the needle darting like a fish for food, hitting the mark accurately and without joy. She darned our stockings, patched our elbows, took up hems, let down turn-ups, turned collars, let out gussets, took in waists. Necks were knitted up or slashed away, sleeves lengthened, whole garments remade. Like Penelope she was never done. With no suitors to court her in her age, no man long at sea to welcome home to his hearth, she nonetheless worked unceasingly, the thread flitting through her fingers as though it were the thread of life she held in her ancient hands. She was a deity of the hearth, but as she sat there with her back to us, black-shawled and hooded, the snipping scissors in her hand, she seemed more like the sisters of Fate woven into one.

'They've been too long at sea, these men,' she would say when my grandfather's boat was slow in returning, 'and I don't like the look of that sky.'

Then she would go back to her sewing, muttering as she worked. The others shifted their feet then, told her not to be a silly old wife, and laughed. But their eyes would wander to the windows, knowing old Leebie's instinct for the weather, they would fall silent, and against their uneasy broodings the harsh humming of the sewing machine sounded sinister and weird, with overtones of fear.

But when we were sick unto death and in direst need of desperate remedies, it was Leebie who administered them—manfully and without mercy. In the unwritten law of Leebie's medical lore there was only one sure cure: the kaolin poultice. It was this I feared most of all.

'It's got to be scalding hot,' she would assure us grimly, as we waited like criminals for all the rigour of the law to be applied.

She put the pot of water on the grate to boil and waited until the water was hissing into the fire, sending clouds of steam out into the room like wraiths out of hell. The poultice bubbled and broke, came bursting over the rim like volcanic lava. She cut the squares of lint according to the size of the boil or blister, or the nature of the ailment. Even a chesty cough meant a portion large enough to cover the front and back, shoulders and ribs. She spooned out the steaming cement as if it were for eating, smearing it over the lint with her knife. I blew on it frantically.

'Stop that, you rascal!' she roared. 'It's got no good in it if it isn't piping. Take off his shirt.'

Kicking and screeching, I was stripped and held down to the floor

43

by a ring of hands, while Leebie held the dressing across both palms, preparing to slam it round my wheezing ribs.

'Lay it on canny, for pity's sake,' said my grandfather. 'It'll take his skin off like that.'

'Don't be soft in the head, man. Would you rather drown slowly or all at once?'

'I'd rather not drown at all at your hands.'

'Away you go back to your boat.'

She slapped it on like a bricklayer throwing his mortar. A dead-eyed doctoring that had me drumming my heels on the floor for twenty seconds while the flames encased me like fiery armour, like hoops of steel. But within the next half minute there came the inexpressible relief of that barely bearable warmth, which dulled down for the rest of the day before turning at night into a feeling of wet clothes gone cold and clammy.

If it was small boils or skelbs, she would mix up bread poultices, afterwards extracting the shards with tweezers, or lancing the boils with red-hot needles held in her pincers and heated in the fire. The two uncles had to submit to these cures of hers for their salt-water sores, ringing their hands and wrists where the oilskins rubbed constantly against their not yet hardened flesh.

But what they refused, with fume and fury, to submit to, was her cure for fisherman's piles, caused by the endless wetness and sitting in cold water. Stockholm tar, heated, and rubbed well into the affected area—that was her remedy.

'A good dollop of hot Stockholm tar up your behind, and you won't be worrying about piles any more,' she said. 'Go on, get your breeks down!'

That was where they drew the line and stayed on the side of their pride and suffering. But sometimes they took the treatment at the hands of my grandfather—or rather at his feet. For he would put on his rubber seaboots, dip one great foot into the solution of tar, and apply the stuff to the afflicted region with a venom.

'It's not that I've anything against your backsides,' he said, 'but I'd be too soft on you with my hands.'

The uncles looked at each other in horror.

'Come on lads, it's time to wet the quarter-deck. Hatches off, bottoms up, and in she goes!'

They were forever on the move, these folk of mine; there was always a going and a coming with them; no-one was idle. And when they were not working they were always off somewhere—the uncles to catch the bus to the Empire and the Regal picture-houses in Anstruther or Pittenweem, with suits double-breasted and acre-wide ties larded with flowers and snakes, such was the fashion; or even, if my grandmother hadn't caught them at the door, curvaceous ladies, as naked as my innocence. But most of their entertainments, I suppose, were found around the fire.

My own first attempts at self-amusement were snatched out of the rolling fun-wheel of the seasons as it whirred past our windows. I played on the beach among the tangles after a sea-cat gale in February, and saw the dead sea-cats in amongst the tangles—still, slippery corpses, not yet stiffened, voiceless things of the sea, which I pulled out by their wet tails, whirling them in circles round my head and loosing them like unchained comets to land with a thud on the bouldery shore. The old folk and the poor ate these sea-cats. Old George in particular used to ask me after a wintry gale to look for them.

'As long as you can see blood coming from them, they will make a good eating,' he would instruct me.

He examined every one I brought to him, trundled all the way up the braes in my miniature wheelbarrow. The sea-cats, he told me, were so stupid that they deserved to be eaten. During the deep storms they clung to the big stalks of the tangles, refusing to let go even though their holdfasts were uprooted from the sea bottom, and so they came ashore still clinging to the washed-up weeds, to take their last journey: a funeral procession in my little blue barrow all the way up to old George's dinner table.

'Take no thought what ye shall eat,' he said to me as he inspected them. 'That's what scripture tells us. Very well then, I make do with the stupidest things in the sea.'

Some he kept, some he returned to me to throw back into the sea. Down on the beach again, I sorted through the tangles for a fair-sized root, which grandfather cut for me into the shape of a pistol. So my first wars were bruited behind the boatbuilding shed with a rubbery gun that had come out of the sea. A gun like this would last for several weeks before it shrivelled and stank. But while it was battleworthy, I walked among the corpses of the sea-cats as among the vanquished slain, treading upon their necks, setting my foot in vicious victory down on their heads. A giant over my foes, I was sole survivor of an unsung epic—the battle for the east sands.

45

On Saturday forenoons during the winter herring I'd go down to the pier and offer myself as a scranner. The custom was that the last herring out of the boat which would not make up a marketable quantity was given to boys to sell for pocket money to the cadgers, who then hawked the fish around the doors, or up at the farms, where the fishermen seldom went.

One year there was a Flanders frost in February.

That was the name the old folk gave to a south-east gale that carried a frost as hard as armour—and many of the smaller craft hadn't put to sea for over a week. My grandfather's boat was in for repairs, but he had been hugging the coast in a hired motor-yawl, the *Jonathan*. I saw them from my bedroom window coming into the harbour, and in balaclava and boots I raced out of the house. The cold smashed the bridge of my nose like an iron gauntlet, its bitter bells ringing in my ears. It nailed my boots to the stones of the pier as soon as I stood still on the edge. I shouted down into the boat to see if they had anything left over that would not fill up half a basket. But every fish was used up. The cold made me shiver.

'Wait a minute,' shouted my uncle Alec, as I turned to go. 'Watch this!'

The yawl had an old-fashioned pump beside the mizzen mast. But it had a brand new one too, for pumping the bilge-water over the side. Alec pulled several times on the handle of the new pump. Nothing happened.

'Hold on up there, don't go!' he shouted again, heaving like a hero at the shining new handle.

After a minute's effort, up there came in a sudden spurt one dozen herring exactly, every one of them as stiff as a dead soldier with the frost. They rattled onto the deck like lead.

'There's twelve apostles for you,' laughed Alec. 'See if you can find faith great enough in all St Monans to believe in them.'

The men in the boat laughed until I thought the stones of the pier would split with the frost and their fun.

But I must have lost my innocence by this stage, for my instinct told me that a cadger would turn up his nose at them. In my wickedness I sold them to a widow woman at her door, and I asked ninepence for them, which I was given. A fearful guilt kept me from spending this money until several days had gone by and there were no reports of her sudden and agonized death. The fact is that she lived on to an excessively ripe old age, though she had not been a particularly well woman most of her days. Maybe, my grandfather said, she had been inoculated by my filthy bilge-herring against every conceivable illness and disease known to medicine, and one or two others into the bargain.

In the bad periods of the south-east gales I sometimes went with grandfather to collect West Anstruther clay to fill up the holes in the back of his father's old fireplace. A long period of south-easters not only set the tangles inshore but sucked out the sand from the beach at West Anstruther, exposing boulders standing on a deep-concealed bed of bluish grey clay. This was the stuff old George liked us to bring, because when it dried it went harder than old Pharaoh's heart, he said. The local saying was 'as hard as West Anster clay', But George used to say that that was not as hard as the hearts of the West Anster folk themselves, hardened against God, a hundred times worse than Pharaoh's.

Just outside of East Anster, in Cellardyke, lived my grandfather's brother-in-law, referred to in our family simply as The Dyker. He used to tell me that the south-easterlies filled Cellardyke harbour so full of tangles that he could step straight off the pier and walk right across the harbour to Shore Street without once having to bend his knee. But the soft south-westerlies always came and sucked the tangles out again, leaving the sand every bit as clean as it becomes now, in our more enlightened times, after the North Fife District Council has spent just a little more of the taxpayer's money trying to accomplish with paid labour what nature does for nothing.

So February passed, sometimes the fiercest month with its frosted flag-rushes by the burn that bled my hands like the blades of fiery-tipped swords, its raw thaws, its needling rains and misty glooms. And its roof-rattling gales. Yet the very gales were a stir of life, blowing red-hot star sparks from Jamieson's smithy right across the harbour in fierce dancing constellations, baring the cold red arms of the country folk as they burned their weeds, drying the sodden clods in the earth. The long silences of the fields were breaking to the high jingle of horse-gear, the early morning cawing in the tall elms. With a wild roar of freedom the burn was unlocked, and twigs and straw continued a journey to the salt sea that had been arrested for weeks. Days came when in spite of everything winter was sowing snow among the spring corn, the fields were white as flour again, and the young year seemed to be turning back to age like an infant slipping through mortality, through frail hands, from darkness to darkness. But the furrows appeared again like strong dark waves on the earth, giving the fields their inevitable shape, while out on the waves of the firth the winter drifting went on.

It was the spawning season in February. The herring gathered in dense shoals in the region of a mysterious triangle whose points were Elie Ness, Fifeness and the May Island. Locked each year within those lines of nature's strong necessities, precise as Euclid, unshunnable as death, the herring teemed with the milkiness of life, pouring it out into the sea. At the early part of the winter fishing the men avoided these spawning parts of the firth, fishing in the softer grounds in the middle, or round the Fidra, or off Kircaldy. But as February went on, the fish went up the horns of the firth on the south side and came down the north side. They were looking for their favourite birth-beds, between Anstruther and Kellie Law, around the May, off Dunbar, or in the stormy Hirst that lay between Crail and Fifeness, where many a fisherman's drowning mouth had closed, on the coarse and rocky ground that the herring loved. The spent herring swam off then; scudding away to deep waters they went, but where after that nobody knew. Nor could I fathom where at that time I was making for myself. Even now, as I return in spirit to my own spawning place, throwing out the net of words, in hope to catch something of my beginning and my end, I am little wiser than I was. Even my grandfather, who hunted something much more tangible than truth, was never sure of a catch.

He had seven men in his crew including himself.

Each man brought with him six nets, making a fleet of forty-two nets for the boat. The white winter nets were preserved with alum, which drew in my mouth like a lemon when I chewed a small piece for fun. Each man also brought with him to the boat six of the big floats called pallets. The old ones in George's bit of the house were made of sheep's hides but the newer ones were canvas. These were tarred inside with two pints of Archangel tar from the ship chandler's, and painted with one pint of linseed oil on the outside.

All these preparations I watched, but never saw the mystery of the catch, for my grandfather went at night to drift. But sometimes on a cold dark night I rose from my bed to look out through frosted glass on a winter firth that had become like a masquerade or moving town— the sea lit up with all the lights from the scores of boats fishing in the Forth. The East Neuk fleet were hunting the herring, and like The Lady of Shalott, I saw only the lights through the glass.

FEBRUARY

For often thro' the silent nights
A funeral with plumes and lights,
And music, went to Camelot.

And had I known them then, I might have murmured the words to the window, melting the frost with the breath of poetry.

'I am half sick of shadows,' said
The Lady of Shalott.

But I knew exactly what was going on from their lights.

They shot their nets before the wind, stopped their engines and put up their mizzen sails. This put the boat's head into the wind, and the wind, drifting onto the boat, kept the nets in line. They shot them down off Crail, drifting away up past the Earlsferry before the tide turned and they came down again. And a whole week on the night tides might earn the boat ten pounds, a single pound for every man, two for the skipper, and two for the boat. It was said they could earn fortunes if they were lucky, but grandfather never did. Sometimes they came in like the sons of Zebedee, he said, having toiled all night and caught nothing. Often only a few shillings tumbled out of the corner of his handkerchief, as he brought home his earnings in the old-fashioned way he followed till he died. I was told about the old days, when the Fifers caught thousands of cran before the war, with dozens of English merchants coming from as far as Penzance for twenty years. And I was told about the *annus mirabilis* of 1913, when the boats fishing out of Yarmouth alone brought in nearly a thousand millions of herring, my grandfather's boat among them.

But I was told many stories.

Sometimes now I wonder if I did not dream them all, as the oil-rigs straddle the firth, grandfather lies in his grave, and the white ghost of the winter herring haunts the harbour of my mind.

MARCH

I sometimes think that in one of his mad March moods, God must have sent out heaven's cherubin, horsed upon the sightless spring winds of the world, to gather up all the strange souls and funny folk that they could find, and to bring them together in one place. That place turned out to be my birth-place: St Monans of the seagulls.

St Monan came to Fife in the ninth century in the company of St Adrian and his monkish followers. Knowing no worse weapon than the Viking axe, beneath which he bowed his saintly skull, he nonetheless prophesied that at the time of the end of the world strange lights would be shot up into space; not as candles to a dying god, but as eyes that would be witnesses to the final holocaust.

As I look before and after, the saint's martyrdom seems as close to me now as the world's end and my own quiet beginning, in those early years when I left the day-long protection of kith and kin, and went out into the wide world of our little village.

It was a fishing and boatbuilding village above all.

In those days the boatsheds rang with the sounds of the adze on freshly cut keels of American elm, and the curing sheds were ecstatic with the reek of newly smoked kippers. A forest of moving masts jostled in the harbour, a Birnam Wood of propitious omen, and the fish gleamed from pier to pier like stacks of silver bullion, breaking the sun a billion times. It was the silver age of the great herring boom, though nothing to what my golden grandfather must have seen as a boy, when a single boat gave work to a hundred hands—a miracle of fishes without the loaves. I soon came to know a good catch—ninety cran, a hundred cran—and the boats that were likely to make them. Today their names ring round the walls of my brain like words out of scripture: *The True Vine, Magdalene, The Shepherd Lad*. The faith of the fisherman is recorded on the old boat like the lettering on a Dead Sea scroll.

And the faces remain, the douce Dutch faces of my ancestors; the Nordic seas that glimmer in a pair of Viking eyes; the suns of Spain that burnish that complexion. The ancestral winds of many voyages have written wrinkles into the faces of the fishermen of today. It was

51

ever thus. History gets worked at last into the flesh, like the lines of passage, entered on the log-books of their parchment skins.

Faces. I remember sailors who are now to coral turned, farmers that are kirkyard clay. I remember old wives who kept the secrets of the town about their scrubbed doorsteps—toothless sybils who sat in the sun to stay alive an hour longer, and weave village gossip on the cracked old looms of their tongues.

And still in dreams I re-encounter some of them, in the cobbled closes and on the bouldered beaches, where their faces and their forms first broke in upon my childhood.

It was Hodgie Dickson who first invaded the blanket of the dark, in those wild nights when the trolls of the town walked the corridors of my sleep like ghosts in technicolour.

Hodgie lived with his brother Frankie, not far from us on the Braeheads, in a house at the West end of the town, right at the top of the Dawsie Brae. The house had a narrow paved yard in front, where Hodgie used to work away with bits of timber. I stopped there often to pick up woodchips and shavings to take along to the burn to be used as boats. The pavement outside the low wall of the yard was always strewn with the detritus of Hodgie's handiwork, though no-one ever saw what it shewed forth, or could remotely guess what it was that he was supposed to be making.

In my dream I saw myself stopping to speak to Hodgie as usual. He was wearing his fisherman's black jersey with neck-buttons, kerchief and cap, and his thick brown kersey trousers. Half bent he was, with his back to me, worrying and whittling at his wood. I asked him for one of his odds and ends. He answered me with a silence unusual for him.

'Hodgie,' I said, 'don't you have a piece of wood for me today?'

He paused in his planing and polishing. The back of his skull was like a closed door.

'No, not today,' he seemed to say, though still he never spoke.

'Why not today?' I asked.

He turned to face me, but with the same unspeaking mouth. Then he lifted his arm and pointed down the steep brae. Following his finger, I saw a small procession of figures at the foot of the hill. As they came upwards and closer I made out six men dressed in black and moving in single file.

'What are they coming for?' I whispered, afraid.

Even yet Hodgie said nothing, but he stood aside from the wall where he had been working. It was then that I started to see, in the insidious insinuations of sleep, what it was that he had been making all this time. Where had I seen that box before, with its terrible solidity and smell? Old Epp floated through my dream and was gone. The men in the boatyard melted through the ribs of their ships and came at me in a shoal, each one with the face of Tom Tarvit, the toeless toothless whaler.

'Aye,' said Hodgie with moveless lips, 'that's my coffin right enough, and it's me they're coming for, as sure as death.'

Hodgie was dead within a week.

If it was precognitive, it could not have been a trouble to my days at such an early age. But the dream itself continues to play itself back in my sleep, over and over, like a silent horror film too terrible for words.

Death that came into the midst of life so soon, with the passing of Epp and Hodgie, now moved through the village like a morality. The hearses and cars wound their way up the green mound of the sea-flanked kirkyard, a procession of shining black beetles that gleamed beneath the sun. I watched them from afar with a wary eye. When there was to be a funeral, an old town-crier solemnly strode the streets like a medieval leper, ringing a deep-throated bell, whose iron tongue accompanied his own, that told you the day and the time and the place.

From the back of beyond it germinated, the distant clinking of the old bell-ringer, beginning like a beating in the blood, like a slow whisper from the sea, stirring in the ears. Conversation faltered and halted as the tolling drew closer, as if the kirk itself, steeple, bell and belfry, had risen groaning from its foundations, and was grinding its way like a gorgon through the town to bid us remember our end; and the memorials marched along with it, the village dead, a conquering army terrible with stone banners of epitaphs and texts: *Behold He Cometh, The Day Dawns, The Kingdom Of God Is At Hand, We Shall Not All Sleep.* Mortality was on the move, hauling eternity in its wake.

'Do you hear that?' my grandmother whispered. 'Old Penman's ringing his bell. Somebody's dead.'

Her words hung in the air like a sudden pall.

All the busy noises of life in the kitchen now ceased at once. The uncles stopped clattering their dominoes on the bare wooden table; the girls' laughter and chatter burst in their mouths like a bubble, leaving the air around their heads empty and expectant; Leebie paused in her patchwork, the needle coming down midway from the machine and hanging there poised, like a stuck sword. For a moment the whole family sat like statues, their marble heads bathed in the flames that suddenly lurched up the chimney as the fire stirred and spat in the silence. A gas-pocket had been picked out of a lump of coal by the searching fingers of flame and a yellow jet shot out its hissing tongue.

'Who is it, do you think?' Jenny asked.

Her face had gone white under her black mane.

'Who can it be?'

'Wheesht,' said grandmother. 'Just listen and we'll hear.'

The clanging of the dreadful bell grew louder, nearer, filling the room, and with it the sounding of that awful voice—slow and harsh and steady as the sound of shingle drawn backwards by the sucking sea. The words broke over the stone heads like waves.

'The funeral of Charles Davidson Marr will take place from Number Five, Elm Grove, at two-o'-clock on Wednesday next, and from there to the old kirkyard.'

The air sang with the sudden silence that surged backwards upon this sentence.

We waited.

'Charles Davidson Marr died of a heart attack at seven-o'-clock this night. Visitors are welcome at Number Five, Elm Grove, between nine a.m. and seven p.m. tomorrow, when the last kisting will take place. The Lord is my Shepherd, I shall not want. He maketh me to lie down in green pastures. He restoreth my soul . . .'

'That was a sudden call,' said my grandfather.

'No, no,' grandmother said. 'He always had a bad heart.'

'Does that mean he'll go to hell?' I asked.

'Hold your tongue, you young scoundrel,' Leebie gasped from her corner. 'Whatever do you say that for?'

'Well, I mean, if he had a bad heart . . .'

Chae Marr's bad heart had meant only one thing to me: infernal wickedness. For old Epp had often called me a bad-hearted boy who would burn in hell.

'Your heart's as black as the ace of spades,' she used to scold me.

Many's the day I had fled from the sight of Chae Marr coming out of the elms near his bungalow at the east end of the town. He was as gnarled and grey as the trees that shaded his dusty windows, and in my imaginings he was as black-hearted a pirate as ever escaped the gallows to skulk among shady groves and sing masses to Satan at midnight. What would he not perform upon a small boy if he caught him? I was relieved to hear that he was gone at long last where the wicked cease from troubling and the fretting worm feeds sweetly. Poor innocent Chae, whose bad heart kept me from brightening his loneliness with a smile.

'That Penman ought to be put down,' my uncle Alec grumbled. 'He ought to be silenced. He gets up and rings that bloody bell before a body's had half a chance to grow cold.'

'He'll be ringing it next before you've even laid yourself down and died,' Billy said.

'Oh wheesht, wheesht!' whispered grandmother.

Grandfather stuck a thin strip of newspaper in the fire and re-lit his cigarette, which had gone out in his mouth.

'He's like a shark following a ship,' he said. 'Nobody welcomes the sight of him.'

Penman the bell-ringer, how easily he became the death-bringer— not in the eyes of children only, but to those who passed him by on the other side of the street, turned down closes to avoid a meeting, or hastily undid knots of corner conversation to break up and gab another time. To a mere mite his grey moustaches, sad eyes and sepulchral step were enough to strike a chill into the bone, even without the aid of his terrible bell. The cherubin had brought him out of Egypt and I shunned him like the plague.

But the consciousness of flesh, and what was done with it, and what happened to it, were very close at hand.

Two doors along from us lived Lisa Leslie, the midwife and dresser of the dead—in a small house surrounded by a huge sloping garden, walled in from the sea. Two twin daughters lived with her, undistinguishable one from the other, and seen only once a week, on Sundays, when they walked together to the kirk, dressed in black, their arms linked, their bent heads as dumb as fishes. What they did for the rest of the week nobody seemed to know. Maybe they sat at home and pondered the coming and going of human life.

Lisa was always out and around. At all times of the day or night she could be seen, in all seasons, in all weathers; never wearing a coat for wind or rain, but her grey shawl flying with her hair about her shoulders, and her long black skirt flapping at her heels. Bare-armed, with head held high, she haunted the roads, always holding the crown of the causeway; eyes without seeing fixed dead ahead of her, as she made her way to houses of mourning, and to those where men and women bred bleakly in the face of death.

But her familiar figure never made her a property of easiness, for no-one ever spoke to her. And the reason was that she never spoke to a soul herself. If you hailed her by name, mentioned the weather, or assessed the prevailing state of affairs in the world, your words passed her by like the idle wind, which either she disrespected, or never even heard. So she simply arched our existences, not as a person at all, but as a gray rainbow across the village; untouchable, elusive, spanning the unmentionable polarities of crib and coffin. She carried the secrets of being and not being in her hands. Speaking to nobody in her life, yet she held all of us as we came into the world and as we went out, washing away from us the blood of our birth and our last day's sweat and tears, and ignoring us in between. She was the iron gates of life and death; she had seen our nakedness and knew too much. No-one would have wanted her to stop and say, 'Behold, I shew you a mystery.'

In one sense she did not walk alone.

In those days dozens of cracked men and women, young and old but mostly old, strolled about the streets, roamed the braes and beaches, or just sat on their doorsteps and studied the sun through screwed up eyes.

HoneyBunch was one who would never wash.

It was a terrible shame for her, because she was a female of truly astounding loveliness. She must have been forty when I was born, but seemed to me to epitomize the willowy wonder of youth. She was just such a lady whom I might have dreamed of meeting in the meads and gone groaning to her grotto. Honey-haired, bee-footed and almond-eyed, she came down from the country, from the Anstruther estate, her mouth musical with a magnificent English in which she drawled and drooled about whatever happened to be in her head, a pealing of broken bells. I worshipped her accent. She fetched her blood and being from men of noble race, whose proud inbreeding had produced a faery's child and a language strange. On summer days she sat on the sands as the blue tides swished backwards and forwards before her, and she pondered the pebbles which she picked up and held in her hands, staring and saying nothing all day long. She walked through woods and long lines of surf, following the curving patterns on the beach; she paddled in ditches, lay on the piles of old nets at the back of the harbour, her bare feet among fish-heads and rotting bait and crabs' toes; she spent long hours at the rubbish dump on the west braes, playing with the joyless jetsam of the community. She combed her hair with bones and broken combs. Then she wandered through open doors into folks' houses, sat down and asked for cups of tea. Or she appeared in church on Sundays, barefooted and bedraggled in the middle of the sermon, placing herself in the pews among coffin-coloured fox-furs and festooned and birds-nested hats; exuding the smells of the waste places of the town rankly among presbyterian polish, pan-drops and moth-balls. She smelled to high heaven. From six feet away you could have adored her; from three feet you could have died.

So Alec Fergusson, the old beadle who had baptized me with salt water, was the man who did out of pure Christian charity what not a single woman in the place would have dreamed of doing—he washed her. Took her through his burnside cottage, out to the back garden and into his wash-house, stripped her bare buff, laid her down like a sleepy queen on a big old-fashioned scrubbing board, and gave her a good soaping and rinsing before he let her go.

The Women's Guild complained to the minister.

'That mad madam with the marble in her mouth! Washes her down, back belly and in between. It's got to come to a stop!'

Kinnear was no kitten, and gave them his answer.

'Cleanliness is next to godliness,' he said. 'She's got as much right as any other body to come to the kirk, and if the godly folk aren't going to make her decent for it, then either Alec continues to do it or I'll damn well do it myself!'

The beadle went on seeing to the bathing of Bathsheba.

Once I saw her come out of his front door, her hair spread out by the wind, her torn dress draped round her tall form like a flag furled about a sun-bleached column. I stood and watched her as she walked past me into the waves, laughing, and I imagined what it must have been like to have washed HoneyBunch. I glowed at the thought. Then I looked over Alec's garden wall. He was still out there in his garden, mending a puncture on his bicycle.

There were other female figures who lacked the fascination HoneyBunch held for me, who were simply there, as part of the moving scenery.

Bella Bonny Socks, like HoneyBunch, lived on little but charity.

She went to the shops with not a penny in her purse, asked for a few simple stores, enough to keep her from starvation, and when asked for the money, would tell the shop-keeper, 'Tam'll pay it, when he gets back from the lines.' And nobody had the heart to break through this simple shield her brain had put up, to tell her what she had long refused to know, that her young man, Tam, was lying where he had lain for forty years—at the bottom of the grey North Sea; caught in a deep-sea fishing-line which had wound round him like a bobbin and pulled him out of her life forever; leaving her newly bought wedding-ring to lie empty on her display cabinet, a barren circle of gold for the rest of her days.

There was Kate the Kist, who went into the boatbuilder's office every morning first thing, lay down on his floor and demanded to be measured for her coffin; Wilhemina Well, who refused to use the sink which the council had put into her house. She drove a pick-axe into the shiny new porcelain and carried on drawing water from the old well at the bottom of her garden; and poor Mad Maria, whose suicidal urges came on her every winter. On freezing cold days she would walk down the slipway at quarter tide, wade into the middle of the harbour until she was up to her knees, and start to wail like a stuck siren. Then she'd slither back to the shore, her feet and legs clogged with mud, shaking her head and saying the water was much too cold today for drowning herself; she would have to wait until the warmer weather came in. But when summer seas cooled the hot stones of the slipway, poor Maria never felt the winter in her blood which turned her old feet to the water's edge at the turn of every year.

As children we seldom laughed at these folk, though they would have made huge walking targets for our fun. But one or two of them we did notoriously abuse.

We went soft-footed after the crazy old sweetie-seller who came round the streets pushing a barrow and carrying an open pack on her back.

'Kate's crystalised candy!' she used to bellow. 'Come and buy, Kate's crystalised candy!'

She had sharp ears and would whip round and box the ears of any lad making for the sweets with all the longing of Tantalus but none of the sureness of the sleuth. In doing so she would be sure to spill some of her wares. Then a dozen small shadows would materialize out of doorways and corners, from where they had been stalking her—a small army of gaunt guerillas, a list of lawless resolutes sharked up for action, their stomachs ravenous for spoil. There would be a quick grim harvesting carried out among kicks and curses, while she wielded a hazel-switch and called upon God to punish the pilferers of the poor old widow's mite. Sometimes the sugar candy was eaten between bloodied lips and sweetened a singing skull.

When we were really bored, we shadowed the deaf French woman, whom we called Jean Jeff. Her name was Genevieve, which we could never properly pronounce. Genevieve Catriona Louise—and something else which was wholly unsayable.

'Jean Jeff's a pickle deaf!' we bawled after her, knowing she was safe inside her silence. She carried on walking, muttering to herself in a rapid machine-gun succession of strange syllables, fired off at whatever phantoms of the past peopled her shuttered mind. She was just another of these weird old widows who walked among us like a caste of priestesses, linking our lives to whatever imponderables reigned outside the sure span of our blue skylines, the much less certain allotment of our three-score-years-and-ten.

But the unseen works the greatest magic.

And in the fairy-tale page which time left long unturned, there lived a princess.

A St Monans mariner and adventurer called Darsie had left home in 1868 and established a trading company in the South Seas. When after fifteen years his boat sailed back into harbour, he carried down the gangplank a Princess of Tahiti, who settled with him in the village, bearing him five children, all of whom died. Then, when she was fifty, she gave birth to one more child, a girl—and died herself on the childbed. The girl inherited her mother's title and became known as Princess Paloma. Darsie sailed back to Tahiti to collect his dead wife's sister, herself a princess, who came back with him to help look after her new niece. He had amassed a vast fortune and they lived in a great walled mansion fronting the rocks at the west end between the town and the kirk. The new princess grew up, was educated privately, was never seen in school or kirk, never attended to over cart or counter; never once walked in the community in which she had been so strangely set, like a jewel in a copper crown. Darsie died and so did his sister-in-law, and they joined the old princess up in the kirkyard. Later, when I could read, I used to go along to their single gravestone, a huge upright slab set in the south-east wall of the kirk, and read aloud their names and dates and strange eventful histories.

A TWELVEMONTH AND A DAY

In Loving Memory
of Princess Titaua Marama
of Tahiti
Chiefess of Haapiti, Wife of George Darsie.
Born at Papetoai Moorea Society Islands
3rd November 1848
Died at St Monans
25th September 1898
The five children of George Darsie and his wife
are also interred beneath this stone.
Also George Darsie
Died at Johnston Lodge St Monans
5th April 1919
Princess Ouiritania sister-in-law of George Darsie also has her ashes
interred below.

Something then of the unutterable sadness of human life came whispering at me from their carved names, out of the stone. St Monans mariner and South Seas princess, their lives and loves spanning continents and oceans, shrunk now to the lettering on a slab, splashed by the spray, stroked by the sun. Gone into the back of the universe, with old Epp. How could any of it be true? Had they ever really lived at all?

Then my eyes wandered from where I was standing to the squarely towering lodge with the conservatory, the shaven sweep of lawn, the dark green flames of the rhododendron bushes, holding their flowers like burst stars. Somewhere inside that building, under these myriads of tall white chimneys, there was a princess of Tahiti: the Princess Paloma, walking free and yet in chains. Though I had never seen her I knew that she was beautiful to behold—with beaded breasts and grass-skirted loins. Inside the house there were palm trees and lagoons where she shaded her dim and dreaming brow and cooled her toes from the heat of the tropical sun which Darsie had brought back in broken bits in crystal chandeliers. I could sometimes make them out through one of the windows, using old George's telescope. Servants fed Paloma with pineapples and coconuts, and she lay in a swoon on beds of leaves, to be fanned by nodding fronds into restless memories of the land of her birth which she had never seen; far beyond the Firth of Forth. I could be like Darsie and take her home again, if she could wait that long. I looked back to the gravestone. But perhaps she too would be slipped like a pearl into the earth's purse before I could live to see her in the light of a brasher day.

MARCH

Then there were the old men.

Men who had been fishermen, many of them, but now with nothing left to keep them active on the tides, they pottered about the edges of their own existence, killing time and frightening little boys.

There was the awful McCreevie who drowned unwanted kittens.

He just dropped them in a pail of water, sat on it, and laughed. Once I watched horrified as the pink blind mouths mewed to the blue sky, looking for the mercy that had found no lodgement in McCreevie's square, grinning head. Tittering softly, he sloshed them out onto the grass like little grey gloves that had lain in the rain for a day. Their wetness and inertness was terrifying. How could such things be and not be in such a short space of time? Why not dry them out, lay them in the sun and let them live again? But as I looked hard for that Promethean heat that might relight their lives, McCreevie picked them up in one spawny fist, opened up his mouth like a well and pretended he was going to eat them. He laughed hugely at my horror, his roars dredged up from the pit of his shaking stomach through that black imbecilic hole in his face.

Only McCreevie knew what he did with them after that. He met me in a wynd once, and with a leer informed me that he would cut my head off. I saw no reason to doubt him and fled screaming for my mother.

There was The Blind Man, whose name I never knew. Everyone, child or adult, simply referred to him as The Blind Man. We tortured him badly, though we let most of the other worthies well alone. That was because he was so bad-tempered, cursing and lashing out if he heard anyone coming his way. So he was followed by troops of youngsters who had at one time been kicked or cuffed by him, and who had sworn vengeance. We catcalled after him, pulled off his cap or turned it round the wrong way on his head, tugged at his rubber-ended walking stick which he used to feel his way about. He swung it from side to side as he walked, to detect distances and guidelines. Any one seeing him coming had simply to get out of his way as fast as possible, for he swung and slashed without mercy as though he were a reaper; or the last of the six hundred at Balaclava, still blindly sabring the gunners in the jaws of death. So we stood in serried ranks and shot at him from our fists and fingers enough shells to have severely altered the battle-maps of all recorded history. But still he came on, his mouth bloody and his head unbowed, and we toppled and died until he reached us, and then we fled.

His coming made for a game of daring in which nerves were tested to the utmost. He used to come home along a narrow fenced lane known to all of us as The Little Path. As he could quite easily bang his stick from side to side of this pathway against its low iron railings, he was able to make exceptionally fast progress home. It was his favourite route. So a bold boy would lie in wait in the middle of the lane, while the rest of us looked on from the safety of the street. We rolled about the pavement like bent hoops, hugging our groins with sheer expectation, our hands held tight between our legs, and our red faces drawn in horrible torture as if we were bursting to go to the bathroom. We smirked and winked at each other through spread fingers, pointing and shaking our heads in utter helplessness. Then from round the bend of the path the sudden clanging could be heard as the railings rang to the noise of the terrible stick. We jumped up at once, our laughing done, awaiting in a skin-pricking silence the expected encounter.

There were many variations to the game. The boy crouching in the path of death could wait until the last possible moment before leaping up with a murderous yell and running back up the lane to safety. Or he could vault the railings and taunt his victim from the safety of cabbage patches, where the butterflies danced in the lost Edens of our innocence. An even braver boy might try to dodge past the old man without being caught by the stick, perhaps reversing his cap in his lightning strike. Breathless at times, we watched with horrified glee as one who fancied himself as an Apache stood bent and barefooted in The Blind Man's path, holding the tarmac tightly between his toes, and by skilful, silent manoeuvring of his person, avoid the swinging stick and the blind boots—the old man passing on his way in total ignorance that one of his foes had foxed him. Few tried that particular feat of courage, and fewer still tried it without bruises to testify to their failure; battle marks which were worn like medals for the rest of the month.

Once on a freezing afternoon I sat on a stanchion on the middle pier and saw The Blind Man coming down for his constitutional He walked out onto the piers with never a thought for danger. He had all their lengths paced out in his head with perfect precision, and could bring himself to a halt with not a single step left between him and a twenty foot drop to a dark drowning. The visitors used to cry out in alarm as he neared the end of the pier, only to be cursed soundly and told to mind their own bloody business. Bigger boys stalked him over the big stones, shouting aloud their classroom sums to confuse him in his counting. But on this particular day there was no-one else on the pier but myself. Just as I rose from my seat a friend called to me from Shore Street. I hailed him and began to walk up the pier. At once The

Blind Man took it into his head that here was one of his torturers making malicious sport. He half bent, his blind head shot forward for scent and hearing, and he started swaying from side to side like a cobra, whipping his stick widely about him and with murderous intent. He came on down the pier like that, while I slowly retreated, unable to find the courage to battle or bluff my way past the whirling weight of his weapon, which would easily have cracked a skull or broken an arm. Whining, I backed down the pier, tripping over the coils of rope and getting caught in the bundles of nets which never seemed to trouble the man with no eyes but with an inhuman sense of smell. At length I arrived at the windy end of the pier where the little waves cracked like black whips. And still he came on.

'I've got you now, you bad little brat, you've nowhere else to go! I'm going to break your head and feed your brains to the fish!'

My heart fairly whacking my ribs, I slipped over the end of the harbour and stole softly down the rusted iron rungs of one of the ladders. There was no handy little boat there that I might have slid into and lain snug and safe from the weather. I climbed down until the black water was slapping the soles of my shoes. Then I waited. The Blind Man's face appeared in the sky above me like a malevolent planet and he rapped the first rung with his stick. He made no effort to descend, but he stood there in a grim silence throughout two hostile hours, until my feet were quivering, my fingers were blue claws, and my jaws jabbering at my knees—jack-knifed with cold and cramp. When he finally left his post, I made my way home in agony, bent and bawling, and an object of derision to circles of hooting children. The Blind Man's revenge was to be remembered.

Some of these people quietly pursued trades of their own, scarcely dimpling the surface of village life.

The Snailer went about the braes gathering slugs and snails which he brought back to his garden in biscuit boxes and bred. He sold them at a halfpenny a dozen as his own country cure for salt water boils. Not many fishermen bought them, but I knew that they worked. I once had a bad boil on my leg that made the limb blow up to twice its size. As I limped along the braes to avoid one of Leebie's kaolin poultices, the Snailer hailed me, refusing to let me go until he had rubbed one of his catches into the sore for nearly an hour. Next morning the leg had gone down like a balloon.

'Just you give your boils a good drink of snail slime,' The Snailer used to say, 'and they'll soon go back where they came from.'

Peter Cleek had a hook for his left hand—hence his name. He pushed a big barrow round the town, holding one of the shafts inside the hook and the other with his good hand. Usually he brought round herring. But in the month of March the cod had huge roes in them, and he would shout along the street: 'Good cod roes! Good cod roes!' Then we'd shout back at him: 'Isn't there any herring in the firth, Peter?' And he'd answer: 'Good God knows! Good God knows!'

George Young went after all the horses in the town, waiting patiently with sack and shovel for them to drop their cargoes of hot compost straight onto the street. The big baker's horse, the milk horse, the fruiterer's and the fishman's, he followed on their rounds, and all the little horses that carted the gear to and from the boats and hauled the unloaded herring up to the station. Not even waiting sometimes for the horses to move off, he reached between their hind legs with his spade and raked away the steaming loads of fertiliser, shovelling it into his bag, which he then swung onto his shoulder, marching off in search of more takings.

'Geordie Young, the King of Dung!' we shouted after his back through our tightly held noses, furiously fanning the air in his wake, and he seemed to revel in the title, his red face lighting up, his eyes crinkling as he silently nodded and laughed, winking and wagging his head.

Now and again these strange figures made disgraceful public exhibitions of themselves. Mansie was a ton of man who, when drunk, became suicidal like Mad Maria. But unlike Maria, he had no immediate hesitations. He took off all his clothes, folded them neatly on the pier, and threw himself into the harbour in a sitting splash. It was only when the cold sea hit him that he experienced an instantaneous change of mind. Wallowing and wheezing whitely in the oily water, he spluttered for help. My uncle Billy dived in once and saved him. Mansie was so fat, Billy said afterwards, that the wet naked flesh kept slipping through his fingers like blubber, so that he was nearly drowned himself in the process of trying to bring him to shore.

'It was like trying to save a whale,' he said. 'I've told him next time to keep his bloody clothes on!'

Other characters were less dramatic but no less memorable.

Philip The Philosopher had only one question for you whenever you met him in the street.

'I'll prove to you that you're not really here,' he used to say.

'Go on then, Phil.'

'Very well then. Are you in Edinburgh?'

'No, Phil.'

'Are you in Aberdeen?'

'No,'

'Are you in Glasgow?'

'No.'

'Very well then. If you aren't in any of these places you must be somewhere else then?'

'I suppose so.'

'Very well then. If you're somewhere else then how can you be here?'

It was bent logic, but it straightened us out for a mind-boggling minute while he went on his way triumphant.

And there was the old cold gold-earringed sailor called Gowans, who drew me conspiratorially into the folds of his sea-waistcoat, pointed his white buccaneering beard at me, and whispered unto me the strangest sentence I have ever heard:

'I've seen monsoons and typhoons and baboons—and teaspoons!'

These were the eccentrics, whom progress has mostly swept away.

One of them would place his hands on his navy-blue lapels, draw himself up to his full height, and announce with a staggering show of pride: 'I stood where thousands fell!' Visitors were given to believe that here was a man who had survived the din of war and all its deadly missiles. The true significance of his claim was somewhat less heroic.

In the old days, which he was remembering, the only public convenience other than the naked rocks, was a brick contraption which jutted out starkly over the back of the harbour wall. A hole in the overhang permitted human excreta to be deposited directly into the sea, as into the moat of a medieval castle. When the tide was out, the old fishermen used to potter about on the rocks underneath, looking for crab bait. This was the inglorious battlefield on which the unbroken soldier had stood unscathed. And thus the age of affluence has purged away the age of effluence. And along with the dirt has gone the gold, and the doodles in the margin, so beautifully inessential to the argument of the text.

Frequently they congregated in front of the harbour, these old men—maybe twelve of them at a time, bunched together like a dozen old herring on a string, walking up and down a small stretch of Shore Street, no longer than the span of an old Fifie sailing boat from stem to stern. Twenty steps then turn, twenty steps then turn again, they made their old men's half strides, walking back and forwards to keep out the cold, or simply taking the measure of the imaginary deck their feet had disembarked from long ago. Or they strolled to the end of the pier, spat into the sea, blew their noses with their fingers into the winds, and sauntered back again; perambulating penguins, with nothing left to do on a cold day but blow their beaks and spit. Time hung heavy on their empty hands.

The working fishermen, their hands hauling on sodden nets, were generally too hard worked to develop eccentricities. All the same, several of them proclaimed their individualities against the rough routine of the life of toil.

One of these was Star Jeems—a man of enormous strength who scorned the use of a hoist or barrow or horse when shifting his nets from boat to pier and from harbour to house. Jeems was called after the name of his boat, *The Morning Star*. On a Saturday morning crowds of boys would gather on the middle pier to watch it come into harbour. After all the fish were landed, the great moment would arrive when Jeems would heave his share of the nets onto his huge shoulders, ascend the iron rungs of the pier wall, using a single hand, straighten himself for a second among his massed admirers who stood around open-mouthed and smiling, then walk half a mile to his home, trailing a long tail of children, and bearing a weight that would have bowed the legs of a rhinoceros. For good measure he would then walk up the steps of his own house all the way up to the garret. This was sheer bravado, for he then flung them down into the yard for their Saturday washing. But he liked it to be seen that he had no need of the hoist and tackle that topped the garret window. Then he would carry on in the usual way, the white nets being dipped in a hot solution of alum and boiled for three minutes before being laid out to dry in the quick March winds.

For now at last the cold brutal winds of February had changed their tone and lost their gutting-knife edge.

But they blew harder still if anything, scattering gulls high and low above splintering seas, tearing the water into white webs of salt; drying out the winter woodpiles, so that up in the country Peter Hughes started to look at his fences. Then the farmers began ploughing in earnest, turning up clods which soon blew dust; and even if they found the right weather in this many-weathered month of the year, the older ones would wait until the moon was waxing rather than waning before they sowed a single seed of barley or oats.

From the Burn Woods and Balcaskie came the harsh cracked cawing of the crows, requieming the brown fields to resurrection. The sound entered the milky skull of old Leebie like a distant wind, dislodging one of her many pieces of parochial wisdom.

> *On the first day of March*
> *The crow begins to search.*

Then she added that no self-respecting rook, on the other hand, would deign to dream of nest building until the third Sunday in the third month.

> *On God's third third the rook*
> *Bestirs himself to look.*

Dog Mercury was now out in the woods, pussywillows appeared, the lesser celandines and coltsfoot were in flower. Pale primroses were born to die unmarried on the braes, and daffodils, shaming the swallow, brightened the breezes with their shining brass bugles, the violets passing like the sweetness of sad music on the sea-winds. The small tortoise-shell butterfly and the first dive-bombing bee droning low over the ground, made me stop dead in my tracks and look and listen, suddenly remembering the summer.

'Can you plant your foot on nine daisies at one go?' Leebie liked to say. 'If you can't, then don't tell me that the spring has come.'

But I was looking for tadpoles, not for daisies or daffodils. The frogs that had lain like blotched stones, sunk beneath layers of mud, now rose like bog kings from their own spawn, the black jellies floating among reeds and grasses to be eaten by anything that moved. Whatever was not eaten spawned, so that soon last summer's jam jars were alive with tadpoles, not one of which ever once performed the much hoped for metamorphosis, but stayed as they were—ugly black shooting stars with just a slow tendency to become quarter-comets, wandering aimlessly about the neutral curved space of their glassy universe.

Down on the shore, in the quieter weather, the tide was creeping up the dry stones of the beach; the water, which had been wintrily muddy in the evenings, in the mornings became clear as glass; and scum could be seen now floating free on the flood-tide. Then the first green water of the year appeared, occurring when there was a fresh wind blowing from the north-westward. The sea turned a living blue, with far out the long strips of vivid dark green which could never be seen in winter. In the rock pools, where baby Porcelain crabs scuttled like loose thumb-nails, the green sleet started to grow, and the whelks to gather in clusters. At low tide the broad blades of the oar-weed tangles were exposed, listlessly lapping above the water like aimless eels, indicating that the tide was going further and further back. And far out on the firth the gannets were ploughing round the Bass, and the birds were threading past each other in the great pageant of migration—the fieldfares flying back to Norway while the settling shelducks closed their wings for the first time on the coast, their arrival established.

I knew for sure that spring had come only when grandfather came in after the last haul of winter herring and took me down to the shallow area called Buckland to look for troonts. These were sticklebacks, which swam into Buckland on a big tide in the month of March. The females grandfather called 'baggies', showing me their distended bellies full of eggs about to spawn. Always they died during the night, and if we came down early in the morning we found them lying lifeless for lack of oxygen in the water, their big upturned bellies like floating graveyards under the sky. But the males, called 'doctors', with their red fronts, usually survived, so we took them home to be kept in jars of fresh water in the house, often for many months, and always outliving my tadpoles.

We looked also for butterfish and granny fish, and for the lumpsuckers which grandfather called 'paddles'. Sometimes they came in shore as early as the middle of February, and now cast their skins and prepared for spawning in the lamb-like days of late March or the calm weather of early April. Grandfather showed me their eggs once in a crack between two rocks, guarded by a male fish which lunged at his pointing hand like a living blade. But when caught on rocks between tides by the suckers on their bellies, they showed no interest at all in their audience, and we left them there to wait for the next sea. Back at home with grandfather, I felt sudden rising surges of desire to get outdoors again. A terrific feeling of well-being drove me up clothes poles to hang there, hugging them tightly between my legs, screaming silently at the sky; sent me racing back down to the sea, where I ducked my bursting head into the waves, drew it out again gasping madly for air, and shook it about wildly, laughing like a lark.

The vernal equinox passed, with daylight now strong in the sky at teatime, the stars of Orion bestriding the Bass at sunset—and with the equinox the terrible storms which had my grandmother and Leebie up at the windows the whole day, and my mother and aunts wide awake in their beds, their minds tossing on the firth, where grandfather and his sons bobbed like human corks with just several spars of wood between them and the bucking white bull of the sea.

MARCH

During the winter fishing the men were sailing in and out of the harbour every night and morning. Grandfather wanted to take me to the night-fishing, but the women held up their palms in holy horror. I asked to be taken to the anchored nets instead to see the fish hauled in. But the anchored nets were shot only by the bauldies, the smaller motor boats. Grandfather did not anchor his nets, as the drift-nets, being eighteen score meshes deep, would have become entangled and torn on the seabed. The anchored nets were less than half as deep, six meshes for the smaller yawls, nine for the bauldies, with the bottom rope very thick to withstand the titanic tug of the tides. By the time I started school, the bauldies were using twelve score nets, with very thick ropes, there being six nets between anchors in a week of neap tides, and only five between anchors on a big tide week. I learned all about this from The Dyker, who never went with the drifters.

What I liked best of all about the winter drifting was seeing the fishermen every day. They seldom took much food with them in the winter, preferring to leave eating until they came into harbour and up to their houses. Still, I sometimes went with my mother to buy a quick round of stores for the night-fishing boats. Eggs at a penny each if they were pickled, sevenpence for a dozen, and eightpence or ninepence a pound for steak. Once, when the men were too busy to come ashore, I took the box of stores down into the boat, and the cook, not much older than myself, fried me an egg. He cleaned the cast iron frying pan with steam from the *Maggie Main*'s boiler, banged it down on the black lacquered stove, and cooked me my first meal at sea, though the boat was only two inches from the pier and was scarcely afloat on an ebb tide. These were my moments of living closely to the work-life of the sea.

But as the shoals moved eastwards along the shore, everyone knew that the winter herring was coming to an end. Old George, standing at his window in the old house, watched the fleet coming home in the last days of March.

'Here come the Ishmaelites,' he said. 'They never died a winter yet, God be praised.'

Some knack of knowing told him that the winter fishing was over, and that when next the men went out to sea, they would be taking with them the spring lines for the deep-diving cod that moved invisibly in their cold soundless shoals.

APRIL

No-one told me about going to school.

I remember no warnings, no cushioning hints that freedom fell away from us at the age of five. One morning I simply woke up and found myself there, surrounded by faces I had never known, voices unfamiliar, shapes that made no sense.

What are the pieces that remain, still standing out in some sort of relief, their definition undimmed by the passing years which have gone out themselves like lights, one by one?

The smells.

The smells remain. Still sticking inside my skull, naked and sharp as electric bulbs, bringing into prominence the dusty old corridors and corners of the brain.

Always the smell of new varnish opens up these closed old cells, not dead as I imagined them to be, but still frighteningly jailored by the turnkeys of the present—the action of a pen upon blank paper, the saying of a name long unmentioned, the echoes stirring in an empty room.

Our desks had been varnished for the start of the new term, but nothing could conceal their dismal and dismaying oldness. Old oak they had been made from, older than Epp's coffin and Epp herself who had sat at them perhaps, these solid slabs of oakwood, brutally banged together to form mantraps for boys and girls, to keep us sitting in rows, two by two, like the animals in the ark; sealed in from the great flood of unknowing that raged around the edges of our lives.

So we sat there, heads upright, faces to the front, torsos and calves perpendicular with the walls, thighs aligned to the plane of the ceiling, feet flat on the floor, toes together. We sat thus, in the shapes of broken crosses, for the next seven years. We sat and sat—and grew into the angles of our desks, and the wood of the desks, dead coffinwood, grew into our souls.

The varnish struck match after match in my mind even then, though I never paused, in those dark little rooms of my head, to analyse the images as they exploded into light. Epp's box floated back into the haven of childhood from which it had been pushed out like a burial ship, and the friendly spring scents of the *Maggie Main*, newly varnished in April, merged again with the smells from the boatshed, where the builders fell like woodworm through the ruined ribs of their skeleton craft. And old Hodgie Dickson worked and worked at his daily death, the back of his head a blank wall and the front of his skull staring with the eyes of Tom Tarvit. The whole classroom was a hot suffocating varnished coffin, newly made—for whom?

> *You will go to hell. Your throat will be like the Sahara.*
> *You will be smoked like a kipper. And not one drop of water will you get.*

Epp's mouth was closed by Lisa Leslie, who bandaged the sneering jaw, placing a knot at the top of her white dead head. Like the bow on the head of the little girl in front of me. Lisa Leslie then varnished Epp for her coffin. Ah, but she could never varnish HoneyBunch and stiffen her like dead glazed wood. HoneyBunch walked tall and free and supple as larch through the waves, and would be washed only by Alec Fergusson, who baptized me with the living sea and mended his punctures in his back garden. They came crazily at me, all of them, out of the grain of the wood. Kate the Kist lay down on my desk and demanded to have her measurements taken.

> *One, two, three, four . . .*
> *Twelve inches one foot, three feet one yard.*
> *Six feet . . .*
> *Six feet long, six feet deep.*
> *Six feet under.*
> *Perpendicular. Horizontal.*
> *The days of our years are three score years and ten.*

'Waken up there, boy! Write this down on your slate with your chalk.'

The smell of chalk.

Chalkdust trapped in the slanted sunbeams that pierced the shades of our prison-house. Clouds of chalkdust from the blackboard settling on the teachers' hair and clothes, powdering their flowery smocks with a malignant moss till they looked like faded old dusters.

'Stop chewing that chalk, boy, it's for your brain not for your belly!'

Down onto our slates went the first words, the first chalk cells of literacy that would multiply and grow.

Fish, star, starfish. Gull, sea, seagull. Verse and universe. God and the Devil—flying over the rooftops, over the shaky slates of the school on his sooty pinions, the crumbs of sinners falling in flakes from his jaws, gouged gobbets of eyes falling like fish-heads into the waves.

APRIL

God is love.

'No, that is wrong. "Love" should be written with a capital. Don't you know what love is, you dunderhead? Take that!'

The first blow.

The first unkindly cuff to the head. Not delivered because of disobedience, impudence or sloth, but because of love spelt with a small letter. *God is Love.* And a red raging rose on the side of my face where my ear was. Miss McNeil's hand rubbed out the offending letter from my slate and replaced it with a rigid right-angled Pythagorean capital. Her fingers were caked with chalk-dust, like the corpse-white unringed fingers of old Epp as she gripped the poker in her anger, as she lay wreathed in white to the wrists, ringless in death as in her life. Flour like a dusting of chalk on Mrs Guthrie's wedding-ring as Lisa Leslie removed it before preparing Mrs Guthrie for the ground. Flour turning into chalk, bread into stones. *God is Love.*

The strange smells of other bodies.

I had never before been so close to so many people in such large and sweating numbers, in such hot and stifling conditions, heavy with varnish and chalk; bodies that carried around with them the odours of antiseptic sinks, bottles of ink, strips of plasticine, pots of glue. The farm boys, on the other hand, reeked of dung, which we thought greatly inferior to our own tar-and-salt smells of the fishing boats. They came clumping in from the country, the children of the farms, wearing huge muddy boots and question-marks for faces. They slammed themselves into their desks, which were much too small for them even from the very first day, and stared dazedly into space. None of them was ever able to answer any questions.

I sat near the bottom of the class myself, next to a farm boy called Bert Mackay.

'What's a young horse called, Mackay?' the teacher asked.

The silence started up at once, cruel as pain. The teacher repeated the question. The silence insisted.

I felt Mackay's head near to mine begin to blow up red with the baffled effort to discover within itself a piece of information that simply wasn't there. The question-mark on his face contorted, became a corkscrew.

'Answer my question, boy. What do you call a young horse?'

I made to help him.

'Be quiet there, boy! Do you imagine that if *you* were struggling with the plough, he would lift a finger to help *you*?'

Bertie breathed like a horse, straining to wrench out of the muddy soil of his mind a question too heavy for him to tackle. He sweated and stank. The rich ripe smells of the earth steamed out of his lumpy carcass with the fury of his thinking. But no answer came forth.

'He's fit for carting dung, that's all,' sneered the teacher.

George Young, the King of Dung.

'All right then, we'll give him an easy one. What's a young cat called?'

'A kitten, miss.'

Blind pink mouths mewing for mercy to the blind blue sky and McCreevie's thick grinning head breaking open with his laughter.

I'll cut your head off, I will.
I'll break your head and feed your brains to the fish.

'What did he say, boy?'

'McCreevie, miss.'

'What? Are you drivelling or dreaming? Supposed to be helping him too. Take that!'

The heavy hand of schooling, beating away the dreams of dawn, day by day.

'How can you prove that the earth is round?'

Prove to you that you're not here.

'What are monsoons?'

And typhoons and baboons and teaspoons.

'Who fell at Flodden?'

Stood where thousands fell.

'Lord, bless our food and make us good.'

Good cod roes! Good God knows!

'Oh Genevieve, sweet Genevieve!'

Old Jean Jeff's a pickle deaf.

'You're snail-slow, boy!'

A good drink of snail-slime and you'll be fine.

'Are you blind, boy? Have you no brains in your head?'

Break open your head. Feed your brains to the fish.
God is Love.

The school day began with the uninhibited life of the playground, where flocks of youngsters wheeled and whirled, diving like gannets in the gladitorial amphitheatre of the sea.

On my first day I was beset by colonies of bigger boys and girls who preyed on me without mercy. I left my mother's hand and walked sullenly through the iron gates of the school. At once they zoomed in on me. Arms spread stiffly like wings, they swooped and soared, their goggle-eyes stabbing as they advanced, their clattering tongues machine-gunning me dead with fear before they closed. Dog-faced dog-fighters, gull-hungry for attack, they struck, tore, bit, clung. They swung from the twin ends of my long knitted scarf till my tongue turned black. They knocked me breathless to the hard ground. Their faces jostled in the sky like bunches of bruised fruits, and their busy hands rifled my pockets to take whatever could be found to be eaten. Then they were off and I was initiated.

The boys of Bert Mackay's kidney, who sat through most of their schooling like dumb bemused beetroots, pulled at and poked by their teachers, made up for this daily humiliation in the cut-and-thrust of the playground. Ink-stained, fat fingers that could scarcely hold a pen let alone form a letter, bunched themselves suddenly into flying fists, delivering punches with all the zest of beings goaded beyond their natural forbearance. Heads bent and bowed in disgrace for most of the day tossed like butting bulls. Tongues that could not articulate a single sentence in class became boisterous bells, pealing out of the dim noisy belfries of their empty heads. And shuffling, heavy-booted feet sent footballs crashing like cannonshot into the wall of the school.

The girls, who simpered through the lessons in a smarter, soapier silence, demure dolls most of them, carried on their sedater games in their own playground, separated from the boys' playing area by a high brick wall and a solid door with a rusted lock. Breaking school rules, we would scale the wall, and watch the girls playing at their beds, their skipping-ropes, their rhymes and roundelays.

> *Salt, pepper, vinegar, mustard,*
> *Miss McNeil's got a face like custard.*

Sometimes, daring the dread of the belt, we dreeped down onto the girls' side of the wall in furtive little forays, and before they knew what was happening, we were among them and upon them. Their shrill silvery screams rippled like summer lightning. We eyed with intent amusement their long white thighs flashing above the rumpled stockings, the flowered dresses, skirts and pinafores.

A TWELVEMONTH AND A DAY

Heaven help me, I'm a martyr,
Kiss me quick or I'll grab your garter.

I never won a garter, but once I watched a successful operation from the wall, my heart thumping with glee at the thought of imprisoning a handful of that white forbidden flesh so as to remove the garter and come home in triumph to the boys' side.

Three of the boys in my class earned themselves lasting immortality in that way. Bert Mackay, the farm boy from Abercrombie, was one, and Gollie Gowans and Peem Peattie went with him on that run. They chose the three nearest girls who had just made themselves dizzy from their ring-o'-roses spin, and were flying towards our wall at a drunken tangent. But these girls were no easy prey—they were not Sunday schoolers and they did not sit smirking at the top of their class under masses of pink bows. Fishergirls they were, with loose salty tongues and rough and tumbling hair. The boys sprang at them, netting them neatly in their own sudden circle. The challenge was then thrown. The kiss or the garter. Capitulation was unknown in that long gone society where death before dishonour was the maiden's forlorn cry. The whippiest of these forlorn ones lashed out at Bert Mackay with a cracking slap, and the other two distressed damsels defended themselves with teeth and talons. Gollie was hauled to the ground by his blonde hair. The two rings closed and crunched, Peem disappearing between them. Fists and feet flew in a furious grapple, and the long white legs kicked against their deflowering as the Battle of the Garter was fought and won. The three heroes of the hour ran for the wall, pursued by the outraged screams of every girl in the school. Willing hands were waiting to haul them to safety, to touch their glory, and over the top they came. They pulled the garters over their tousled hair, stretching them across their victorious brows for headbands, and now, whooping like braves who had taken their first scalps, faces scratched, lips like bleeding berries, shirts and trousers torn, they war-danced round and round the playground to the hysterical hootings of the jubilant male tribe.

The bell rang then, hammering us into submission.

'Line up!'

A hundred unruly voices stilled and the conflict of bodies came miraculously together in two long lines, the animals going into the ark.

Eternal Father, strong to save,
Whose voice hath bound the restless wave.

The headmaster barked an order and in we went, like mice beneath his hawkish nose and eye, the bristling ginger moustache, the sharp jaw. Heads down, staring at his checked plus-fours for which we were quickly to discover an unrepeatable name, we filed into our classrooms.

'Good morning, boys and girls.'

'Good morning, Miss McNeil.'

'All stand. Our Father...'

> *Which art in heffen*
> *Hallo pee thigh name*
> *Thigh kinktom come*
> *Thigh will pee ton*
> *On earth as it ish in heffen*
> *Giff us this tay our taily prett*
> *Ant forgiff us our tetts*
> *As wee forgiff our tettors*
> *Ant leet us not into temptation*
> *Putt teliffer us from eefill*
> *For thighn ish the kinktom*
> *Ant the power ant the clory*
> *Foreffer*
> *Amen*

'Amen.'

Miss McNeil. Highland Miss McNeil. Amen for Highland Mary, who taught me my ABC on a broken slate by the strength of her chalky ringless fingers, fleshless now in the ground, where Mrs Guthrie smiles on.

She taught me to know mine end and the measure of my years, how frail a thing I am.

'What is the chief end of man?'

'The chief end of man is to glorify God and to enjoy him forever.'

'With a capital H.'

'Yes.'

'And say "Miss McNeil".'

Enjoy Him forever, Miss McNeil, now a spinsterish skeleton sprinkled with daisies in that green mound by the sea.

Enjoy Him Forever.

Amen. Amen. Amen.

Miss McNeil, with the thick tweeds and the thick chestnut shoes and the thick-ribbed stockings like the sandbars on the beach when the tide has ebbed, how quickly your tide went out, Highland Miss McNeil!

'Miss McNeil's dead!' buzzed Gollie Gowans as he bombed his way past me at battle-speed across the playground, loosing off bullets at the Red Baron, who went into a nose-dive and revealed himself as Peem Peattie fighting in flames at my feet.

'What do you mean?' I shouted after him.

Gollie tilted his wings, banked dangerously, and came bombing back up the playground to make sure Peem was dead.

'Miss McNeil's dead!' he screeched again.

He whizzed by on the second run, his hands juddering on his guns. Peem went into paroxysms.

'Died in her sleep last night.'

Died on the air as Gollie headed for home and became a speck in the fields. Peem gave a final convulsive twitch, giggled at the sky and lay still, his grinning jaw hanging open like McCreevie's.

Dead.

I muttered the word to myself several times over, standing quite still in the heavy silence Gollie had left in his wake. The Red Baron bundled his books back into his schoolbag. How could those ribbed stockings and those hairy tweeds be dead? Someone had been inside them all the time, Miss McNeil whom Lisa Leslie would wash, gone now with Epp and old Hodgie into the black back of beyond where the children never come.

Dead, dead, dead.

It had the sound of a heavy door slammed shut in my face, that word, behind which lay the lost unknowable lives of people, their echoes reverberating out of time.

Amen Amen Amen

Miss McNeil was replaced at short notice by Miss Quinney, an Englishwoman who, I now realise, was young, though her thick-rimmed glasses and gravel-lined larynx concealed this fact from the eye of childhood. She hated our local accent, thought it brutish and vulgar, and tried to beat it out of us in class. Keep your gutter-tongue for the gutter, she used to tell us.

'What am I pointing to on the map, boy?' she asked me.

'Ireland, miss.'

'I know that, you clothead. What part of Ireland?'

I saw a problem here, and muttered into my boots the term which so amused us.

'The Erse of Ireland, miss.'

'Speak up, boy, I can hardly hear you!'

Just a little louder this time, the laugh quivering like a bubble in my mouth, the class stirring with anticipated pleasure.

'Are you talking Scots or what?' she roared. 'Shout it at me in English, you mumbling little moron. Go on, shout!'

'The Arse of Ireland!'

The bubble burst, the class erupted.

There was a boy in my class who had moved to St Monans from Buckhaven, further down the coast. My grandfather, like all the other fishermen, rather despised the Buckhaven men as a timid lot when it came to going to sea, and so their sons had to bear the sins of the fathers shouted in their ears as insults. Buckhaven folk were known to us simply as Buckers. But when Miss Quinney heard me shout across the playground to this boy that he was 'just a stupid Bucker', she quickly arrived at the not unreasonable conclusion that I was a bad-mouthed brat, beyond saving. After that she ignored me.

We were passed on to Miss Hughie, whom we called Shuggie.

Shuggie was a religious maniac, who had weighed the Old Testament in one hand and the New in the other and found the latter to be wanting. So she threw it away. She measured Zion with a ruler.

A stuffed stork stood on one tireless leg in a long glass case in the corner of her classroom. She directed our attention to this bird at once.

'Now children, there is a silly superstition that little girls and boys are brought to their parents' homes by the stork. That, of course, is just an old wife's tale. You can all of you see this stork in the corner, can't you?'

We looked at it.

We looked at it every day of our lives. We looked at it for the first time that day with special interest.

'Now does that bird look remotely capable to you of bringing a baby boy or girl through your mother's front door, or down your chimney?'

We had to admit that it seemed improbable.

'So where do little boys and girls come from then?'

My hand shot up.

'Lisa Leslie, miss.'

'Don't be so stupid, and pay attention to the question!'

Silence.

Then suddenly I remembered.

'Please, miss.'

'Yes?'

'Boys from the Bass and girls from the May, miss.'

The class collapsed while Shuggie raged.

'You blasphemous young brat, it's perfectly obvious where *you* came from, and where you'll be going to!'

> *You will go to hell. And not one drop of water will you get to cool your burning tongue.*

Lessons all came to the same thing in Shuggie's class.

History: *In the beginning God created the heaven and the earth.* Art: *And God saw everything that he had made, and behold it was very good.* Biology: *And out of the rib which the Lord God had taken from man, made he a woman.* Geography: *And he placed at the east of the garden of Eden a cherubim and a flaming sword.* Arithmetic: *Six days shalt thou labour and do all thy work.*

All the humanities she gave us in one sentence.

> *For dust thou art and unto dust thou shalt return.*

So Shuggie kept us in the wilderness; we never came near to Canaan. But a retiral further up the school brought a new teacher to the village, and Miss Balsilbie came like a daughter of Zion to give us glimpses of the promised land.

When she swept through the pale green door of Room Five at the start of the new session, I felt my toes tingle and my tongue cleave to the roof of my mouth. HoneyBunch walked into the waves and the sea washed her clean to the bone. She never came out again. Miss Balsilbie was taller, taller far than HoneyBunch, and needed no beadle with a scrubbing board to mend her between punctures, to baptize her into acceptance by the twitching noses of Class Five. She was all sweet in my nostrils, Miss Balsilbie, carrying continents in the scented palm of her hand. The perfumes of the east were flung from her black hair, scattered by the corn-sowing wave of her arm as she welcomed us to her new kingdom, the garden of delights, and we her open-mouthed subjects, too tattered and untaught to say a word.

Roses are what I remember.

White ones.

Miss Balsilbie's blouses were white roses that fluffed and fell as she breathed, and the merest puff from an ungallant infant might have blown them clean off her back. What would happen should all those soft and snow-crimped petals fall fluttering to the floor of the classroom?

But Miss Balsilbie carried her white roses all round the room, visiting each desk in turn. When she came to me I was beating my head against the blind brutal wall of my sums, which I could never do easily or well. My jotter was a mass of erasions and errors, filthy with ignorance. She leaned over me, reaching for the page. I hid my inky, nail-bitten fingers between my knees. The rose-petals brushed my cheek, whispered against the scarred lid of my ugly, lumpish desk. I held my breath as tightly as I could. Miss Balsilbie reached out her white, swansnecked, swansdowned arm, and her hand touched my exercise book. She held a long, beautifully sharpened pencil between her fingers, a red pencil. Her nails were polished a vivid scarlet, like strawberries, like blushing blood-red moons. No scars from the gutting-troughs warred with those milk-washed hands of hers.

> *How should I your true-love know*
> *From another one?*

Her pale blue veins ran like dim rivers in an undiscovered country, the land of lost content, the land of milk and honey. Georgina's wounded fingers were plucking music from the salt and glimmering strings of the sea, and I felt a hard knot tighten in my chest. But the scents from Miss Balsilbie flooded the firth, bathing HoneyBunch's bleached forgotten bones. Georgina was betrayed. My head swam.

'No, no dear,' she drawled, 'you don't know how to divide, do you? Here, let me show you.'

She squeezed herself into the desk beside me, tucking in her shimmering silk skirt. It rustled mysteriously like the quiet turn of the tide, fell over my knees in cool waves. It made me shiver.

'Goodness me, you are shaking, my poor boy. What in the world is the matter with you?'

She put down her pencil on my desk and placed her arm around me.

'You don't have to be frightened of me now, dear, do you? Even though you can't divide.'

She gave a tinkling little laugh and hugged me close, drew me towards the dazzling white world of the snowdrift. I sank into it, through the fluttering flakes and into the heart of the rose. When I came out of it, the day had changed irrevocably; another terrible beauty was born; my heart was as cold as ice. It belonged to Miss Balsilbie, Miss Balsilbie now my Snow Queen, queen of my crystal heart, why was your reign so short? Too short to let me understand the heart of the rose, you froze me until the day I could divide.

But by then it was too late.

Miss Balsilbie read us poetry.

> *Have you seen but a bright Lillie grow*
> *Before rude hands have touch'd it?*
> *Ha' you mark'd but the fall o' the Snow*
> *Before the Soil hath smutch'd it?*
> *Ha' you felt the wooll o' the Bever?*
> *Or Swans Downe ever?*
> *Or have smelt the bud o' the Brier?*
> *Or the Nard in the fire?*
> *Or have tasted the bag of the bee?*
> *O so white! O so soft! O so sweet is she!*

'Does that poem remind you of anyone, boys and girls?'

We gaped.

'Doesn't it make you think of someone?'

My heart beat hotly in its case of ice. I wanted to melt, to tell her. The voice continued, dreamily wooingly demanding of us the required response.

Do you think I'm slim, class? Write down in your jotters the word which applies to my complexion. Whom do you know whom that poem perfectly describes?

My hand rose shakily.

'It's you, miss.'

The roses in her bosom fluffed and she blushed.

'Only one clever boy in the class. Now tell me, why does it remind you of me?'

Words failed me then as I reached for understanding and fell back into the heart of the rose.

At bible reading time she recited portions of The Song of Solomon.

> *I am the rose of Sharon and the lily of the valleys.*
> *I am dark but comely, O ye daughters of Jerusalem.*
> *Stay me with flagons, comfort me with apples: for I*
> *am sick of love.*

It was on one of these occasions, when she was crooning the Song of Songs, that Mr Gourlay, the headmaster, came into the room. He saw the open bible on the teacher's desk and stopped what he was about to say.

'What's this?' he asked quietly.

'It's bible reading, Mr Gourlay,' said the teacher.

'Do you mean to tell me that you have actually been reading to your class from . . . from that?'

Miss Balsilbie gathered up her roses haughtily.

'Yes, Mr Gourlay, I do tell you that. And I can tell you what it is that I have been teaching from it, too.'

'No, don't bother. I shudder to imagine. Would you step outside a moment, please?'

The headmaster went out, and as Miss Balsilbie followed him, we heard him knocking on Miss Sangster's door, and his voice echoing along the empty corridor.

'Miss Sangster, would you leave Primary Six for several minutes, please, and come and look after this class? Miss Balsilbie, follow me to my room, if you would.'

We had our first encounter with the much feared Miss Sangster, the terror of the school, whom we had not expected to meet for another six months. She smirked at us sourly from behind her gold-rimmed glasses. Then she noticed the open book still on the teacher's desk. Her cheerless lips curled into a vicious sneer. She shut it slowly and deliberately, clasping it under her arms to her brittle bosom. Closing her eyes then, she rocked backwards and forwards on her thick polished heels, trembling in the throes of silent hysterical joy.

And so, Miss Balsilbie, you ravished my heart with one of your eyes, with one chain of your neck. Honey and milk were under your tongue, and the smell of your clothes was like the smell of Lebanon.

You were too good to last.

A garden enclosed, a spring shut up, a fountain concealed.

She had given us the apples of the trees of the wood, Miss Balsilbie, when our understanding was not yet ripe. So the headmaster banished her from the garden of delights, and the flaming sword of Miss Sangster's vengeance guarded the school gates. We never saw her again.

But Miss Sangster was waiting for us.

She was a long frozen leek of a woman, Miss Sangster, standing straight and hard as an undriven nail. From her coat-hanger shoulders her smock hung like a faded flag, covering her bony, crepe-stockinged shanks almost down to her ankle boots.

Even on her own head she had no mercy. The thin grey hair lay like ash on the pink skull. She parted it simply, without a shred of pity for her womanhood, shearing it just below the ears on either side, and leaving bare the reptilian nape of the neck. Her eyes were glittering pin-pricks under her glasses, her lips were pursed prunes. Vinegar ran in her veins and chalk in her arteries. She blew on the embers of dead days with her dusty breath, warming her cold fingers before the tired fires of life. These fingers of hers were always ringed with warts and plasters and little bandages. They were the broken hands of a loveless lady, the sex within her denied and defeated long ago. But with these very hands Miss Sangster beat us into daily submission.

She had a whole panoply of punishments in her armoury, every one of which we had learned to fear. The warty fingers would close on an ear, or a nose, or on a tuft of hair, and for relentless minutes at a stretch she would be tweaking and tugging for an answer. She slapped our faces, banged our heads against the wall, beat us on the backs of our legs if we did our sums wrong; she pressed our foreheads down onto the lids of our desks until our flesh took on the grain of the dead oak, and we wore it in our faces for the rest of the day.

Knuckle-jabs were her speciality, delivered to the vital organs with a hissing insult. She crept up from behind on an unsuspecting boy or girl, taut as a tiger. Bending one warty forefinger until the bone shone whitely through the parched skin, she drew back her elbow and let fly. Her arm thrust forward like a piston, dug deeply into a sleeping back. She had three favourite body blows: she attacked the spine itself, or the flesh just beneath the ribs, or she went for the kidneys. Rabbit-punches she threw out ten a minute, striking with the heel or the battle-axe edge of her hand sharply across the backs of our bowed necks.

It never once occurred to us to consider the moral or educational grounds of all this; it was her teaching style and an intrinsic part of the lessons she gave. Questions and answers were punctuated by the punches she landed, the smart slaps of her ruler, the stinging whiplash of her tongue.

Eleven sevens are seventy-seven, whacked across the knuckles. *Darnley died at Kirk o' Fields*, dented upon our heads. *Sheffield gives us steel*, hammered out on our hides. Miss Sangster was fists and fingers and feet.

But her worst instrument of torture was the belt.

At school, belts acquired the mythical fame of Notungs and Excaliburs, and teachers became legends in their lifetimes for the highly personalised styles in which they wielded their particular weapons. Annual belting averages were calculated, record punishments totted up, committed to memory, and passed from mouth to ear like the heroic deeds of yesterday. Mothers, fathers, aunts and uncles—all showed their scars obtained at the hands of teachers still in possession of that very same ground on which the older generation had been taught by the force of the tawse. Present fears were worsened by the horrible imaginings which preceded them and which continued to colour the truth long after it was plain and clear.

For instance, Miss Sangster's belt was generally agreed to be at least six yards long, the length, perhaps, of the average dragon's tail, hard with agony. But all of us could see that it could hardly have been more than twenty-four inches. It was a leathery lizard's tongue of a thing, forked at the end, the two thongs having split themselves in turn to form a four-tailer. It was popularly believed that she kept it steeping in a stone jar full of vinegar, which she kept in her room just for the purpose of increasing its bite. But I once looked into that stone jar on the window-shelf, only to discover that it contained nothing more than a jumble of broken coloured chalks.

In any event, the belt never left her person, because she wore it under the frayed flowers of her smock, draped across the shoulder and down her back. It was thus within easy reach, and when stung to an anger that could not be assuaged by the application of a finger-jab or a punch, she shot her hand between the two loose buttons of the smock, and whipped out the belt as if she were pulling a gun. Then she fired. She never even bothered to ask questions later.

So in many a playground battle, where tense gunfighters faced one another for the draw, the invisible weapon turned out to be Miss Sangster's tawse, the terror of the imagination, and instead of an air cruel with cordite fumes and the whang of bullets, we watched the last scenes of such dramas turn to farce. Wyatt Earp and Buffalo Bill held out their hands in mock misery, and each flogged the other to within an inch of his life. The glorious heroes then thrashed the air wildly with their palms or tucked them tightly into armpits or groin while they moaned and intoned.

> *Jessie James he died a gangster,*
> *Served him right for kissing Sangster.*

In her application of the belt, Miss Sangster's dedication knew no horizons. A girl would normally be let off with a straightforward licking on the open palm, executed without frill or flourish. The boys had no such maimed rites. For them she retained a repertoire of hoary tricks which she had been practising since the year dot.

She made us place one hand beneath the other, so that something of the sting would be felt even by the unbelted palm. Then the hands had to be switched around so that the bottom one could receive its proper due, even though it had had a foretaste of pain. Sometimes she told us to place our hands on the hard slabbish lids of our desks, knuckles against the wood, palms upwards. Then she brought down the belt side-on with a heartless thud.

She had a nasty trick of flicking it in such a way that it curled up around the wrist and arm, producing long red snaky weals. We swung our arms aloft like flaming windmills, desperately trying to cool the burning, and because we could not hold our pens properly after that, she thumped our heads with dictionaries, complaining bitterly about our inability to write, even with the benefit of a good belting behind us. We heard tales of astonishing atrocities carried out on boys who could not put pen to paper in the proper way. She jammed a pencil crossways between their fingers, the pencil resting on pinkie and forefinger and held fast by the two middle fingers. Then she thrashed and thrashed until the pencil broke. I never saw that done—but I believed in the story. I had to.

Occasionally a boy who had taken enough would jerk his outstretched hand away just as Miss Sangster's belt was coming down for the fifth or sixth time. If the belt struck her on the knee, she would be galvanized to uncontrolled fury like a machine gone mad. Then she would be lashing out with the leather at legs, arms, body, backside, head and ears, anything that could be reached—chasing the victim round and round the free standing blackboard until he was caught and beaten or ran right out of the door and into the fields, not to reappear until her white-hot wrath had died down once more to a slow constant smoulder.

What do I really remember from her? What are the roots that clutch out of the stony rubbish that she gave me, what fragments to shore against my ruins, torn down by time?

A few spellings. A few capitals and kings.

Open your sum books at the end. Put your hands behind your heads. What is the capital of Norway? Tell me the time on the clock. Tell me the date of the Battle of Pinkie. Tell me the sixth commandment.

Tell me where is fancy bred,
Or in the heart, or in the head?

Poor, lonely, unloved, unwed, unmanned, unwomaned, suffering Miss Sangster, who taught me compassion years too late—what was the point of your time spent in the classroom, beating banalities into us by the sweat of your brow, by the blood of our stripes, by six of the best, by the denial of your sex, by all that was uncouth, unholy, and utterly uneducating? Dear, dreadful, sweet and sour Miss Sangster, you passed on, out of Room Six, out of our lives, out of your own life, into the classless coffin-desked kirkyard, into the sea-bound ground that swallowed up your answers as of no account and left behind you only one eternal question.

So we were passed on from miss to miss, year by year; booted and balaclavad, coughing and cod-liver-oiled in the winter, shirt-sleeved and sweating in the summer; harelipped, stuttering, gap-toothed, warted and all. We threw up our bean-bags and caught them on our heads. We sloped our writing towards the door. We chanted our tables, touched our toes, calculated the price of carrots, parsed our nouns, prayed for our king, suffered under Miss Sangster, brass voices and the belt, and came out into the light at the end of that dreary tunnel relatively unchanged. We had grown skins, perhaps, to make us insensitive to dreariness without vision. In the coarse curriculum that we followed there had been little to awaken the sleeping imagination, and those bunned and bespectacled old dears who administered it unto us and belted us about the bare legs—they knew nothing of love and all their lives were rehearsing for death.

We rarely rebelled against them.

But when I was a very small arrival at school, I heard stories from further up the tunnel concerning the deeds of the terrible One-Gallus Gang. Galluses were braces, which we wore if we were unlucky enough not to be the owner of a striped, elasticated belt with a snake-clasp. The members of the One-Gallus Gang resolutely proclaimed their individuality by snipping off one of the two front straps of their braces, and pulling down the remaining strap crosswise down the chest. This simple sartorial alteration lent them an air of astonishing disreputability which they studied to deserve.

They did no homework, brought no books, gave no quarter. When they came to school, which they did only when they chose, they beat up the headmaster and held hostage their classmates in the bathrooms. They turned on taps, redrew the map of the world and drank ink through straws. But most of their time they spent well away from school avoiding the Whipper-in, which is what we called the school Attendance Officer.

One day they lay in wait for him as he pursued his rounds up in the country. When they ambushed him near Balcaskie, they sank him up to his head in Peter Hughes's dungpit, tied him up and brought him back to the village in a wheelbarrow. There they tied his shoelaces together and tossed him into the harbour at low tide. Then they returned in triumph to raid the school gardens. In broad afternoon they dug up every dreel of potatoes planted by Primary Four, pelting the teachers with clods when they tried to save the field from spoliation. The headmaster had to call the policeman, who arrived transporting a dripping Whipper-in on the back of his bike.

The One-Gallus Gang fought a valiant rearguard action all the way. They bore off all the potatoes in their wheelbarrow, built a huge beacon on the beach opposite the kirk, which burned for three days and nights, and there they roasted every last potato, consuming the entire school harvest of that year. Worse: they cut off dogs' heads for fun, crucified cats and roasted them along with the tatties. They dug up the bones of buried teachers who had belted their great-grandfathers, and they drank rum out of their skulls, washing down their seventy-two hour long supper with contraband spirit.

What was truth and what was fantasy in these local legends is hardly difficult to say. What *is* true is that the gang ended up at the court in Cupar, was disbanded and sent to Borstal. My mother told me that two of them went to the Marship. There had been nine members in the gang—each of them ten years old.

After that it was forbidden even to mention their name or the fact that they had even existed, for fear that even a whisper might confer immortality on so diabolical a crew. But whispers indeed worked the much feared miracle of resurrection, for the stories about them are as alive in my mind now as they were many years ago. Maybe more so.

When the spring madness entered our blood all of us were tempted to play the truant. The yawls were hauled up the brae and into the field opposite the school, ready for tarring. It was then that Gollie and Peem and myself heard the call of the sea, and answered.

At play-time we stole out of the gates, following our shadows. The yawls were high up on trestles like wooden horses, their hulls higher than our heads could reach. They were cratered with barnacles and slimy with weed. We clambered up the rough ladder, sliding under the tarpaulin that kept the April rains out of the boat. Then we hauled up the ladder after us and curled up in the boat's belly, sealing ourselves off from the world. We let in just a single blue chink of sky. There we lay for the rest of the day that had become a secret shared between ourselves, playing cards, eating our jam pieces and waiting for the night to fall, when we would drop out of the boat in a wicked litter, swing open the school gates, and signal to the sails waiting out there in the darkened firth. They would glide inshore like sharks' fins and the towers of Troy would fall in flaming ruin.

The yawls had been hauled up all the winter from storms, and were cleaned out in April and made ready for sea. The Dyker came along on his bike and took me back with him to help him prepare his own little sailing yawl for the spring fishing. It was a warm day, just right for spreading the tar thickly to the insides of the boat. But first it had to be washed out and wiped dry, and that was my job. When he came back with the tar, the Dyker pulled a long face and said that I had scrubbed and cleaned the yawl much too thoroughly.

'It'll leak, laddie,' is what he said. 'Dust and tar holds a yawl together. You've left no dirt at all.'

We painted the outer topsides green to finish with, which is the way he liked it to be done, and then we left it to dry. The next day I went back with grandfather to help the Dyker move the boat down to the shore. They used pit-props as rollers to slide her down the East Green and into the water. As soon as it touched the spring tide the Dyker was in on all fours busily hunting for leaks. As he had prophesied, some last touches of tar had to be applied to patch up the damage caused by my keenness with the scrubbing brush. At last the Dyker pronounced himself satisfied, and grandfather hurried home with me to see to the spring cleaning of the *Maggie Main*—a much bigger job.

Spring cleaning was always a great occasion.

My head among chimney-pots and the cold sunlit breezes, I perched high up on a mountain of white nets which were being bumped along by horse and cart to the mouth of the burn. There they were spread out among bubbles and boulders in the clear fresh water to wash away the weed and scum of a winter at sea. They were wheeled up the brae then to the backyard for boiling and mending. The *Maggie Main* had to have her boiler cleaned out and overhauled, the gear was polished, the stove lacquered, the cabin revarnished and its roof white-enamelled so that it caught the sun in its flight and threw it up the firth. Grandfather handed me a scrubbing brush and said he would give me a shilling for cleaning the main deck and hatches and the commons round the hold. But he told me he would

89

take off a farthing for every single fish-scale which he found on board after I had finished. I spent two days scrubbing and wiping and picking clean, and at the end of it I searched the deck malevolently, my blood thirsting for the merest stray scale which might deprive me of the smallest part of a copper. I earned my shilling intact. The boat then took on new ballast, tar was applied, and she was left to dry.

Grandfather was seldom at rest.

But on some brief day between the herring and the line fishing, when the *Maggie Main* was drying and April was greening the ground, he took me for a long walk up into the country.

We went up the old Black Road to Balcaskie, through Chae Marr's elms that were starting now to make some little show of green, while Chae himself lay white and anonymous in the black earth, not to come into colour ever again, except when he walked my dreams. The Black Road was lined with ash trees, their sooty seeds rattling in blackened bunches—the keys to a year that had groaned shut like a prison door. But their new leaves were springing open, unlocked by the light, and the lime trees too were putting up their green window panes and the sun was pouring through, emerald and gold mingling in the morning light. Oak buds were drops of blood spilt on the blue, bird's-egg sky, against which the chestnut's quiet fingers were already moving. Up in Balcaskie the silver birches stood like sea-gods among golden waves of flowers which they showered back to the ground like spray. And beyond Balcaskie grandfather took me further than I had ever been before from the sea—to Balcormo Den, deep and high upland into the country, where the firth itself was just a bright lane in the distance between fields and sky, the short springing turf was bedazzled by the yellow suns of dandelions, and marsh-marigolds were spilling steeply into the burn.

We came to an old wooden gate in a drystone dyke.

Near it was a kingly beech, spread out across a hundred years. There were no leaves on it yet, but its strong smooth bark was engraved with dates and initials, bound by arrow-pierced hearts. Young folk, their fancies lightly turning to thoughts of one another, had come up here in Aprils long trodden out beneath the floor of the fields, and had carved on this tree the fragrant wounds of love. Time had taken away the sweetness of their suffering, and had given them darker griefs to bear. They had married, had children, worked all their lives, grown old and died. But the wounds in the wood refused to heal, as though the tree knew that love was the most tragic thing in the world and its loss cruel as the grave.

On the other side of the gate from the beech the burn slipped under an arched bridge. Between its curved keystones and the fly-dimpled surface the swallows flitted like darts. As we stood there between the beech and the bridge, we saw an old man come walking over the fields towards us. He was bent with the burden of his years and seemed to be carrying the sky on his back. His eyes were fixed on the ground. We waited and waited until he reached us. He propped his walking stick against the beech and leaned heavily on the other side of the gate, out of breath. The three of us just stood there while the birds whistled and the occasional bee buzzed by.

'Aye,' he said at last. 'Aye, aye.'

It was not a greeting. He was simply recognising that the world and its ways altered and men and women grew older, while the things around us never changed. He was half sharing that simple recognition with my grandfather, and something of their understanding touched me then, at once and forever.

'Aye,' said grandfather.

That was all he said, my grandfather who loved to talk.

I looked at the two of them secretly as they nodded to one another, smiling and looking away. The old man's eyes went back to his feet. Friends of his had gone out long since like the ghosts of these dandelions—faces fading till only the sky showed through, their time ticked round to the last breath and their golden heads drifted like seeds across the fields. I stared hard at the old man. He seemed to me to be seeing not the flowers at all, but that dim mustering-ground for immortality where all those young lovers who had heard the cuckoo and made daisy-chains for slender necks were gathered now, waiting.

But he said no more, and grandfather uttered never another word himself. The two of them were at peace, communing with the afternoon, their share of the world. So the three of us waited while the sun crossed the sky and the great beech bore a century in its branches and love in its bark like lichen, and beneath the bridge, where the light-footed lads and the rose-lipped girls had stood and kissed each other, the swallows sped like vanished thoughts, quick bright things come to confusion. It was in that one extended moment, spread out in time like a tree, that the first anxiety was born, a twinge from a nerve deeper than that touched by the weird old men and women of our town, an aching and a sadness without a single identifiable object. Wouldn't it have been better to have been Miss Sangster and not to have known love at all, than to have lost the world?

A TWELVEMONTH AND A DAY

With rue my heart is laden
For golden friends I had,
For many a rose-lipt maiden
And many a lightfoot lad.

By brooks too broad for leaping
The lightfoot boys are laid;
The rose-lipt girls are sleeping
In fields where roses fade.

When we came back home in the late afternoon, a secret corner of me had grown as old as the very old man from Balcormo Den, whose name we never knew, and who had said nothing—yet who had been perfectly at ease with my grandfather, and who had passed on to me something of those thoughts that lie too deep for tears.

With the glass high on old George's wall and easterly winds coming in from the firth, the thick weather now swept along the shore. But instead of the brooding banks of grey that lingered in the winter months, the fogs of April were white and patchy, with bays of clear weather between the horns of mist. The stirring fields felt the restlessness in the air, with its haars and clear weathers catching nostril and eye. Under the strong winds the sea became very dark blue, the horizon sharp as a razor.

Early in the month a hazy purplish-brown streak like thin smoke formed itself into a line just above the horizon's edge, from the southeast up to the north-eastward, and the cold became very cutting, so that the old men sought the shelter of the dykes and the thick harbour walls to carry on their conversations. All during the hours that this haar lasted there was a splendid clearness. George took down his telescope, opened his window, and pointed the glass at the May Island, its cliffs like blue icebergs in the choppy sea. The lighthouse keeper was standing at his cottage, and his shadow was sharp and black on the whitewashed wall.

'In this sort of weather you can see the shadow of a seabird on the water thirteen miles away,' said George.

One morning I was standing in the yard with grandfather just as he was preparing to go off to the lines. It was the first day of the Easter holidays, just before nine-o'-clock. I realised that I was not at school and started to shout for joy.

'Ssh!' whispered grandfather suddenly gripping my arm. 'Listen.'

A second later there was a very slight splash from the rocks a hundred yards away.

APRIL

'It's the tide-cry,' he said. 'That's the first time I've heard it this year, and that's the tide I'm going on.'

When there was low water and a big tide and the sea was flat calm without a wind, the silence would be broken in this way by the rustle of a small wave moving the tangle-blades or running up the slope of a skelly to fall back over the steep landward edge of the rock. This was the tide-wave's first arrival as the ebb changed through slack water to flow. That split second in which the tide turned could never be heard in the winter time. My grandfather had heard it in his blood a single second before it happened.

By the time Easter came round there were no men at home, so my mother took me along to the braes to roll my egg, which she had boiled in very strong tea until it had gone a golden brown. We sent it spinning along like an old broken sun through the paler galaxies of primroses bewildering the braes. It cracked apart on the sea-bleached boulders at the bottom, where the violets were. After I had sat munching my egg among ladybirds and straw-gathering sparrows, there would be a bar of Highland toffee and a bottle of lemonade.

I ran down to the rock pools before going home, eyeing the cold clear water for shrimps and blennies. We took home a bunch of bladder-wrack. Jenny and Georgina separated the buds, laying them on the embers of the fire late at night to see if they would pop when the names of their true loves were whispered to the dying flames. A silent hissing consumption by the fire, with smoke and steam sent dismally up the chimney, was a sad affair. A sudden explosion was greeted with gales of laughter.

But as the fire settled into a dead white ash, old Leebie quietened everybody by telling us that it was St Mark's Eve, and that if we were to go along to the old kirkyard and keep watch there all night, we would see the apparitions of all who were to be buried there in the coming year. The wraiths of decayed old men went up the chimney from the burning seaweed and drifted out among the spring stars to the kirkyard, where Miss McNeil lay breastless and without a grin for Shuggie's stern God. The room was marble cold. I shivered and wished my grandfather had been at home, to tell me in his warm, kind way what silly blethers these old wives talked.

But by that time grandfather had been three weeks at the lines.

MAY

It all started with a hook and a line, let down into the blue water.

After the first barbaric bits of flint and bone, and the sharply shaven shards of wood, barbed, baited, and hung beneath the waves from lengths of gut, there came the net and the trap, putting meshes into the sea. In modern times the purse-seine nets have taken the silver out of the firth and made for a quick spending; the close-mesh trawl has committed infanticide upon the nursery grounds; the suction pump goes down like an obscene worm to the ocean bed, and gorges up the fish greedily, indiscriminately, and without skill. And fish can still be caught by spear or even by hand today as thousands of years ago. But a hook in the water is the oldest permanent symbol of the fisherman's hope.

When grandfather was away at the line fishing in the spring, I went oftener along the coast to Cellardyke to see the Dyker. He had the burgh coat-of-arms painted brightly on the side of the *Quest*. It showed a man in a boat with an enormous hook let down over one side, and the motto rippling underneath in golden lettering, following the curve of the wave: *Semper tibi pendeat hamus*: 'May you always have a hook in the water.'

As a small boy I used to steal old Leebie's needles and pins from her brass box by the sewing machine. Stuffing into my pockets some of her strong packthread, the kind she used for sewing together the men's thick sea blankets for sleeping-shrouds, I would slide out of the house and whistle down to the slipway to fish for dergies, the tiniest fish in the harbour. The needles always broke when I tried to bend them, but the pins proved more pliable. A whitened, wave-worn stick for a rod—and some bait was then all I needed.

Bait was never difficult to pick up. The scrapings of flesh from an old crab's hairy pincer lying broken on the pier, a shrivelled segment of lugworm, a fish-scale through which I could see the sun—it hardly mattered that the bait failed to meet its own definition. For the catching of a particular fish was not what was important in that first May when the boys brought out their rods and lines, making them out of the debris and detritus of house and harbour. To have a hook in the water—that was what the sudden bleeping in the blood demanded after the long winter, when the life of the child and of the year suddenly sprang together.

So I lay down on the tarry, sweet sun-warmed stones of the slipway and started to fish. It was high tide in the harbour; the water was clear and calm. Ignoring the alien reflection of my own face, I studied the stabbing slashes of the dagger-thin fish as they cut the water without a scar; silver shadows flitting inches from my eyes, gliding away among cool boulders and weeds, which just a few feet of sea made somehow so mysterious. I let down my silly hook into that crystal element and entered the world of the hunter. The waves of the firth began to lick gently at my sides. I held my breath.

When I was a little bigger I took the old brown twine from the rafters in the garret and fixed on some small metal hooks, real ones, from the handlines. For a sinker I used two washers tied together, and a round flat cork from a herring net as a float. This simple tackle I took to the pier end, where I tried for poatlies and flounders. But now there was no seeing what was happening beneath the float. Through the looking-glass water at the slipway I had watched the dergies threading themselves around my own drowned face, the real remote me which I could never come near. The pierhead was a greater height and the surface of the sea was a blurred ripple of chords. Whatever might come to my hook would snap out of the dark unseen. When it happened for the first time, the sudden tug sent a shuddering up my arms and down my body, setting my groin on fire. I was sickeningly glad that they were hidden, these blind dumb mouths that could not see the sky, that could not cry for mercy as I pulled and pulled at the live umbilical, my hands aflame and McCreevie howling in my ears.

I'll cut your head off, I will.

Disengage from the hook then the taut rubbery mouth, bang the soft hard head twice on the square stones of the pier, wrench it with an expert twist of the wrist till it comes off—then throw it bloodily to the other fishes, or to the swooping gulls.

I'll break open your head and feed your brains to the fish.

The terrors faded as the blood ran from my fingers and was washed away. And the spring cracked open like a blue-and-green bird's egg.

The next stage was to be digging in the soggy, tide-cleansed sandbeds for lugworm, or to be tearing mussels from the scoops near the mouth of the burn. After that I learned to tie a baited line between two rocks close in to the shore. Offshore fishermen, when fishing for codlings in the summer months, used the harlins, or handlines, with two hooks hanging below the lead sinker, each of them stuck with crab. Or if they were drifting instead of lying at anchor, they used the sprools or the jigs, relying on the shininess of the scraped metal and the jerking motions of the lines to attract the instinctive snapping jaws.

Leaving behind the rocks and skellies and setting further out to sea, they used the small lines. These were strangely named, I thought, when grandfather first showed me one, for they were fifty fathoms long, and each one carried a hundred and twenty hooks. Baited with herring, they were laid down for haddock, or for flatties and cod.

But the highest class of all was the great lines, or, as we called them, the gartlins. And although these could be shot in the firth, they were often taken up to two hundred miles away, to what the old folk called 'the far-aways', or even as far off as the Faroes, and there they went down over four hundred fathoms into the sea, searching for cod.

From a bent pin at the slipway, dangling in four feet of water, to a hundred-hooked line four hundred miles away sweeping the bottom of the world—it was quite a progress from boy to man. But the hook in the water was what counted. My grandfather, not inclined to think the Dyker superior to himself, often gave it as his opinion nonetheless, after a season at the great lines, that the Cellardyke fishermen were the most intrepid gartlin fishermen on the whole of the east coast. Certainly their coat-of-arms had served their burgh better than most, and its central symbol had dominated their lives.

'I'm a net man, not a line man,' he used to say at this time.

> *Of all the fish that swim in the sea*
> *The herring it is the fish for me.*

But the Cellardyke motto, he told me, was often quoted by his crew when the nets were being shot for the first time in a new herring season, as if the driftermen acknowledged the sharper reality of the hook as the badge of the fisherman's calling. The Dyker himself would always have the saying on his tongue as he shot his first fleet of creels after a hard winter. And I have heard it in my head over and over since then, this great admonition and expression of hope.

> *Semper tibi pendeat hamus*: 'May you always have a hook in the water.'

A TWELVEMONTH AND A DAY

I saw very little of my grandfather in April and in May when he was at the gartlins, and too far from the firth to come home for more than a sore night's sleeping in between the long hard hauling on the lines. After the spring cleaning of the boat, the bustle and breeze of the new fishing season moved through the house, when we all put our hands to the preparations for his going.

The winter nets were stowed away in the garret and the narrowest bait nets were brought out for setting down on board. These would trap the smaller herring to be used as bait for the lines, that would in turn catch the cod. The lines were dragged in heavy, stiff coils from underneath the benches, where they lay stacked for ten months in the year. Grandfather examined every coil before they were hoisted down to the yard for mending and carrying to the boat.

A great line consisted of six strings, or taes; they were made of Spanish hemp, about the thickness of the pencils we used at school, and each of the six lengths was seventy-five fathoms. This meant that a great line reached four hundred and fifty fathoms into the water. Each man carried with him five great lines to the boat. And so, with a crew of seven men on board, grandfather's boat had over fifteen thousand fathoms of gartlin to be paid out.

Each one of the six main lengths had twenty snoods — finer sections of hemp with the hooks attached to them by pieces of cotton tippin. The entire line thus carried up to one hundred and twenty hooks, three and a half fathoms apart on the line. This again meant that each man brought nearly six hundred hooks to the boat, which would be putting down over four thousand hooks in all into deep water every time they shot.

The hooks themselves were a ferocious four inches long. Tying them on by whipping the hook to the tippin was what our fingers did in the spring during the week before grandfather went away. I first helped with this task on a brilliant morning when the sun was a gold-scattering sower in the sky. I was sitting on an upturned basket down in the yard, in a dark circle of old men, all of them long retired from the sea. They used to come up to the house sometimes on their slow quiet walks to see George, and they each grafted for themselves an even slower ounce of tobacco, mending the nets and preparing the lines on which their hands were now too old to take the strain. But as they worked, their tongues talked a little now and then, telling stories of sea and sail; and their old remembering hands saw giant cod on the newly fitted hooks, felt the shuddering shrug of the huge halibut hammering on the line, the long hauling on the Spanish hemp, sodden and heavy from the grey North sea.

'You see this gartlin hook?'

One of the old ones laid in my palm the four inches of iron he was about to whip on.

'How big a fish do you think it can hold?'

I shook my head.

'I once caught a halibut of sixteen stones on a hook like that.'

I held it between my finger and thumb and tried to imagine the terrible thrashing torment of the thing.

'That's more than twice your weight, I'll be bound. Do you think your gums would hold if you bit on it and I started pulling you up?'

The old one spread his lips in a grin. There was not a tooth in his head. Tom Tarvit changed places with him and went away again.

'Do you think you'd be lippy enough to hold on?'

The old one persisted.

'I think your jaw would come off and you'd go back down to the sharks.'

I handed him back the hook, my jaw dropping.

'Leave the boy alone.'

George had come down the transe and into the yard behind us.

'There's worse things than sharks,' he said.

'There's nothing worse in the sea,' said the old man. 'But I've never seen anything fight like that halibut. Sixteen stones if it was an ounce. It was the last hook on the line. We were so close in to Peterhead we trailed it behind the boat, and it was sold alive on the scales, still twitching.'

'George will have seen greater sights than that at the whales,' said another of the old ones.

George was like the black book in which he spent his days. Sometimes the breath of talk would turn one of his quieter pages, and he would open out.

'The greatest sight I ever saw was not at the whales,' he said. 'It was when I was an ordinary fisherman on the small sailing boats, and it was turbot that took my breath away.'

'Now what's so great about turbot?' asked the one who had caught the halibut. 'I've never heard of one that took the scales at sixteen stones.'

'It wasn't their size that impressed me,' George said slowly. 'It was just because of the way they lived in pairs—the way God had ordained that they should live.'

'And in their deaths they were not divided,' he added quietly.

He told us how the free partner always followed the one on the hook just as the great line was coming out of the water, so that the man hauling could often scoop up the loose one, if he was quick, when it swam up into the air beside its doomed companion.

Blind pink mouths opening and closing on the blue sky.

'Yes, they were like Saul and Jonathan, these fish,' said George. 'Lovely and pleasant in their lives, and in their deaths they were not divided.'

Grandfather had told me the same story about the turbot.

I thought of the great lead-weighted gowking stick silencing them as they came thrashing onto the wet slippery deck. George I could see in his youth as a cold killer who went on to wrestle with leviathan, quieter now in the coldness of his age. But I wondered at the thought of my gentle grandfather slaughtering such fish in their great faithfulness. Could he not have thrown them back into the waves for the beauty of their love?

But he was a fisherman.

'We live by the sea,' he said.

And I locked away in my head a fast gladness, which I did not dare tell the old men, that the fish were not separated at the end, but came aboard together to die out of the sea where they had been so lovely and pleasant in their lives.

The firth flashed like a bright brass plate in the morning sun, the old hands worked seeingly, the eyes half-shut as the story telling was passed like a pitcher from mouth to mouth, and the pipe-smoke hung in the windless air—a memory lingering.

'And in their deaths they were not divided,' George repeated once more, still remembering.

He stared out over the red roofs, past the firth and the still skyline that held its secrets. Then he walked back upstairs to his bible.

Once ready, the lines were looped into the sculls, separated by layers of dried grass so that they would uncoil cleanly, and the hooks were arranged with great care around the borders of the basket. Everything had to be lugged through the transe, where my uncle Alec was waiting with a horse and cart to take the gear down to the boat. The bait nets and the lines were put in first, carefully, and the rest of the equipment piled in after them—dahns and lamps, tins of paraffin, bundles of corks to be used as floats. I carried down from the garret that terrible gowking stick which they used for stunning the big fish when they came aboard—sixteen stones of living silver clubbed brutally to a dumb dull stillness till they drowned in the bright blue air.

On the Saturday before grandfather was due to leave, I went with him to Gerrard the fish merchant to collect two tons of ice. Inside

Gerrard's cold store was the North Pole, reachable without sledges and huskies and berg-breaking ships. The ice lay in huge blocks as high as the mizzen masts of the drifters and smouldering cold emerald in the green sun that leaked through the thick frosted windows. Gerrard's men attacked with picks and sledgehammers, as though they were being challenged by Greenland bears—they were fighting for their lives on the giant floes. The ice was splintered and smashed to size in the struggle. Crushed and sparkling, it was shovelled into boxes, swung into the cart, and jogged smartly down to the east pier, to grandfather's favourite corner for mooring his boat.

Some of the crew were waiting to load the boxes into the hold. Each box was then covered with a layer of coarse salt and stacked neatly away. I stood for a moment in that frozen space, shivering, and staring into the empty wings. There the fish would be buried in ice after they had been caught and gutted—black brutal coffins where the dead shoals would lose their lustre and be freed from the flux and flow of tides. Terrified, I saw them all lying there—Epp and Hodgie, Chae Marr and Miss McNeil, they all came back at me again—and Shuggie too, breastless and gutted and packed in ice to be kept fresh for roasting in hell. And we would all have to join them on one tide or the next. Grandfather took my arm and brought me up into blue space.

After that we went to Agnes Meldrum's for the stores. Tea, tinned milk, tatties, ox-tongue, beef, mutton, pork, flour, butter, raisins, suet—the list seemed endless and enormous—and dozens and dozens of eggs. The outby boats went off to very distant waters, taking on much more ice and even greater quantities of stores. They were bound for the far-aways. But by the time I was born, grandfather was an inby man, staying at sea for eight or nine days at a time in the spring before coming into port, and he never in my lifetime went to the far waters.

But it seemed far enough to me.

It seemed far enough to me that they were going as I stood on the pier watching the black and yellow funnel of the *Maggie Main* bobbing and ducking in the choppy waves of the firth, the boat growing so small that it was soon nothing more than a seabird specking the distance. And I never once went with them on their constant goings, though I often begged to be taken along.

By the time I was old enough the day of the drifter was done, and another day had been written into the calendar, a day not in the twelvemonths of the year. Not in the year that my grandfather knew.

But I could see in my head the *Maggie Main*'s progress all the way up the North Sea, and all the business of her crew. I knew it from all those murmured reminiscences told to the firelit faces, or heard at the head of the pier, which was as far as the feet of the old men went when they headed for the sea.

So grandfather cleared at last the brisk fluctuations of the firth, and reached the deeper waters of the North, with its longer slower swell. Then he waited patiently for the light southerly which he knew always provided them with plenty of bait.

'A cold east wind is no good at all,' I have heard him say. 'I've gone back to harbour in an east wind after casting nets all night long—and I've never shot a single line.'

The lines were baited with one whole and one half herring time about going onto the hooks, and shot across the wind from the quarter starboard deck. When fully shot they stretched for twelve or thirteen miles, each man paying out nearly two miles of great line in a curving zig-zag, the true vines of the deep, awaiting the sudden growing of the great silver grapes and the hard harvest of the sea. It could take six hours or more to haul a whole fleet of lines. With the wrong wind or weather it might take a whole day. Grandfather talked about the times when the wind changed to dead ahead for days at a stretch, and became thick with rain, the boat sliding through endless curtains of wetness and not a single fish on the lines, so that the shooting had to be done again, and maybe again and again and again.

'It got to the stage where you couldn't shut your fingers,' he said. 'Even us old ones had to steep our hands in hot water to help the blisters. And as for the young men, I've seen them just cry with the pain, just greet like any bairn.'

And at the good times their hands were blistered with the even greater strain of bringing in a bumper crop.

'A herring in every mesh—that's just a myth,' grandfather said. 'A haul that size would sink your boat. But a fish on every hook, that I've seen with my own eyes. A hundred and twenty fish on a line, and not a gartlin hook missed out.'

The great line grew a shoal of the deepest vintage, and came up heavy with harvest. Not just cod, but haddock, ling, skate, turbot, halibut, and the big eels—all kinds of eating.

And so they fished the North Sea throughout the spring, coming into the harbours on the ebb tides, and landing their catches at Shields, Aberdeen, Newhaven and Dundee.

MAY

The start of May, grandfather being gone, found me cycling along the coast road to see the Dyker, first thing in the morning on Saturdays, or just as soon as the school bell rang.

The Dyker had a great many sayings in his mouth about the month of May, most of them to do with the sea and the weather.

A misty May and a leaky June
Brings the corn home soon.

That saying sprang to his lips as brightly as bluebells at this time of year, because misty Mays were very common in the East Neuk of Fife when the wind fell quiet and came in from the sea, and fogs were very frequent from May onwards when the wind was in the east.

Once I sat through a whole afternoon with the Dyker and another much older man while the *Quest* lay at anchor just offshore, They were at the harlins, and as the sun wore slowly across the sky, they argued quietly, seriously, about the meaning of the words 'a leaky June'. They were bleached, bronzed old statues murmuring into their graven beards as the boat bobbed softly on the swell. The very old man spoke out of the wisdom of whiter hairs than the Dyker, and he maintained with sage shakings of his head that the expression meant an exceptionally hot and dry June.

'Why would they have called it leaky then?' demanded the Dyker, unhooking a silvery sliver from the dripping line.

'I'll tell you why, if you'll just listen to me.'

The old man took the shivering fish from the Dyker and it gaped and gulped at him as he talked dreamily.

'In a very hot month, you see, the staves of the old water barrels used to shrink, and if the month continued hot then the water used to leak out between the joins, unless they'd been made by a first class cooper—and that's the reason, and no other, that it's called what it is.'

The haddock gaped wider at him, disbelieving, and he knocked its head on the gunwale. It lay still.

'Don't you pay any attention to what he's saying,' the Dyker warned me, as his line hit the water again. 'His head's full of old nonsense, like all men of his age.'

The Dyker laughed out of his seventy years.

'A leaky June means nothing more than what the word says,' he told me, 'and that's a wet one.'

The older man gutted the haddock and threw the streamer of redness to the birds. He shook his head.

'No, no, no, a wet June will hold up the harvest.'

The Dyker insisted.

'You get mist in May followed by rain in June and you'll always get a hot July. The corn will be all cut before the middle of August.'

He turned to me as I sat staring at the fish, which had lost its silveriness, its secrecy.

'You just remember, lad, it's the simplest explanations that are usually right.'

Many's the year since then I have seen the two best months of the year spoiled by mists and rain. And the early harvests have left me remembering the strength of the Dyker's simple saying, told to me time out of mind as the *Quest* lay quietly off Cellardyke, and we kept our hooks in the water.

If there were very strong easterlies in May, they sometimes lasted the whole month through. The cold winds, thicknesses and drizzling rains set in so severely, that the wetness seeped through the hollows of our marrowless bones, and the limpet-cold locked on grimly to our chilled ribs. My feet were leaden lumps clumped in the bottom of the boat, part of its ballast. This was the dreaded weather which the Dyker called the 'coo-quawk', when the farmers used to say that whole fields of cattle would just stand in black huddles of misery and quake uncontrollably with the cold.

'Keep two pairs of gloves, lad,' the Dyker often said to me. 'One for the winter, and a second pair for the month of May.'

But even in the East Neuk, where the sharp east winds have kept a scalpel edge on nostalgia, Mays were more often memorably idyllic.

There was nothing the Dyker loved better than to be hauling his creels or trying the sprools off the Billowness near Anstruther on a May morning, with the sea a soft powder-blue silk, and the sun standing still in the sky; or to be lying at anchor at the harlins on a calm drowsy evening, using shore crabs as bait, and the fish coming sedately to the lines.

For these occasions, in the sudden silences between the pulse-beats of the year, even if we were fishing in June or July, or even into August, the Dyker had a favourite saying.

'It's the Broughty Ferry man's way today,' he would say. 'A morning like a May morning—and all the Buckhaven men at sea.'

Whether he was quoting from something he had read or heard, or had maybe made up the words himself, I shall never know. But he shared my grandfather's disparagement of the Buckers, who wouldn't go to sea, he said, if there was the least hairline of a ripple cracking the calm mirror of the firth. But no doubt the Buckers said much the same kind of thing about the fishermen of Cellardyke or St Monans.

So for all its failures to live up to its reputation as a time of beauty, May remained the Dyker's favourite month of the year, and he always blessed the first fish he ever caught at this season with another of these sayings which have gone the way of the men who said them and the skills they knew.

One drink of the May flood
Makes all the fish in the sea good.

It was the time in the year when we were able to tear off our socks and shoes and go guddling about barefoot in the clear pools. It was the first month of the seashore for playing games on the beach and discovering the lore of the rocks.

The first thing we looked for was a peln.

Pelns were shore crabs about to cast their shells, and it was at this stage in their lives that they made the best possible bait either for the harlins or just for boys with rods. We preyed on them pitilessly.

Shuttering up the pictures in the rooms behind my eyes—the partans boiling redly in the iron pot—I learned how to grab the hard crabs from behind and snap off the small joint of a big claw. Curiously, I felt no guilt on behalf of these crabs when breaking their limbs, for they knew the demoniac trick of growing again the limbs they lost. Clearly they could feel no pain, I told myself.

When the jointed claw was snipped and the nipper came away cleanly, the crab was no use as bait. But if the flesh stuck out like firm white velvet, then it was a peln and doomed to die. We set it down on one stone and smashed it with a blow from another. Then we scooped it out of its own armour and cut it into segments, keeping the flesh of the toes for the finest bait. Crabs that had just lost their shells we called bubbles; after that they were softies until they grew their suits again, and we spared them, as they brought no fish to the hook.

Catching the pelns was easy once they were found, for they were quiet and comatose when the shell was about to go, and never nipped our nervous fingers, unlike the large ballycrabs that would bite out of badness at the nearest opportunity. They gave crabs a bad name. Sometimes we relieved them of all their pincers just out of our own badness, so giving boys in general a bad name.

Female pelns in their quiet condition were an especially easy prey to the rampaging male ballies, who scuttled about the shore like the bad black knights that they were, looking for these half-drugged damsels in distress, clasped them to their jointed breastplates, and mated with them mercilessly. During mating the ballies carried their prize pelns around with them like the spoils of war. As soon as we saw this double-act, we knew that one of the crabs was potential bait, and in any case we enjoyed putting an end to the male's horny fun, so we drove a sword-stick of chastity between the two; or we disentangled them with a flick of the fingers, and hurled the marauder into the sea with howls of triumph. The poor female peln then became our bait. But we had saved her from a fate worse than the death which then befell to her as the fairer lot.

Groping about in this way among the warm pools and puddles of the shore was how we really began our summer, and the find of the first peln was the surest sign that the long winter was behind us, and the warm weather on the way. My grandfather always had an expression for it himself.

'It's Tammie Limie time again,' he used to say.

Tammie Limie had a small sailing yawl called the *Fisher Lass*. His wife Jess ran a draper's shop in the basement of a huge house in East Shore Street. Her constant complaint to her customers, regularly rolled out across the dark counter with the bales of linen, was that the awful spouse would never wash his feet. And as the year wore into winter, and Tammie dived out of one pair of sweaty sea-stockings into the next, shrinking from the merest glimmer of water in between, poor Jess's song of wifely suffering took on the plangency of a dirge.

'Sleeping next to him is the cross I've to bear nightly,' she sighed as she snipped and measured with precise white fingers, and with tight little tremblings of her neatly parted head.

'And he'll not even wear slippers in the house.'

But when spring burst over the coast, all became bright again in the dark little draper's shop where Jess lived among fabrics and feet.

'Never mind, Jess,' Tammie would say to her. 'It'll not be long now, lass. It'll soon be the time for pelns again—and clean feet in the month of May!'

So this man's feet succeeded in giving him a legendariness in his own lifetime, and a local expression to a time of year.

Tammie Limie time.

Tammie Limie time brought to our shores all the summer migrants—the willow warblers, wood warblers, the chiff-chaff and the Black Cap; and swifts and swallows now flashed about the town buildings like painted paper aeroplanes, zooming under the old men's benches, where they sat stiff-legged; bending gravity round corners and between streets and chimney pots.

Down at the water the baby mallards and eiders were already active, the weird whooings of the eider ducks bringing the music of a different planet to the quiet coast, where the wheatear and the ringed plover alighted. Like an alien being I stepped out secretly from Buckland among the whispering seaweeds and new sounds of the morning. I was looking for sea-urchins. Grandfather called them Hairy Hutchins, but once I had scraped off all the spines, they fitted the Dyker's chillier description of Dead-Men's-Crowns—as bald and brittle as the skulls of Chae and Hodgie, stranded up there in the kirkyard in their single fathom of earth. Sometimes they broke as I scooped out the stuff of life from the inside, and I threw the cracked skulls to the birds and fish.

Break open your head . . .

Only whispers in the wind now, in those calm hours, with summer stealing on.

The jellyfish started to come up on shore. Bloodless blobs on the sand, masquerading under the sign of the cross, I hated them for the pain they inflicted on swimmers. Once on a breathless May Sunday, I took off all my clothes and plunged from the rocks into a high tide, only to come under their ugly purple whiplashes, which stung me into a frenzied retreat to the land. As I hoisted myself painfully out of the water, I saw, to my amazement, a guillemot's egg bobbing in the waves, tapping the edges of the sharp rocks. My legs and thighs on fire under me, I ran crying home with my hurts, and holding out in front of me the lovely turquoise planet which had swum so strangely into my ken.

Leebie told me that the Lord had punished me for bathing on the sabbath, but my grandmother dabbed me with paraffin to burn out the stings. If the jellyfish were the instruments of God's wrath, my own anger knew no bounds. Later in the year, when they came ashore in battalions, I led Peem and Gollie against them in reprisal, armed with the long rubbery rooted tangles, with which we whipped them vengefully to shivers.

I showed the guillemot's egg to the Dyker. He pointed to the small hole in one end and told me what had happened. A bird had pecked at it on the May island, meaning to make a full meal out of it. But it had rolled right off the edge of the sheer cliffs and landed unbroken in the sea, floating right across the firth to where I found it because of the jellyfish.

His old friend was with him at the time, and waved his words away, as he did with most of the Dyker's explanations.

'Have you never wondered,' the old man asked me, 'how it is that these very young birds manage to fly from the May to the mainland at this time of year, and them hardly a week out of the egg?'

I looked at the Dyker, who was already shaking his head.

'Well,' the old man said, 'they don't fly over here at all at that age, you see. The egg is laid at sea and the mother bird catches hold of it in time and tucks it under one wing. Then she swims over here to hatch it out—and that's how you found that egg of yours.'

The Dyker's simpler version was easier to believe. But what mattered was the telling.

The first lightning flickered over the firth, where the gannets now flew out in long files to feed in deeper waters. For many days at a time, mornings and evenings, I stood watching them through George's powerful spyglass, and I saw how their route never varied. They described a great arc from the Bass Rock in the morning, outward to the North Sea, and so back to the Bass in the evening. Always on the way out to their feeding grounds they passed to the north and eastward between the shore and the May island, and always they came back again on the other side, the far side of the May, the two arcs from sunrise to sunset forming an invisible circle, unshunnable, strong, distinct. In January and February the sky was unbroken, but in March and April the first flakes began to drift, and from May onwards the Bass was a blizzard of birds, snowing hard all through the summer months until October thinned them out and November and December were quiet again.

Standing in front of George's window, open now all the time, or at the green vantage point of the Braeheads looking eastwards on the sea, I could see the long files coming from far off Fifeness, flying low above the waves. It was best watching for them when there was a hard south-east gale blowing along with dull gloomy weather. Then they showed up against the purplish-blue water like white-clad, sea-bound pilgrims moving on their eastward course, so close to the surface that they would be disappearing from moment to moment in the deep troughs between the snow-crested mountains of sea, and rising again on wave-wet wings to head for their haven, that great rock of ages far out in the firth. The cormorants and shags rose high into the air when passing over the land, but the gannets in their great beauty kept to the sea, flying right around the jutting jaw of the ness rather than cross the land as the crow flies. The Bass Rock alone was their firth-girt castle and they left it only to pass over the blue ploughlands of the sea. So they remained the lords of the waves, the keepers of the rock, bright beings of distance and air.

Inevitably the dreams began, and still go on years later in the time-passing, moments before waking.

There were two distinct dreams.

In one of them the long flying files became the 'beauteous files' of the hymn we had sung for Shuggie without a flicker of understanding—and the Bass was the kingdom of heaven.

> *My soul, there is a Countrie*
> *Far beyond the stars,*
> *Where stands a winged Sentrie*
> *All skilful in the wars.*
>
> *If thou canst get but thither,*
> *There growes the flowre of peace,*
> *The Rose that cannot wither,*
> *Thy fortresse, and thy ease.*

In the second dream the incorruptible rose became the flock of gannets that I sometimes saw feeding closer in to shore, west of the kirk. The huge white flower fluttered out in the firth like Miss Balsilbie's blouse as the birds hung low over the water, hovering between sea and sky, a mystic shroud. The flower burst and sprang apart, the snowy white fragments plunging seawards, wings closing into the dark blue waves; then upwards to the sky, a bright fountain of joy, droplets turning to stars, constellations cascading into the sea. And so the dream goes on, the snowy white flower opening and shutting, Miss Balsilbie's roses, rising and falling like a milky fountain, like confetti in the firth, speaking to my wide-awake spirit while my body lay asleep, of that unknown country far beyond the stars.

A dream that remains. A month to remember.

But most memorable beyond everything else in May was the quality of its light. On a sunlit morning when I looked at the new leaves, at the young plants and grasses, they exuded an unearthly luminosity, as if all the light were liquid. And this clear film of brilliance on the moist fresh foliage, though lasting for only a few short weeks, is what lingers in the memory like music. Music when soft voices die.

It was this quality of the light which led my spell-bound feet up from the shore and through the milk-yielding fields into the country, where the uddered cows lowed soft and swollen among buttercups and daisies and clumps of purple clover. Blue vetch was out by the roadsides, along the hedgerow the raspberry and the wild rose were in leaf, and the spiky strongholds of the thistle patches were running up their butterfly pennants, the Red Admirals fluttering among the green spires and towers like blood-red banners.

The first hum of insects was beginning to be heard. But in Balcaskie, where I sheltered from a shower, the bluebells hung in a dim and misty silence, ringing to the rain. Coming out of the trees, I heard the scents from the splashed hawthorn blossoms go through my head like memories of all the Mays that ever were. On the way back home I broke some of them off in sprays for my grandmother to put in jars and fill the house with fragrance.

So the month moved us into that magical period of time when there was no astronomical night, when the sun swung like a dimmed lamp not far beneath the horizon. I stuck my head high out of our skylight window, looking out over the roofs at the green and red harbour lights; and turning to the west I could see the afterglow hanging like a mist of hawthorn flower powdering the sky. I knew then that the time was near when grandfather would be bringing back his lines and taking down the black nets from the garret, ready for the early drave and for the summer herring.

JUNE

At the end of May grandfather came home from the great lines, littering the piers with hundreds of cod. There were no boxes for them in those days, so they were arranged in scores on the bare stones, each score divided into fives: four with their heads up, and every fifth fish with its head down, tail pointing to the boat. They lay like legions of soldiers lapped in lead, exhumed from their four hundred fathoms and the ice-cold hold of the *Maggie Main* to be stripped of their armour and turned to fodder by the fiery suns of June.

After the war the new steel drifters proved to be such fast and efficient fishers of the cod that some of them flung out their great lines all the summer long, carrying tons of coal on their decks during the windless sun-blistered days to take them further afield and go for the unseen armies, the outposts, the ninth legions of the giant cod. These boats did not go to the summer herring drave at all, but pursued their deep-sea fishing right to the end of September, when it was time to sail to Yarmouth. The corn grew and ripened and was cut to stubble, but to the crews who ploughed the wave-blooms six days a week, and sleeping every seventh, there came no autumn.

As for the smaller motor boats and the older wooden steam drifters like the *Maggie Main*, they headed every summer for the drave. Some of them sailed to Shetland at the end of May, slowly following the shoals south throughout June and July. But grandfather's favourite place in the summer was Peterhead, and most of the St Monans fleet went with him. All through the summer months they fished up and down the northern half of Scotland, landing their catches mainly at Peterhead, and then they came back to the firth in August.

But there would be the space of a week, maybe ten days, while the gear was being prepared for the drave, during which grandfather remained at home. It was at this time that he used to go out with the Dyker in the *Quest*, some days fishing out of Cellardyke, some days out of St Monans, depending on how their luck was running. They shot creels for partans mostly; sometimes they sprooled for cod and whitings, went out with the harlins or the small lines for codlings or haddocks; now and again they tried the herring jigs. As the fish never moved much in the middle of the day, and were mainly caught between six and seven in the morning and in the cool of the evening, this meant that they were able to take me along with them before and after school.

That was when I learned about 'meads'.

'Meads' was the word they used to describe their way of establishing their position at sea when they were not far from the land, and the commonest question I heard asked on the pier when a fisherman had just brought in a good catch, was: 'What meads were you on?' It was a bearing on the land, enabling them to keep on returning time and again to the same patch of sea-ground where they knew they were sure of a good shot. At the drift-net fishing, the sprools or the jigs, exact meads did not matter so much to them. But when they anchored nets, laid lines, or shot messenger creels, the meads had to be precise so that they could haul hours or days later.

Grandfather and the Dyker were dead-eyed demons at the meads.

Their method was simple. For an informal meads they took any large object on the land and steered the *Quest* until it was lined up with it in conjunction with a second object in front of it. The East Neuk countryside was mostly flat farmlands, and for the St Monans men and the Cellardykers its one high green point was Kellie Law. It was well up in the country, beyond Balcaskie, beyond Balcormo, by the Carnbee loch.

After Kellie Law the kirk steeples of the villages offered the most obvious landmarks, pointing like thinly tapered fingers into the sky, some of them needle-sharp spires, and others like distant pyramids rising in the blue deserts of space. When we were well out towards the May Island from Cellardyke, the Dyker showed me how Kellie Law loomed over Anstruther Easter kirk and Chalmers Memorial kirk in one perfectly straight line.

'Kellie over the kirks,' he said simply.

That was his favourite meads for herring, with net or line.

When grandfather went sprooling for cod out of St Monans, he lined up the Law with the Old Kirk, and that provided him with his rough meads.

'Kellie on the kirk,' was his term.

But for a more accurate cross-bearing on the land, the two of them used what they called a sharp meads. For this they took two pairs of objects in transit, waiting until the known four were lined up, two and two, and when the boat arrived at the apex of the imaginary triangle, they let go the anchor and started to fish.

When they were taking a sharp meads their favourite objects were the lums of certain houses or any of the bigger buildings they could fix on. Looking for lobsters, the Dyker's favoured meads was: Watson's oilskin factory chimney over Tom Melville's kippering kiln *plus* the big lum of the gasworks in line with his own cottage chimney, which he had painted bright orange, right down on the shore. He called this meads 'oilskins, kippers and gas', and it brought us to the hard rocky ground where the lobsters were caught. But if we wanted crabs on the sandier ground, he took the *Quest* a mile out from this meads, and instead of his own chimney, used the steeple of St Adrian's. He called this 'the back of the kiln', and it was there we caught the partans.

Grandfather's lobster meads was a simpler one. He lined up both sets of the chimneys of Johnston Lodge, where the Princess lived, with the kirk steeple, and called it 'Johnston on the kirk'. For the partans he used the chimneys on either end of Tammie Limie's house and took them in conjunction with the ones on the lodge. He called this 'Darsie and Limie' but sometimes referred to it as 'Limie's lums ringing'.

Tammie Limie's old yawl, the *Fisher Lass*, lay so low in the water, that the Pittenweem fishermen had christened her 'The Plank', and the name had spread along the coast. One morning in June Tam came into the harbour loaded to the gunwales with herring, which were not caught in large quantities in the firth at that time of year. The stupidest and also the most inquisitive fisherman in the town was a man called Patchie. He shouted down to Tam just as his boat was bumping against the pier.

'Hey, Tammie, that's an uncanny load of herring you've caught there—I've never seen the like! What meads were you on?'

Tammie, who was famed for his feet, was also known for his sprooling, and for his keen eye's ability to take a very sharp meads. But he was also known to be very close-mouthed about his successes.

'Meads?' said Tammie, as if he had never heard of the expression.

'Aye, meads!' roared Patchie. 'What meads were you on?'

'Ah! Steeple over the kirk,' replied Tammie after a pause. 'Yes, that was my meads—steeple over the kirk.'

Patchie took off his cap and scratched his head. He walked back up the pier to ask for guidance from the old men, and it was left to wiser minds to explain to him that the steeple is always over the kirk no matter where you are, on land or sea. Tammie at once considered this remark to be one of his triumphs. But as soon as he had uttered it, he came up the steps onto the pier, and when he saw just how little of his boat was left above the water, he had to be taken up to the Sun Tavern and revived.

These were the days when the sounder was a lump of lead on a length of twine, when the only instrument on board the boat was the age-old compass, and when the skipper, though achieving less certainty and a greater sense of mystery than the modern seaman, worked his fishing grounds, managing wind and tide, labouring through sea and shoal, with a rule-of-thumb accuracy that could not be emulated today. Years on now, in these times of radar and echo-sounders and computers in the superstructured hulls, I fall asleep in the same old June sun, in front of the same old sea, and I see the Dyker and grandfather sitting in the *Quest*, looking out across the firth, grandfather with the golden brown sextant of his eyes, and the Dyker with the bright blue measuring-tape of his, scanning the spires and steeples and all the lums of the town; calmly, efficiently, and with a steady stare, taking their meads.

Crabs were their main catch from May until the end of June. When the drifters came home at the end of the great lines they sometimes brought coal saithe to be shared out as free bait for the full time creel fishermen. The partan creels needed fresh bait every day, and when they invaded the lobster creels the partans ate the bait, which the lobsters did not do. By the end of July these big crabs had become an increasing nuisance, for they were casting their shells, and semi-hard partans, which were unsuitable for eating, and for which there was no market, were a trouble to the Dyker right through till October.

But in June I saw some huge catches come over the gunwales of the *Quest*, usually on a north-east swell, which made the water thick above the sandy ground. Once I counted fifty dozen partans hauled on Darsie and Limie, though grandfather said he had seen one hundred and twenty-four dozen brought aboard as a boy on the same meads.

We took our crabs to Burgon, whose men measured the doubtful ones. They had to span at least four and a half inches across the largest section of the shell, and Burgon paid us a price which never varied, between one shilling and threepence and one shilling and sixpence per dozen. On the wall of his shed there was a yellowed and dog-eared prices chart which had been printed by an English buyer when he came up the Scottish coast in the 1860's to do business. Incredibly, the figures for partans read thus: 'Partan crabs: $4\frac{1}{2}$ inches: 1/3 per dozen; 9 inches: 1/6 per dozen.' Burgon was offering a sum which had not altered by one single penny of inflation in nearly seventy years. A reasonable span. A more than reasonable state of economic stability.

On days when there was a south-east swell they decided against the creels and took me to the harlins. We used two hooks baited with pelns hanging below the lead sinker and hauled up a fathom after the sinker hit the bottom. I had to be in school by nine o'clock, but on a summer morning by half past seven the bottom of the boat would often be shivering with fair-sized fish, and the Dyker took the yawl at a leisurely lilt along the coast to sell the catch at St Monans. On those mornings I had for breakfast a hot fry that had been swimming in the cool blue firth not much more than an hour earlier.

It was out there on the sea, in the early summer hours, that I saw for the first time the burghs from a distance, spread out along the coast—crazy old castletowns they were, with their clutterings of red roofs tucked into the hazy tracts of countryside, and above them the spires and steeples: fingers pointing from the green fists of the kirkyard mounds, where all my people lay. And as the *Quest* wore quietly homeward on the wordless waves, the fingers beckoned out of all the humped green hands, the songs of the hearth rose from the white chimneys, and the dead folks and the living folks were one, claiming their kin in that first conscious corner of belonging cut for me out of time.

On other mornings we tried our hand close in to shore, where many old men used to fish in the early hours following the dawn. Sitting in the boat, we were often close enough to talk to them as they stood on the rocks, swung their lead-weighted lines around their heads, and cast their peln-baited hooks into a gap among the tangles, waiting until the corks sank before hauling in their red codlings with intent faces, and taking them off to fry for their breakfasts or their tasty bites of supper.

Blue days at sea, these were, that came to an end when it was time for the drave.

Grandfather followed the old traditions. When he went to the early drave fishing he used his oldest nets which the years of tanning or barking had made narrower. These caught the younger and smaller herring, though they were not the tightly-meshed, woven purses of greed that rake in every smallest particle of silver. As the drave wore on, the herring grew bigger and the spawn began to form, so he brought ashore his old nets and set down on board his widest and best, which had not endured so many seasons of immersion in the barking boilers or the tanning tubs.

Barking the nets, though it narrowed them down over the years, lengthened their life by preserving them from the corrosive action of the salt sea and all its weed and scum, especially bothersome at the height of the summer. So the great lines and the bait nets were pushed back beneath the benches in the garret, and the black summer nets were pulled out and hoisted down into the yard. I sat astride each bundle as they swung it down onto the flagstones, running up the stairs again in time for the next load.

George usually left his bible and came down for the barking.

'There's no substitute for the true bark of the oak,' he would say. 'Melt that down and you've got the best solution for a herring net.'

Instead we filled the barking boiler with water and poured in the cutch, which was the resin taken from one of the Burmese acacia trees. When the mixture was hot enough we dipped in the nets, boiling them for several minutes before hauling out hot and dripping and stretching them on the galluses— poles and crossbeams—to dry out in the wind and sun.

George never failed to crown the process with this pessimistic forecast.

'They'll last you two or three tannings like that—and then they'll go frush.'

'What's frush?' I asked.

'They'll go too dry,' he said. 'Then they'll rot and tear. You need the true bark of the oak.'

Grandfather asked him how many of the Balcaskie trees he thought he could strip of their bark before he was caught and prosecuted. But he did the best by his nets, grandfather. He had a passion for order and precision which I have inherited.

Many of the driftermen did not take the trouble to bark their mizzen sails when they were preparing their nets. But even in the age of the steam boiler grandfather wheeled his canvas in a large barrow to the barking pan in the fields across from the school, where the last of the old sailing skippers made ready their sails for the sea.

The first steam boiler to be installed in a fishing boat in St Monans was in 1895—the *John and Agnes* was the name of the boat. When the century turned it was like the turning of a huge tide. After that very few sailing vessels were built—they were nearly all steam drifters, the noisy lords of the fishing grounds for nearly fifty years. The sailing boats then started to be a nuisance and a peril to the powered craft, like grand old men, despised at last by the bustling, prosperous youth of the day.

But there were still three Fifies sailing out of St Monans when I was born. They were the *Barbara Beattie*, the *True Vine* and the *White Rose*, all of them skippered by men who refused to give up the sail which had brought them through their working lives.

The skipper of the *White Rose* was a friend of grandfather's called

Adam Innes, who had named his boat, he told us, after the large white rose on Gladstone's coffin.

'Local feeling ran high against me,' he said, 'for calling a boat according to the emblem on a coffin. They said it was tempting Providence. They said the boat herself would be a box—a dead-kist that would take her crew straight to Gladstone by the first tide she took. I couldn't get a crew together for near on six months.'

The old captain remembered how the launching of the *White Rose* had been marred by the town drunkard, Andrew Robinson, who as usual that day, was affected by the drink.

'He had more in his belly than was good for his head,' Adam said simply.

The wife of the Free Kirk minister was just about to break the bottle against the boat as it started its slide into the harbour, when Andrew Robinson tried to snatch it from her and she missed her chance. The boat went off the pier and into space with the bottle swinging alongside on its rope, still unbroken.

'It was your grandfather that saved the day,' said old Adam Innes. 'He sprang onto the boat when it was still in the air, pulled up the bottle and smashed it over the stemhead just as it was hitting the water and the spray flying over her bows.'

'Was it champagne?' I asked.

'Champagne or salt water—I wouldn't have known the difference,' grandfather said. 'But I was well christened with the mixture myself.'

It was a poor start to a boat's life. But the *White Rose* and her two sister ships saw out more than one succeeding Prime Minister, and right up to the day I left the school, they remained the greatest sight coming into St Monans harbour.

Barking the sails for boats like these was not something that could be carried out in a back yard. There were three hundred and fifty yards of foresail weighing nearly a ton when dripping wet, and two hundred and fifty yards of summer mizzen sail. At the end of the line fishing the winter mizzen mast and sail were taken down and the mast was hauled up by horses and rollers to the rough moorland where the women spread out their washing on a blaze of whins. Here the summer mizzen mast had lain all winter like a fallen tree.

Gallons of water were hosed into the barking pan and fires crackled underneath until it bubbled like broth and the steam rose into the sun. I was sent running down the brae to the butcher's to ask for seven pounds of butcher's fat, which was added in a solid sticky white lump. One of the old men suggested throwing me in next so as to enjoy a mouthful of good soup before the rest of the ingredients made it uneatable. But they poured in instead twenty-one pounds of tannin and fourteen pounds of oakum, and everything was allowed to melt and then stirred with a large stick. The sails were spread wide on the grass and the liquid brushed well in, like old brown wine, thick at the dregs. After that they dried in the middle-of-the-day sunshine and were turned over for the same treatment. Grandfather brushed in what was left of it into the *Maggie Main*'s mizzen—a woman's handkerchief, he said, compared to the giant canvasses of the old masterpieces.

They too came at me in dreams—all that is left now of these slow old tuneful times.

On the wall opposite the window in George's room hung a painting which we had inherited with the house. It had been painted in the very room in which it was hung, we were told, by an artist called Lorimer, of Kellie Castle. The picture was a study of the view from the window, quite some years ago, looking out on the sea.

In the painting it was blowing a full gale of wind from the west. The whole firth was a single white sheet of spray and scores of sailing boats were turning up the Forth from east by. I counted more than sixty boats in all. Their huge foresails were reefed down to the smallest bit and the smallest bit of the mizzen sail, which the Fifies used to turn to windward in case they failed to stay. One of the boats nearest the harbour had caught the full weight of wind, and she was heeling over on the crest of a sickening second of fear, perpetuated in paint—her gunwales and lee deck dipped in the churning sea right up to the commons, the white waves licking the main hold. To the west of her a bunch of tiny wild faces was staring from another boat at the whole exposed length of their comrades' keel. It was as if someone's entire backbone were on show. Their features were too small to be made out, but the sheer horror was written into the rigid thrust of their heads.

A flood tide was running. But the sea was not so heavy close in to the shore, as if the artist had felt the merciful grip of the wind on the land—the jutting tip of Elie Ness always allowing that small benefit to St Monans harbour when there were westerly winds. So some of the boats had already made the weather side of the harbour, and with both sails lowered, down before the wind they were driving fast, their bare masts of magnificent pitch pine that would not bend growing austere and tall out of the blossoming white breakers, while further out, the supple yards of knotless larch were bending to the set of sail as the skippers took their chances, hurrying to haven through the eye and teeth of the storm.

I stood in front of this picture often, and George told me that once he had stood on the braeheads as a boy and counted three hundred ships like that sailing up the firth. How I wished I could have seen such a sight!

So, when the thick theatre-curtains of sleep swish open nightly on my dreams, sometimes the three last sailing boats that ever were in Fife become the three score of Lorimer's picture, and the boats in the picture multiply into the three hundred of George's youth. The paint begins to flow then, and the ships to move, and flying like a gull again, I am sailing before the wind—the firth a milky fountain, the flung froth of the clouds, the spray bursting up into my face like white roses, like sweet salty champagne.

Struggling out of the spun yarn of my dreams on these early summer mornings, I looked out from my window and saw an empty harbour. The fleet had sailed to the north, leaving a population of old men and boys to be threaded into the lives of women, and I would not see grandfather now until some weekend in August when all the men in the town would reappear.

It was the time of year when I headed for the rocks with Peem and Gollie, and on Saturdays we would be combing the shore for what was to be found. We raked between the skellies for gartlin hooks, new nails, and lumps of lead and copper to sell to the boatbuilder for a penny if the weight was good; we hunted for the little glass balls from the old lemonade bottles, to use as marbles; we sailed paper boats made out of stiff old school jotters, using sand as ballast, and if there was a westerly wind and a jabble on the sea, we watched them sail out of sight before they became waterlogged and sank; we ran to the Golden Strand, where at this time of year the grass was covered with the haikes—wooden trestles on which the salt cod were dried—and we snipped pieces out of them on the sly, chewing them like gum, a good strong salty mouthful; we rodded for dergies and whiting, not killing them, but keeping them alive in pools, putting them back into the sea if nobody needed cat-meat—we had little use for them ourselves, but we were afflicted by a feverish desire to fish after the winter, when the perennial question was, 'Are there any in yet?'. Sometimes effluence obscured the water, and if not breaking peln toes, or cutting wriggling segments of lug, we would be biting off pieces of limpets in our mouths to make them small enough for bait. The practice must have immunised us against many infectious diseases, not having killed us in itself.

Or we made our tinny fires.

For this I preferred the larger size tin of Lyle's Golden Syrup. My grandmother kept back her empties for me, and after I had scraped them clean, she washed them out and put them on the sink. They were useful for holding lugworm and most people collected crabs in them, though I hated the scrabblings of their claws on the bare metal, and I always gathered my pelns in an old stocking leg, maybe because that was just the way my grandfather did it.

When making a tinny fire, we took a clasp knife and a flat stone, and punched a neat hole like a tiny door, one inch square, out of the lower part of the vertical curved surface of the tin, sometimes enlarging it with a piece of strong iron hooping from a broken barrel. This sucked the draught through the fire, which we built inside the tin itself, with the lid off, the hole being placed to face the prevailing wind.

Our fuel consisted of brittle bits of stick from the remains of old herring baskets, crumbs of cork, small nuggets of sea-coal, and coke from the gasworks. The poker was a gartlin hook heated in the fire until it was a red-hot worm, and then hammered into a crinkly straightness between two stones.

On the top of the glowing tin we placed a slightly smaller size of tin for the cooking pot. It was invariably a cocoa tin, or a Fowler's treacle empty, filled from the sea where it came in cleanest. In this we cooked our first bachelor meals—potatoes from the fields later in the year, but at this summer season mussels and whelks. When they were scarce, we knocked the limpets from off the barnacled rocks, removing their excretory centres and roasting them three at a time on the upturned top lid of a tin of Cherry Blossom shoe polish. The limpets were not so tasty, but had the advantage of always being there.

Who is to estimate the long-lasting effects of so Robinson-Crusoe-ish a diet?

Mussels were my favourite.

They could either be eaten or used as bait, but they always seemed in my mouth too good a morsel for a haddock or a cod, even though thousands of them were shelled for the lines. At one time horse-drawn carts had brought home huge blue mountains of them from the mussel beds in the River Eden estuary, and our fishing crews had put them in stone circles between the skellies at the mouth of the burn, to keep them alive and fresh for use as bait. Nets were put over them to prevent them spreading and to keep out the oyster-catchers, which grandfather always referred to as the mussel-pickers. The remains of these old artificial beds were still to be found here and there among the west rocks. They were called the mussel scoops, and so, while we 'gathered' whelks, we went 'scooping' for mussels. Either of these sea-dishes could be greatly improved by a splash of Grimble's Malt Vinegar, which we took it in turns to raid from our mothers' larders.

There were bad times when whelk-gathering became a matter of bare necessity. That happened in those black seasons when the fishing failed. Then every boy and girl and man and woman in the town would be lifting every available stone along the coast searching for whelks for sheer poverty. In better times we gathered them just for a few coppers to rattle in our pockets and spend on Lucky Bags and liquorice and sherbet dabs. It was a laborious job because the whelks clung together in the freezing wet weather, when gathering them was a cold and miserable business. In the spring and summer months it was a blue and golden time on the rocks, but then the whelks scattered, and bringing them together in a pail or a sack was slow work—unless there was summer mist, which brought them all out like snails in the rain.

We sold our whelks to Joe Smith and Eck Birrell, who had a shed on the east pier. Joe had been in his time a master navigator, and now in his seventies sent down shellfish to the English markets.

Eck was a dunce.

When the harbour was being modified one year, poor Eck was in a state of genuine fear for many months, because he imagined that the coffer dam which they were building would cause the waters of the firth to rise up over the east pier and float their shed like a second ark, flooding Shore Street and sending us up the steeples to talk to the weathercocks until God saw fit to stretch forth his arm upon the sea. He told everybody, man or boy, who came to the shed, that the end was approaching, and Joe spent long hours trying to explain to him by means of patient charts and diagrams that since the area of sea throughout the entire world would also have its level increased by this little elbow of the firth not being allowed to nudge the inner harbour, the rise of the water level of the east pier would be so slight that he would never notice it.

'There's no instrument made on earth could measure it,' he told Eck. 'It won't even be seen in heaven.'

'I don't get it,' groaned Eck, 'I just can't work it out. It's such a big body of water that comes into the harbour every day. Where's it all going to go to?'

Joe and Eck were very particular about the whelks they bought from us. When we set down our buckets outside their shed, one of them would emerge, grab a glistening black fistful at random, and throw the shells onto a sieve. If a single whelk fell through we were sent away.

'Only whelks the size of black striped balls go down to Billingsgate from here,' said Joe.

We soon learned to bring them the best. A black striped ball was a humbug that could be sucked through one of the Reverend Kinnear's most substantial sermons.

In the month of June the whelks used to climb the weedy walls of the east pier in sky-aspiring squadrons, and the temptation was irresistible to clamber down the ladders after them, or to swing on the mooring ropes in twos, one holding the bucket, the other picking off the whelks. They were easy prey like that. But Joe refused to accept whelks which he suspected had been taken from the harbour wall, of which he had a good view from his shed. Their standards were high, he boasted, and the oil and refuse from the boats in the harbour made such specimens unhygienic.

'No contaminated whelk goes down to Billingsgate from here,' he said.

But Eck accepted the bad whelks gleefully, so long as they were of the acceptable size.

'Poison the bloody French,' he gloated, smuggling them into his shed under Joe's sharp navigator's nose.

For some reason Eck had a pathological hatred of the French, which took a dangerous turn whenever Genevieve Catriona Louise happened to pass by the east pier, muttering in staccato. If Eck spied her out of his small window he rushed out of the shed screaming and snarling after her till his face nearly burst.

'Bloody foreign snail scum!' he roared. 'Eaters of dee leetle frogs! Aw haw haw haw haw! You dirty traitors!'

Jean Jeff passed on, through the voiceless vistas of her past, not hearing her own soft-throated curses, and paying less attention to Eck's. The real danger lay in the likelihood that Eck would cause himself some irreversible injury in the physical fury of his loathing. As to why he hated the French, or considered them to be traitors, he hadn't the wit to explain to anybody who bothered to ask him. The fact is that although the whelks went down by train to London, Eck believed there was a chance that some of them might be shipped across the Channel, and in any case he associated the sea-snails with those peoples of the earth who found the earthly variety so disgustingly delectable.

One year I was allowed to go down to the boat with grandfather to see him off on a four a.m. tide to the summer drave. We came two hours early to check the stores and the gear. As we walked along the pier we saw the dim gaslight from Joe and Eck's shed, and when we looked over the pier we saw a dark figure standing in a yawl quietly filling a bucket with whelks from the wall.

'There's Eck poisoning the French again,' grandfather said.

We went on down into the boat.

But when the dark figure, surprised by us, stole up the steps and into the shed, we were struck as dumb as the whelks. It was not Eck— it was Joe.

Strange the surprises that come in with the tide by dark. The tide that took grandfather away.

When he had a day to spare before going off to the drave, he took me up to Kellie Law under a soft blue sky in which the stray clouds floated in silvery wisps like lumps of bubbles out of the backyard boiler. The warm silk of the south-west breezes stroked the fields, scarcely stirring the stalk-still corn. By the sides of the hot bright roads stone-crop dripped like honey along the tops of the lichened dykes, the wild roses were in flower, the hips and honeysuckle in the hedgerows, and the long avenues of elders were putting forth their rich creamy blooms—billions of brides holding their virgin bouquets, untouched as yet by the time turning. Masses of thistledown floating like white old heads whispered to them, drifted across the footpaths where the deep green mosses covered the fallen stones.

On the high slopes of Kellie Law we sat and stared at the landscape stretched out beneath our feet. From the sprinkled farms and cottages we could see the tiny people, etched and embroidered like figures on some vast green canvas. Some were at their work, some were moving out in processions. One of these was strung out like a trail of bright flowers scattered from the Carnbee kirk; another was a long narrow black file, and the memory of Hodgie came and went through the sunlight in my head. But except for the colours of the folk there would have been no telling whether the far-away files were marrying or burying parties—no noise or movement came from them, and their laughing and their tears suddenly became irrelevant, surrounded as they were by the sheer simplicity of green. I wondered if the old man whom we had met up in Balcormo was still alive. At that moment the packed patchwork of people's lives frightened me for the first time. These fields had taken the thousands of folk who had tilled them down the years, and had spread over them like a great green bedcover. Even those who now worked the floral fields would be ploughed under before they saw the trees look any older, or the fields any different from what they were.

'The country boys are seeing to their brides and their buryings,' grandfather said.

We sat and looked at the printed processions of people.

'One way or the other there's always ploughing to be done.'

Fisher marriages were usually left until later in the year, and I recalled old Leebie's saying about marrying.

Marry in March and you'll bend like the larch
Marry in Lent and you'll surely repent
Marry in May there's the Devil to pay

She had more lines of it, which stayed locked in her head when she laid it down for the last time. According to Leebie the chances of a good marriage were one out of twelve. As I write this now, the chances of a quick divorce are one in three.

'Any time's a good time for marrying,' said grandfather. 'But I've never heard tell of a good time for dying.'

He took me to the stile by which we had crossed over to the summit of the hill. Exposed to sun and wind, the wooden spars were like bleached bones, the shiny step smoothed hollow by the feet which had passed across to the other side, time and time over, fleshless feet which had journeyed to the undiscovered country, from whose bourn no traveller returns.

Back on the shore the blue spaces never frightened me as did the green.

It was the culmination of the year.

Grandfather always referred to the solstice as Milner's time (after Milner's *Gallery of Nature* which he read avidly) when Altair, his favourite summer star, was a dewdrop in the south-east, and the afterglow so strong that the sea was a silver glimmering all through the passing dusk. He told me that George claimed to have sat on the summit of an Orkney hill at midnight on the solstice, one of a rum-filled ring of wild young men, and seen the sun's upper rim flaming just beneath the horizon.

The green sleet was arriving at its fullest growth in the sea, making the rocks into mountains of slippery green eels, but we prided ourselves on being able to skim like birds along the shore and not to stumble once; while a bad bruising or a soaking was the lot of the visitor boys who came at the end of June and the start of July, and whose feet went sliding from under them on our rocky coast.

At low tide in the mornings the steam rose from the tangles in a gentle mist, the whelks crawled out onto the rocks, and the waterpools lay like broken mirrors among the black crags. Now the eiders had stopped their whooing; only the whisperings and strange hissings from the laminaria broke the silence of the shore, depopulated of its waves like a town on Sunday as the tide held its blue inaudible distance. The rest of the seabirds too fell quiet for a space, as if they could almost sense that summer was tilting. The black-headed gull was already beginning to shed its executioner's hood, and its winter white-cap was coming on; and the cormorant was just starting to lose the white thigh-patch on its black-green glossy feathers.

Only a narrow and a quiet eye could see those things, the wintry decline of life begin even at the height of summer, death stirring in the midst of life as all the May moisture in things began to dry up. Summer seemed, in fact, to grow stronger still for a space, the orchestral chatter of insects increasing while the birdsong declined, the bluebottles sunning themselves on the sunny sides of the dykes, the invisible point of life expanding.

I made my way in slow motion to the harbour.

In the tar-and-tangle of the afternoon the old remaining boats creaked on the still tide, resting at last from the sea, and as I lay on my belly on the warm pier, the moored mind kept time with them, rubbing and bobbing against the sleeping stones and the pier's moss-grown gentleness. The June sun beat like a golden gong in the sky. But from the creels stacked along the harbour wall there crept the deep cool smells of unseen seas, fanning me out of sleep.

Opening my eyes again, my poppy head hanging over the edge, I watched the flatfish flapping slowly in and out of the harbour mouth, taking the sun on the sandgreen bed of the bottom, where the seagulled sky was superimposed like a dream—birds and fish mingling in an impossible element. Around me drifted the tall tobacco tales piping blue and easy from the after-dinners of the old salts, who sat with their backs to the stones, caps shading their eyes; and off the harbour walls and into the golden drench of the firth they lingered and faded, into the thin and insubstantial air that they were.

But I could not take the trouble to listen to their stories. I closed my eyes again. The smell of centuries was everywhere, and the rocking voices of the old men, as drowned and dead as dusty fathers and their grandfathers and their great-great-grandfathers, as the yellow grains the waters wetted for a tide, then left—then drowned again, over and over: through the smell of sun and salt they came alive. Summer was outstretched in a blue stupor on the pier. In the bright darkness of the old afternoon the village slept, and all my ancestors rose from the waves, preserved in the tang of my sea-dreams.

Time was at anchor here.

JULY

When the janitor clanged the school gates closed behind us for the summer holidays, it was sweet bells jangled, out of tune but not harsh. Pleasure lay on the outside with us for the next seven weeks, no longer torn through iron bars. But how could we take our pleasure when there was no-one to stop us? At once we found ourselves with nothing to do and the whole oyster world to do it in.

Inevitably we looked for trouble.

The harbour master was an old wrinkled kipper of a man called Harry Watson. He had an office at the head of the middle pier, not much bigger than a drifter's wheelhouse. There he dozed and dreamed all year long, lost in a cloud of black tobacco that smoked him through all the earthly stages, past all the known frontiers of preservation, until he was cured for eternity and beyond. Inside this office there were three items of furnishing: a sloping desk for his feet and legs, a high chair on the tilt for his back and behind, and a coke stove to deepen his tobacco tan until his face was as tough and leathery as his ancient brown shoes.

On winter days the harbour office was a haven of warmth, and as many old men as could squeeze inside stood bunched together like strings of herring smouldering over the sawdust. But in the hot summer weather only Harry could bear it. He lay back in his chair, his pipe lolling slackly out of his sleeping mouth, snoring like a funnel in the engine-room glow of the coals. Standing on Gollie's shoulders, I hoisted myself up the tarred wall of the hellfired little howff and onto its hot corrugated roof. Peem threw up a handful of old netting which I stuffed in fistfuls into the saw-toothed tin chimney. The last of the black feathers drifted across the harbour and were gone. We waited behind a barricade of fishboxes for Harry to emerge.

It always amazed us how long it took.

On the one hand there was the sheer wonder of it that the white-bearded old Satan inside was breathing freely in his own infernal element; and on the other hand there was the growing conviction that we had asphyxiated him. Then the door was flung open and Harry flew out with the fumes, toothless, spitting and snarling, his eyes streaming and his arms waving wildly as he tried to scatter the clouds with his battered old cheesecutter. We shoved over a few fishboxes, ran a circle round him three times, making malicious mockery of his wheezing attempts at rage, and made off along Shore Street with Harry spluttering at the pierhead and shaking his fist and invoking fate and metaphysical fury to fall upon our heads.

'The wicked fleeth while no-one pursueth!' he wailed.

We reached the west pier in triumph and staggered about with horrific and helpless satisfaction as his cabin belched blackly over the water like a ship on fire, till some supple-jointed seventy-year-old mountaineered his way shakily to the roof and freed the choked funnel. With most of the able-bodied men in the town away, we ran wild like this for days with the first taste of freedom.

We ran down to Buckland, where Bella Dunn's back garden came tumbling in green waves to the shore. When we lit up our tinny fires on the beach, Bella came running over the grass and danced on her dyke, frantically shooing us off.

'I boond from the Bass!' she screeched like an hysterical hen.

Over and over again it was the same thing from Bella.

'I boond from the Bass! I boond from the Bass!'

Her fue duty was one coffee bean, and for that, she maintained, her property rights extended over the dyke, down the foreshore and right across the firth in a straight line to the Bass Rock itself. As for the fishing boats—so she argued it out on the pier—they were constantly crossing and re-crossing between the shore and the Bass that narrow strip of unfenced blue water that was rightly hers; and in addition to their harbour dues they ought to be paying her an appropriate fee. She came down to the pier frequently to demand it, and was usually quietened with a fish from one of the skippers. Otherwise, she boasted, she could make them steam right round the other side of the rock and be well on the way to Leith before they could come back to port.

When Bella chased us we went barefooted into the water looking for snoaches, and when we had trapped a few of the sea-scorpions we dropped them in a bucket and came back with them to the harbour, where we fixed a good-sized cork to each one, jabbing them onto their spiny backs, tossing them into the water, then standing back and waiting for the gala to begin. A humble cork, the lightest of loads, proved to be a deadly burden for these short-spined fish, popping them skywards when they tried to dive, and so preventing them from leaving the surface in order to feed and breathe properly.

In their desperation they performed galleries of agonised aquabatics, drawing cruel whoops from the spectators. They traced lightning zig-zags about the harbour like daft drunken dancers, markers gone mad, shooting stars fizzing out sherbet bubbles in their wake. At their wits' end they stopped dead, and summoning all the strength in their prickly scales they went down deep. Seconds later they shot up like balloons and landed back on the surface with a spash, ridiculously defeated. In the holiday weather, when we went swimming in the harbour, we chased them in dolphin droves, hunting them down with screams and splashes, only to free them in the end from their comic crucifixions, and let them return to the sanity of their cool cellars among the rocks and weeds, well away from the first regrettable frenzies of boys on holiday.

One summer a much bigger sea specimen came into the harbour.

I saw it from the back yard first thing in the morning, swimming between the May Island and the shore—a black boomerang that ripped open the firth, shot up higher than the lighthouse, crossing the white orbits of the gannets, and crashed back into the sea with mountains of snow cascading to the clouds.

I ran up the stairs to George's house.

He was standing at his open window, already fully dressed, and the pages of his bible fluttering in the blue breeze from the sea. His spyglass was at his eye.

'What is it, Gramps? Can I see?'

He handed me the glass, and I looked, and saw for the first time, close, the savage cut and thrust of that living scimitar slashing and thrashing the waves, the battling bull head, the powerful fin, and the tigerish tail that mauled the water, churning it like a propellor.

'What is it?' I shouted. 'Is it a whale?'

'Aye, they call it a whale,' George said, 'but it's liker a wolf.'

'Is it like the ones you used to hunt for?' I asked.

'No,' he said quietly, 'that's a killer out there. And compared to the beasts I went after, that one is a butcher, let me tell you, a bad black butcher.'

He told me how he had seen a pack of killers tear out the tongue of one of the great blue whales.

'It was nearly ninety feet long,' he said, 'and its tongue in its jaws must have weighed a ton. They just ripped it out and fed on it while it was bleeding to death from the mouth.'

'Didn't you catch killer whales, Gramps?'

He turned, and I saw his back making for the door.

'Come with me,' he said.

I followed him down to the lumber room of the old house. It was like the interior of a shipwreck—everywhere there were broken bits of everything that had to do with the fishing. He clambered stiffly over the piles of torn nets, long since mouse-eaten, dog-torn and condemned, throwing aside shredded baskets and boxes and punctured dahns in his struggle to reach what he was after. I frisked after him on all fours, sniffing at this and that. He was in the corner, tugging heavily at a stiff tarpaulin draped on a long pole.

'Pull it off,' he breathed, 'you that has so much life in you.'

I had the eye to see but not the understanding to know that my great grandfather was no more the man who had taken the Jehovah's Witness by the throat.

He tilted the pole and I pulled at the faded green sheeting which came away—and my mouth opened wide.

It was his old harpoon.

Nine feet of lacquered larch and a further foot of solid iron, tipped with the most brutal barb that made even a gartlin hook seem like a bent pin. The everyday working weapon of my great grandfather's youth, unveiled after half a century—now standing upright and shining in the bright windowed corner of a local museum.

'Can you handle it?' he asked.

He did not wait to see.

I followed him through the transe and into the yard, amazed at the sheer weight and size of the arrow that hurt the whale to the heart. We looked out at the killer, still wounding the firth like a vicious vandalizing ploughshare.

'That fish wasn't made by God,' the old man said, buttoning his jacket as the wind came up stronger with the brightening sun. 'Do you know what it will do? It will slash open the bellies of seals for sheer sport and leave them dying among the rocks. It will bite the heads off their bairns just out of its badness.'

He steadied himself against the galluses and reached out for his old weapon.

'I'll tell you this, too. If I had seventy years off my back I'd take that harpoon and a boat, and I'd go out there right now and bring about the death of that brute in the name of the Lord.'

I looked at him as he stood beside me white and trembly, putting up his hand to his blurred old eye.

'But this is the nearest I'll ever come now to a whale.'

The first surge of sorrow for one of my own family. One whom I should never have dared dream of pitying. But just a few short years of my life had begun in him the slow stiffening which was a rehearsal for his death.

I looked away from him and out again at the whale, still whipping the waves into a welter of white foam.

'I think it's coming in, Gramps!'

He peered hard over the rooftops.

'So it is,' he said slowly. 'It's coming in to shore. It's coming in to die.'

The killer came in with the forenoon tide and the ebb left it stranded in the harbour by the late afternoon, stuck in the mud between the middle and the east pier. Everyone that was alive and walking that day came down to stare at it. Strung out along piers and street, the galleries of folk scrutinized its immobility, its utter possession of agony. The old men said that it was being slowly crushed by its terrific weight, the vanquished victor victim now to its own bullying bulk; the pitiless unpitied.

When they saw its helplessness the swaggering boys began to descend the steps, plodding soggily across the mud to within a few feet of it. The whale ignored them. Trapped inside its carcass, and netted in air, it could do nothing. Only its tail flapped idly like a tangle at low tide. Closer they came, the brave ones, till they could reach out and touch the torpedo itself in its defused, defenceless state. They landed puny punches on the very tip of the slumped warhead, jumping backwards with cracking halloos as though expecting an explosion. Undetonated, it seemed as invulnerable as the air around it, and their vain grimacings as grotesque as their blows.

Then the first of the boldest clambered onto the big back, near to the tail end, clutching at the hulk with his hands and feet as if he were hanging on to the edge of the Himalayas by a hinge of hair. The whale gave no reaction and the boy was joined by two others. They stood like victorious climbers on their cheap-won summit, arms aloft, cheering. The crowd did no cheering at first, but someone threw them down a flag to stick in its back. Mad matadors mocking the bull. So some people started to laugh.

This was what gave me the sudden glorious idea of bringing down George's harpoon. I ran home fast and stood outside the house taking slow deep breaths before creeping in soft-footed to the lumber room where the mighty arrow was back in its green quiver. But George's hearing was not what it was. His ears were filled with fog. I hurried back to the harbour, frightened in case everyone had gone.

They were in full attendance. The game had reached another stage, and the whale was now crawling with boys, who were taking it in turns to drop pennies down the blow-hole. Seconds after being dropped in, the pennies were shot high into the sky, to the roars of the crowd and much hand-clapping. Many of them were now openly appreciating the sport, to the extent of taking small bets on heads or tails. And each time it sent the coin spinning into the air, the stung whale smashed its tail madly into the mud, sending a boy or two slithering to a soft but dirty landing.

Then people started to notice my harpoon, and a small circle of grinning faces formed itself for me in the crowd. I brandished it clumsily, shouting to the boys down below to watch out for it.

One man climbed onto a pile of fishboxes.

'Thar she blo-oo-ows!'

He flung back his head and pointed.

Great was my encouragement.

'Gangway, there, out the road, you folks! The boy here is going to let him have it, aren't you? Right between the eyes.'

The size of the stage, the audience, and the real life prop which I found myself holding, suddenly made me into a pygmy.

'No,' I said, sullen and blushing. 'My Gramps will do it.'

They all laughed hugely.

'What, old Geordie Marr? He couldn't throw a fit these days! Let's see how you can throw.'

The picture of an enraged silver lion flashed behind my eyebrows, gripping in his bearded jaws a wolf in sheep's clothing, heaving him down the steps and out of the fold. I saw my great grandfather's withered white arm, seventy years of sap taken out of it, bend suddenly like a sapling to the renewed gale of his youth and fury. My own arm knew then what it was to be his. It uncoiled, and the harpoon spun whistling like a javelin from the pier, travelled through space for a terrible eternity of sixty feet. It sang in the skull of the whale for a brutal bone-crunching second, ending its misery, swayed there like a pine tree in the wind, creaking in the held breath of the crowd.

The crowd released its voice then, and I opened my eyes and saw the harpoon sticking stupidly in the mud. I had achieved a throw of maybe five feet.

Hoots and jeers all round. The whale lay like a black Christ. Loathing opened in me like a wound, the seepage from the stigma.

A coarse drunkard called Bert Mackie leapt onto the whale and shouted to the people that he would now spend a different kind of penny in the blowhole.

'We'll see if it survives my harpoon!' he brayed boozily.

The women shrieked, demented, and the air cracked with the whinnyings of the old men.

That was when the minister arrived.

In a kirk silence he materialised in the mud and told Bert to come down. Instead Bert began to execute a vulgar parody of the hornpipe on the whale's back.

The Reverend Kinnear heaved himself up. Without wasting another word he drove his fist straight into the slack side of the drunkard's leering jaw. Bert teetered on one leg for a fraction, then he crashed crazily into the sucking slime, where he lay like a log.

The minister was still standing on the humped whale, quieter now without its tormentors. Everybody waited to hear what he would say. He was breathing fiercely through flared nostrils, his eyes like live coals. His huge fingers were clenching and unclenching, white and red.

But he could not speak for rage. He jumped down and sank up to his ankles. Nobody laughed. Then he strode with soiled shoes and red face across the harbour bed.

'Get me a hose!' he roared as he came up the steps.

A long hose pipe was produced within seconds.

He attached it himself to the tap outside Harry's office, drew it along Shore Street, and pointed it over the wall at the silent whale.

'Turn it on!'

A fountain of fresh water flowered brightly in the sky and fell. The whale was engulfed in a well of life. A great sigh rippled through its whole slow length and everybody seemed to sigh along with it, seeing its last need fulfilled.

But the Reverend Kinnear stayed there himself all through the rest of the afternoon and into evening, hosing down the grateful killer until the first fingers of blue tide touched its dying sides. He made two men with motor yawls tie ropes to its tail, and he went along with them, towing it slowly out of the harbour and releasing it a mile off shore.

And there it died.

But for weeks after that it was washed up at different places along the coast, haunting one harbour after another on the flood tides. Finally it came to rest on the west rocks, just where the Old Kirk spread its grave-green skirts down to the sea. By this time it was stinking.

Kinnear preached a sermon about it.

'O, thy offence is rank, it smells to heaven!' he told his congregation.

One that was helpless had come to them lacking water—and they gave it gall. The dog returneth to his vomit, and wickedness winds its way back to the nostril of the sinner, the owner of that foul disease, indifference; hardness; lack of charity.

When George heard what Kinnear had preached he grunted and grumbled.

'He should go to the whales,' he said. 'He'd not come back with a bleeding heart for killers.'

'You could have harpooned it, Gramps,' I said, siding with him, and remembering my own sorry throw. 'You could have killed it when it was stuck in the mud.'

I looked at his quiet arms.

'No, I couldn't,' he said. 'It wouldn't have been fair that way. But if it had been seventy years ago it could have taken its chances with me in the sea, and I'd have brained it stone dead.'

It wasn't until the drifters came home in August that we were finally rid of the whale. But it keeps on returning, on those tides that ebb and flow within the brain.

The sea was always bringing in something or other, to provide an hour's fun, to give us pause for longer, or to last for a lifetime and never go away.

Out at the waterline one summer, hunting the choicest whelks for Joe's Billingsgate demand, we stumbled over a half sunk crate. It had no markings on it that we could see, and it was seemingly intact, but it proved to be as immoveable as a gravestone. We scooped and threw, flinging off sand with our red stinging fingers, until we were able to lift it free and carry it to the foreshore. There we stove it in with boulders, prising away the splintered spars like wooden teeth from the shrieking, rusted nails.

Wordless, ringed-eyed, ringed-mouthed, we stared, the three of us, into a full case of Spanish white wine.

'We'll cook mussels with it,' announced Gollie, astonishing us with this instinctive grasp of epicurean principles.

We ran to the scoops and tore away tough handfuls, shredding the tips of our fingers in our haste. Not possessing a corkscrew, we burst the neck of a bottle over a boulder, filled a large treacle tin, lit the fire, dropped in the mussels, and sat around inhaling the fumes.

Twenty minutes later we were tasting Neptune's nectar, turning our mussels to the forbidden ambrosial food of the sea-gods. After that there was nothing to stop us. We took the treacle tin by turns and emptied it to the drains. A second helping, then a second bottle burst on the boulder, boiled up without the ambrosia this time, drinking it hot and bubbling from the blackened tin. The goodness of it grew all the way down to our heads and up to our feet. We were ravished. We decided on a third bottle unboiled.

The first cold sweetness of the white wine grape touched my tongue, cooled a long age in the deep undelved saltness of the sea's cellar. It was more than ravishing, it was unbelievable, it was utter ecstasy, it was our only drink from now on.

'We're the One-Gallus Gang,' said Peem solemnly.

Drinking out of the dead heads of the dominies, our long ancestral enemies, gorging ourselves to glory on the embattled edge of the sea.

Gollie picked up a big scallop shell and filled it with a pale glimmering of gold.

'This is Sangster's skull,' he tittered, swigging off his libellous libation with a flourish.

He clapped the shell on his head and went staggering about the beach with long prowling strides.

'Open your sum books at the end! Open your mouths wide, you stupid wee beggars! Open another bloody bottle, boys!'

The tinkling of broken glass and Gollie waved a golden waterfall over us while we lay back catching what we could in our spluttering faces. Sangster's skull fell emptily to the shingle. We kicked it around till we were breathless before smashing it to white splinters.

'Go and meet your maker in hell, you lemon-faced old nanny-goat!'

'Have one for the road!'

'Up your behooky!'

How we hated her.

'We're Spanish sailors!' cried Peem.

'No, no, no.'

I lectured him heavily.

'Drake beat the Spaniards. We're British sailors drinking the Spaniards' wine.'

'And having their women too!' roared Gollie.

'And kissing them!'

Unutterable and inexplicable. We laughed as loudly as we possibly could, out of our undefined pain, at the thought of kisses that lay beyond the Spanish seas.

'Get out your Oxford Song Books, you drunken dunderheads! *You're tone deaf, boy, you're dumb as the devil made you*! You're dumb as they come! *Get your hands out of your pockets*! Get your hands off these girls! *Off these garters*! Off these Spanish ladies, I say! Are you ready then? One, two, three . . .'

One, two, three.

> *Farewell and adieu to you fair Spanish ladies,*
> *Farewell and adieu, all you ladies of Spain—*
> *For we've received orders to sail for old England,*
> *But we hope in a short time to see you again.*
>
> *Now let every man drink off a full bumper,*
> *Now let every man drink off a full bowl,*
> *For we will be jolly and drown melancholy,*
> *With a health to each jovial and true-hearted soul.*

We stood up.

The shore was rolling underneath our feet and the skyline tilted. So we stood splay-footed on the bouldery deck, sea-legged, as the beach battled through the gathering clouds, the earthship spinning in space, we ranted and raved like true British Spaniards while the wine whirled round and round in our heads. It was a wild crossing.

> *Blow the man down, bullies, blow the man down.*

As we tossed and pitched and lurched and heeled, struggling to make it back to port.

> *And away-hay, blow the man down.*

We scuttered and slid about the deck, slipping in pools of seawater, clinging to one another in the teeth of the wind that tore at our hair.

> *The gale she is raging far out on the deep,*
> *Away-hay, blow the man down.*

The waves pounded us.

But we stood upright again and our heads flew from our bodies, soaring into the bellowing blue like lumps of spray across the surging sea.

> *So give us a chance to blow the man down.*

We blew mightily on one another.

I blew on Peem and he dropped like a tree in the storm. Gollie blew on me and I fell alongside Peem. From where we lay the two of us blew at Gollie where he still stood, swaying like a maniacal mast in the force of the hurricane that now raged. He righted himself, riding out the blast, his shirt tails flapping like the winter sails of the *White Rose*. We gave one last whoosh of our combined wine-laden winds—and he toppled and rolled, crashing into us with a splintering of vocal chords. We became insensible as spars. The sea broke over us.

When we woke up we were dead men.

Mewing and puking, we reeled homewards, running the gamut of eyes and faces, jabbering tongues and jabbing fingers. We were totally disgraced. Leebie threatened to knock me back into final senselessness with the leg of a chair. My aunts laughed till they had to lie down for the soreness of their sides. So it was my mother and grandmother who brought me through my first hangover. They used aspirins, soda from a siphon, hot sweet blackcurrant drinks, hot water bottles, window blinds, eyeshades, smothering blankets; some sober whispering and a great deal of sympathy.

Jenny assured me that she had put forward my name for the next meeting of the Fishermen's Mission. I would have to say that I had learned my lesson and the error of my ways, and I would then be called upon, so young a reprobate, to give my testimony.

There was another cargo which intoxicated me in a different way, though I did not consume it as I did the wine. It was washed right up onto the shore very early in the first liquid light, before even the old men were stirring for their solitary constitutionals and their shots at the morning handlines.

It was a crate of oranges.

They were of unbelievable size when I ripped away the roof of the packing case—giant planets they were from comic cuts of the solar system, juicy Jupiters plucked from the sky's best and packed together brightly in a close constellation of their own. I took one in my hands. They were unspoiled, as fresh as if they had just been tossing on green trees, taken as they were from the white surf-flowers by the plucking fingers of the morning tide. I brought the fruit in my hand closer to my face, my nose. It was a burning cannonball, golden, gorgeous. We saw very little of oranges in those days.

I made to peel it. As I did so I hit on my extraordinarily amazing plan, so inspired that it took off my own breath. I would not eat a single orange. These fruits were not for me, they were for someone else, someone who had been starved of them for years, a being more exotic than Spanish ladies and cases of white sea-cooled wine. They were for the Princess. Who else? They were meant for her, and I was the mysterious messenger, her deliverer. With this cargo of glorious golden roundshot I would assail the unassailable Paloma, she the unseen. I would take them to her door.

I put them on my shoulder and walked along the deserted beach, past the kirk, over the brae and up to the great ornamental gates, which I opened with one hand. I went straight as an arrow across the trim lawn and pushed apart the front doors without hesitation. The butlers were asleep. I knew where to go. I fingertipped a glass-paned door and found myself in the tropical room, a bronzed buccaneer with bandana and paired pistols in both sides of my swashbuckled belt, ready to pirate my desire.

And there she was. The Princess Paloma was bathing like a lily in the pool, right up to her neck in her morning green coverlets of water. As soon as she saw me she stood up, throwing off the rippling covers. She was dark but comely, O ye daughters of Jerusalem, and as she came naked through the water to me, with webs of light winking on her skin, I knew the language of love, and my lips formed the words that I had read and heard somewhere before, spoken to her water-beaded breasts and her dripping hair and her sandalled feet as she stepped out. Red roses of Mrs Guthrie withered in the kirkyard, Miss Balsilbie banished far beyond the Bass, where the white roses fall— and the furious flame of Miss Sangster's vengeance burning in her thin and brittle bosom where she stood at the iron gates of life.

> *How beautiful are thy feet with shoes, O prince's daughter!*
> *the joints of thy thighs are like jewels, the work of the hands*
> *of a cunning workman.*
> *Thy navel is like a round goblet which wanteth not wine:*
> *thy belly is like an heap of wheat set about with lilies.*
> *Thy two breasts are like two young roes that are twins . . .*

The Princess Paloma bowed low before me, her lord and master, the bringer of her native succulents. I set down the crate at her feet. Her skin glowed in the orange light of the rising suns, assembled for her pleasure. She offered me the first fruit in her hands and I tasted desire. Her lips were a thread of scarlet and they dropped as the honeycomb, the smell of her nose was like apples, honey and milk were under her tongue and the roof of her mouth was like the best wine for her beloved. We fed among the lilies.

> *Eyes like the fish-pools in Heshbon by the gates of Bath-rabbim . . .*
> *Nose like the tower of Lebanon which looketh toward Damascus . . .*

For she knew my uniqueness, knew what others could not yet see, that I was specially picked out to provide for the mysterious needs of such a one as she. I would marry her without a bible in my hand and her flower would never fade. We should not grow old like a photograph. The *White Rose* would carry us off on our eternal honeymoon, my grandfather breaking bottles of champagne on the bows, my great-grandfather standing in the crow's nest with the glory of youth aglow in his soul, the spray flying in our faces as we rolled and rolled far into the far-flung skylines of our lives.

But by the time I put down the box of oranges by the front door, I had lost the courage to ring the bell, with the strange faded names on the brass plate, Darsie, Titaua Marama, Ouiritania. I walked quickly back to the gates without looking once over my shoulder, then I ran to the safety of the kirkyard and hid by the grave of Darsie and his bride. I stood there all through the day, reading the lettering on the slab, the same faded names that were engraved on the brass bell-plate, and that were carved on the brass plates of their coffins, beneath the butterflies, beneath the bees. I waited and I waited for the child of that fallen flesh and bone to emerge and accept my oranges. Never a curtain stirred in the big old windows, not a blade of grass on the lawn. The box began to look smaller and sillier as the day wore on, and when I went home for tea I could not bear to look in its direction. But when I returned in a smoulder the next morning, my gift had gone. The Princess Paloma had kept her silence, her sanctuary. She remained inviolate, invisible.

So I followed Peem and Gollie to the crumbling old castle to watch the courting couples.

The castle stood in ruins on a green-caped crag less than half a mile west of the kirk. A great stronghold in its time, its positioning was superb. On the south and east sides it was approachable from the town only by one who toiled breathlessly up the steep green slopes. On the west and north sides was the sheer crag, dropping a hundred feet to skellies and sea. But the killing times were past. Three centuries had assaulted its walls, and people walked in through the gaping holes, unchallenged. The blue sky was its roof and the sea came in the windows; the floors were carpeted with tussock and turf; dogroses decorated the green tapestries, the cold hearthstones.

In winter time the ruins were deserted. But every summer it was once again a field of young folk fresh and fair. It was where the local boys took their girls when they had at last grown tired of tinny fires and had started talking to mirrors instead. When we saw them heading west the braes, hand in hand, secretive, shy, we shadowed their slow feet through the tall grasses of July, allowing them always ample time to disappear between the castle walls before closing in fast and frantic, giggling guiltily, afraid of what we would miss, afraid of what we would see.

And what did we see, drawn in the summer grass?

Boy and girl no longer but broken into parts—their eyes, their lips, their heads and arms and legs, lying intermingled in the great green hand of the hill, where the castle kept their secret and the sea and sky stood guard. So private and impregnable they were, so utterly alone—oblivious to the younger eyes that watched from castle walls and wondered. Wondered at the closeness of a kiss. What happens when it happens? What quivering flame of knowledge burns between two people when that fragile point of contact is arrived at, when lips converse without words? Where was the girl who would sooner or later tame these wild uncertainties which sometime grew so great? Shaken and stirred by this, we opened our mouths wide and bawled in hollow mockery of the bigger boy who had broken from the life of the shore and reached that unknown strand, who had found the country we knew nothing of as yet.

We brayed our hatred of him. We threw down handfuls of grass and stones, letting them know that we had sullied their secret, and we ran hooting and howling across the fields, breaking the too terrible beauty of silent union. For the next five minutes we kicked the heads off daisies and dandelions, savagely smashing stones off rocks in our frustration. Then we ran to the castle doocot.

The castle dwellers had long since left the torments of the flesh to dwell with dust; and whatever love-lorn heads had sighed across the salt stretches of the firth were now anonymous with stone and bone.

But the doves were still in evidence. Their feathers had downed the pillows for those lovely heads; their meat had stuffed pigeon pies for amorous appetites; their wings had borne the billets-doux and their billing and cooing soothed the summer-tired ears of the castle ladies. And the doves were still breeding after three hundred years where the stones of men had fallen, love run dry, and only the dogrose sprang to flower.

The doocot was rather like a miniature broch, a fifteen foot round-tower with a wide base, tapering to a small grassy top, on which two or three adventurers might stand, as if on a bastion, and take a survey of the land and sea. A single door led into a curved blackness of tiered ledges in which the pigeons nested several scores at a time. At the end of our tethers for something to do, we usually ended up at the doocot. One of us climbed the outer walls and sat perched on the summit with his jumper off, crouching over the small eyelet through which the doves came and went. The other boys went inside and sang out so suddenly, so abominably bad, that there was a fluttering of invisible wings and the first bird out of the eyelet was caught in the trap. As soon as we had calmed it down we tied a luggage label to its leg, bearing some silly or scurrilous scrawl.

> *Straight to Sangster, say you're mine,*
> *Tear her knickers off the line.*

And bravely we added our signatures, wondering if there was any chance that she would ever read our scribbled messages. Then we let the bird go.

The grass around the doocot was another well-flattened courting area. Though not so private as the castle, its height and openness allowed the lovers the luxury of being able to spot an approach from miles in any direction, and there were no hidie-holes from which younger folk could gawp at the serious romantic gestures of those who had crossed over into their teens. From that viewpoint it was a more strategic position from which to advance the war against the female and play the game of love.

One summer a great burly bully called Scott MacDonald threw up his job at the fishing and joined the army. After two weeks he was back on crutches after wounding himself in the knee with his own bayonet. For all the toffees he had stolen from us, and all the cuffs and kicks we had had for payment, we punished him now with taunts and jeers, hurled at him from a carefully assessed distance outside his huge reach and the swing of his crutches. He limped painfully along, cursing and swearing, but he could do nothing except reap in sorrow what he had sown in our tears.

When the Glasgow Fair began, the visitors arrived by train and the town filled up with big-eyed girls whom we followed at discreet distances, despairing of ever arriving at a destination that was years away. Scott was pitied at once by a blonde and buxom beauty of his own years, whose short dresses and extreme décolletage caused the tongues on Shore Street to buzz like wires in the rain. The bold Scott now threw away his crutches like one whom love had healed, and taking this girl by the hand he led her west the town. The old men chuckled and winked underneath their sun-shading caps, and they sucked their pipes knowingly.

But we had not yet run our passions' heat. We crept after them hungrily, in and out of shop doors, behind the boatshed, along by the rocks. We wove ourselves round gravestones, crawled the whispering green cities of corn, threaded our way through the fumes of poppies and daisies and pineapple weed. Our hands were sweaty and our faces red. We tried to keep quiet but the giggles kept on coming up from our groins and we held them down hard. Still we had not been seen.

Frustration. Scott was making for the doocot and not the castle. There was no cubby-space, no chink between stones, no eye-widening crack through which we might see the unseeable.

Until Peem arrived at his brave decision.

'We'll climb right up the doocot on his blind side,' he said. 'We'll spy on them from the top.'

A venture fraught with hazard.

So we went like snakes in the grass, without our feet. Accursed beasts of the field, biting the dust on our bellies, we slid quickly but quietly towards the sanctuary, touching at last its oldness, its innocence. We lay still for a few moments and breathed secretly, knowing the man and the woman to be there, somewhere on the other side. The doves were murmuring and moaning, immemorial in our ears. We took off our socks and shoes then, gripped the old stones with white fingers and toes, and hauled ourselves up with held breath.

Once on the top it was frightening and weird. The sky was all around us, no longer a sky of earth, the firth was a far blue field in the down below, and the terrible Scott was just fifteen feet away, full of hot hatred and stupidity and a need for love. If he heard us we were dead. He was built like Goliath and needed no cubits added to his stature to take him up the doocot walls in three quick steps, lame leg and all. And we had no wings of doves to carry us safely to heaven.

The silence was unbearable. What was going on down there? Carefully, in case we dislodged a daisy that might drop its warning to the lovers, we lowered ourselves to our knees, hid from the sky, and squirmed to the rim of the tower. Six unwinking eyes rounded, held for one unending second of time the wide-lashed wonder of the bleached sea-goddess, as she lay half-wreathed in the green seaweed tangles of her clothes, turning untidily in the tide. The white shock of her flesh burned our vision, she screamed, we went rigid, Scott screwed up his face in the sun and saw us: a taut tableau.

Then the Philistine was on his feet, his lame leg looking dangerously fit and well. His mighty fist clenched and he flung his mouthful at us from where he stood.

'I'm going to bloody murder you!'

And he was on the doocot like a bear on a beehive.

I didn't calculate odds or damages, I simply shut my eyes and jumped. Never grass felt so soft and sweet, even after fifteen feet. Then I fled from the fight without a thought for my friends. One for all and all for one was forgotten and there was no stopping until I had reached the kirkyard wall and was standing among the safe familiar gravestones. From there I looked back, panting, and saw the devil on the doocot, blackening the sun, a flimsy criminal silhouetted in each outstretched arm, ghastly burlesque of Golgotha. Scott was banging their heads together as though he were doing chest-expanding exercises, and their concertina cries carried far across the fields where I lay and sweltered and slept.

But they were the lucky ones. Their penance was paid. For weeks and months I had to step warily about the town when Scott was around, and even years later I had to run from him, for his elephant brain never forgot.

To elude Scott for the rest of that summer, I took long walks to Cellardyke, where the Dyker was busy with his partan creels. He brought these ashore at the beginning of July when the crabs were about to cast their shells and were not worth the catching. The weeds in the water had reached their fullest growth and did to the fishing gear what they did to rocks and stones, covering meshes and messenger ropes with slimy green-and-brown sleet. Ropes allowed to lie in the sea for too long became as slippery as live eels.

The creels had to be stood out in the sun to dry. Once the slime had shrivelled and crisped, we scraped it off the meshes, and then it was tarring with the thin tar from the gasworks. This we did on the pier on hot sunny days, using a sock on the right hand to avoid smears and stings. If the week carried the sun with it for the whole seven days then the entire fleet of creels would be completed. Alternatively the Dyker tanned them in the hot cutch to bark them. It was more expensive than tar, but I preferred it, as the sun seemed to bring out from the barking that strangely haunting smell of the sea that stays in the head like a tune that will not go away.

This took up the middle of each day. In the mornings and evenings the Dyker still fished for creel bait for the last shots of the partan season, mainly using the haddock lines. He handed me a steam drifter's shovel which the blacksmith had pruned and told me to dig for lug. If we caught dabs or the black-backed flounders with the white bellies, we used them as bait, but if they were good eatable fish, plaice or lemon soles, we sold them instead to the visitors on the pier.

The visitors hated the conger eels which sometimes came up on our lines. They were savage and greasy, and no amount of slapping them on the pier seemed to kill them—they were insensitive to this treatment, like lengths of black brainless rubber. But if the Dyker caught a big one, he used it for bait, killing it with one crunching bruise of the boot on its sharp, ugly skull.

When the quiet July weather was broken by rains and rough seas, the Dyker would still go out if he thought there was the chance of a good catch, and when going to sea in the *Quest* in conditions such as these, he sometimes used the dreaded words, 'Two rings to the stellum today.'

Two rings to the stellum. Few could understand today the power these words had to impress.

The *Quest*'s sail was the dipping lug sail, and when fully set, the bottom ring on the sail was fastened into a hook which hung from a chain, which passed through a hole in the stem. The Dyker called this taking the tack forward, and in this way the boat could sail close-hauled straight into the eye of the wind. But when the wind darkened and blew strong, the sail had to be reefed, and there were rings set into the weather rope so that a smaller amount of sail could be set. When this was done, the sail was fixed into a hook bolted into an oaken thwart which went from gunwale to gunwale, and into which the mast was stepped. It was this thwart which the Dyker referred to as the stellum. An urgently small quantity of sail was set only two rings from the yard arm, and so the phrase was coined out of the Dyker's mouth, two rings to the stellum. The words tied an elastic knot in my stomach, for they told me that in all sanity we oughtn't to be out at sea at all, even so close to the harbours.

I can still see us running from the storm after a great shoal of summer cod had set in off Pittenweem and scores of boats were sprooling there. We were on a tack towards the shore in a westerly half gale, racing along on the sickening upslope of a sea, awaiting the ghastly lurch that came when the snow-tipped crest was reached, and, our bellies bobbing up to our necks, we slid down the slope on the other side, only to be gaping up the green hill of water that was the upslope of the next sea. The huge flans were chasing us like the wraiths of wrathful seagods sweeping the waves. But the mast stood and we managed the Pittenweem harbour. 'Slacken the sheet!' the Dyker shouted through his teeth, the wind tearing at the words—and I cut desperately. The *Quest* had gone down by the stern but came up like a bubble, and we sat looking at each other in the unreal waters of the quiet harbour, an old man and a small boy.

JULY

July was a blaze of wild roses, heavy with the smell of meadow sweet and tall with willowherb waving at me from the dry ditches and byways. A gooseberry bush burst like a galaxy, hanging out its furred green planets, and strawberries lay in the gardens, fallen sunburnt moons to be conquered in illicit fistfuls to sweeten a walk down the lane.

Yet it was a sad month too.

Towards the end of it the swithers and bladderwrack and the green sleet were coming in on the tide in large quantities, the slack heads of the tangles coming ashore in the south-east gales and heavy rains.

'There's a lot of sea-waur in the harbour this afternoon,' the old men said, when they saw the tangles coming in. 'It'll be winter before you know it's here.'

And as I looked at the debris of the sea, I could see summer slipping away and life going back. The whelks that had mated in April and spawned in June, now began to disappear back underneath the stones. The oyster catcher had come back, but the shelducks were the first to go in July, and would be first to return. But that would not be till the beginning of February. The afterglow was dimming fast by midnight, the sea darkening during the lengthening nights, and the air full of the crushed, powdery dust of life drifting like seeds and stars over the fields.

Old Leebie came back to the house after one of her rare summer visits to the braes.

'Summer comes with a white flower and goes with a white flower,' she said.

She was holding a daisy on her right and a bindweed on her left—life and death in either hand.

AUGUST

By August the North fishing had become played out and the drifters came down to the Northumberland coast and landed their herring at Shields during the week. On Friday nights they shot their nets in a northwards direction, hoping for a modest catch which they could carry straight home and sell on the pier on Saturday mornings for anything between twelve shillings and twenty shillings a cran. But if they made a heavy catch when shooting on the way back to port they had to turn about and steam all the way back to Shields with them, for only small shots could be handled by the St Monans buyers at that time. Either way made for a noisy harbour at the weekend, all fish and funnels; and on a Saturday or a Sunday I had Northumberland herring for tea. They were the biggest and the best that I ever saw taken out of the sea.

But towards the end of his fishing career grandfather reverted in August to fishing in the firth. He was in the company of boats which were skippered by some very old men.

'I'm going to the Lammas Drave,' he announced.

The other skippers laughed at them for living in the past. At one time the Lammas Drave had been the great local fishing in the Forth during August, and tremendous catches had been taken from two stretches of water in particular—the area known as the Traith, off Pittenweem, and the Old Haikes, round Fifeness. But all that had come to an end more than fifty years ago. Nobody referred to it any more as a drave—the shots were small and sporadic for any but a tiny boat such as the *Quest*, and nearly all the steam drifters had been going to Shields for many years. Grandfather trying his Lammas luck at the Haikes and the Traith—it was like an old timer returning to a haunted mine, long after those who had been caught up in the great gold rushes were voices in the empty shafts, bullet-ridden bones in paupers' graves, where the gold no longer shone. It was silver grandfather was after. He himself had never stayed in the firth in summer since his first days at sea when he was a boy. But for some reason the memory surfaced as a kind of anxiety, affirming its grip on him near the end of his life.

147

'Have you taken leave of your senses, man?' my grandmother asked him, she who was always so mild-mouthed. 'The silver's to be had at Shields, you know that well enough.'

'I've gone to Shields for fifty years,' grandfather said. 'If I can make money at home this summer, why go away?'

That summer stands out in my mind's stained windows as perhaps the brightest bit of the old mosaic.

Grandfather came back from Peterhead to a fishless firth, in which he hauled back his nets as empty as they had been shot in the water. After two weeks he came back to the house in despair.

'I've dropped it,' he said simply. 'I'll go to the lobsters with the Dyker. There'll be a penny or two in that.'

But the next morning he was sitting in his fireside chair in front of white ashes, the only time I ever saw him not active—either with his hands, or with that slow quiet talking that was always going on in his mouth—when my mother burst through the door, breathless, her red headscarf falling soundlessly to the floor as she stood spent and gasping. We all looked at her as though she were announcing Armageddon. She gulped several times before she could say the words.

'I've run all the way up the brae . . . It's just come through on the phone from Anster . . . The Dyker says to tell you . . . There's herring in the Haikes! Shoals and shoals of them!'

I never knew then how unique and never-to-be-repeated was the thing I was witnessing.

Grandfather ran from the room without even lifting his cap from the nail by the door, and my mother and grandmother went shouting after him to put on his jacket and take a bite of breakfast in his hand. I ran out into the road. He was halfway down the street, and round his flying figure the words were ringing like bells.

'There's herring in the Haikes! There's herring in the Haikes!'

Workers in the fields at Balcomie had looked up to see the gannets diving in their thousands and had run to the farmhouse to break the news. Soon every little boat that could be floated was fishing off Fifeness. The *Maggie Main*, and the handful of drifters that had stayed at home that summer, lorded it over the others, the lions at the feast. I never saw the scene, and have no picture to remember it by, but grandfather put it vividly for me, just as he hung so many memories in the rooms I go back to now in sleep and sometimes in waking.

'The shoals were so dense,' he said, 'you could have walked on their backs right across to the Bass.'

He remembered it over and over.

'Yes, you could have walked on the water, that you could—right over to the other side.'

I see behind shut eyes the busy boats and the plummeting white shards of the gannets striking the shoals, bombing the waves around them, and I hear in my ears the shouts and screechings, and sense the wonder of the moment—man and bird and fish brought together in a miracle of sudden abundance, the whole cosmos killing and creating itself in a circle of sacrifice and sustenance. And grandfather walking on the water.

For the rest of that week they never stopped. They landed at Anstruther and at Pittenweem and at St Monans in turn, sharing out the catches among the saturated buyers, even steaming across to Newhaven and Dunbar and right back again to Fifeness, round the long clock of the week. And though I never managed to see them hauling in the Haikes, I have one blinding image of St Monans harbour glittering in the morning sun with a million fish; bullion in boxes stacked and lying loose; silver scales everywhere littering the pavements, in folks' eyes and hair and clothes; herring spilling out into the street and slipping back into the water, the gulls going mad as they swooped and swung; gorging their feathered bellies with no-one to stop them. I waded through drifted piles of herring, kicking them like harvest leaves, a glittering sea-god hooting on a horn of plenty to the blue glad spires of the sky.

There was little need for grandfather to go to the lobsters that year.

The lobster season started on St Andrews' Market day, the second Tuesday in August. The creels had already been brought ashore and barked so as to neutralize the seaweeds which grew like the grass on the land, reaching their peak period at about the same time as the hay was cut.

As a matter of truth the lobsters could be caught all the year round, but the Dyker believed in letting things lie for a while, and in allowing nature to count the clock.

'To every thing there is a season,' he quoted, 'and a time to every purpose under the heaven. And the best time for lobsters is in August.'

They cast their shells in June and July, coming inshore when the increasing temperatures of the sea told them that the time had come; and as they provided tasty bites for fish with their armour off, they sought the seclusion of the holes in the rocks rather than engage in an unequal jousting on the sea bed. But they were easily caught by the fishermen in August when they needed food to build up the calcium in their new shells. By September their flesh was at its sweetest, when the Dyker usually gave me two small ones to take home at the weekend. The meat grew tougher later in the year, when the wintry tail in particular became difficult to eat.

Grandfather liked to go to the creels with the Dyker at the extreme end of the summer, before he left for Yarmouth. In the slack days of the firth fishing he showed me how to make a lobster creel. It took twelve hours from start to finish and put patience to the test.

But we always did it in stages. We began with old fishboxes, picked up from the beach for their best spars, and we hammered away at the bottoms for the first day, weighting them with large flat stones.

Then another day would come when grandfather was clear of the boat.

'Let's go up to Balcaskie—I think we'll look for boughs today.'

He knew where all the ash trees were growing wild.

'No, no, not that one, that's willow. We'll get fewer breakages with ash.'

If someone had beaten us to the ash-boughs and there were none to be found without seriously vandalizing the tree, then he took dog-rose stems, whittling away all the thorns with his knife. Only if his hands were filled with time did he trouble to take the stems of the whins. These were the best, he said, because they were the strongest of all, but they refused to bend until they were steamed first over the backyard boiler.

'Great creel boughs, the whins, if God's given you too many hours to spare.'

We tied them across their two ends and brought the bundles down from Balcaskie, stacking them in the garret for the morning when he would say, 'What about putting the boughs on today?'

After we had cut them to size, bent them, and nailed them to the bottom boards, we fixed over them the creel cots, for which we used netting of our own. Last were the creel ends, the ropes attached to the creels, and the painted corks to distinguish our lobster pots from anyone else's. We used the Dyker's colours—green and brown paint, the colours of the *Quest*'s sides and deck. Then they were ready for the new season.

Before thinking about baiting his creels the Dyker nosed round the gardens like a cat, looking hard at the blackcurrant crops.

'If the blackcurrants are ready early,' he said to me, 'you'll know there's as good lobsters to be had for your creels.'

I crammed my mouth with bursting black fistfuls of berries till he was satisfied that I was enjoying myself. Then he pronounced it time for the bait.

The Dyker went to great lengths to find creel bait. Fish heads did not satisfy him. Sometimes he stretched a herring net across the harbour mouth to the loud annoyance of the other fishermen. We weighted the net with chains along the bottom, and that way he caught flounders for his creels. He dropped fresh herring guts into muslin bags and pinned these to the bottom of the creel; soft partans with their claws broken off; congers, dabs and plaice. The bait he liked best were the black-backed flounders with the white fronts.

But grandfather always insisted that stinking mackerel was good enough bait for the lobsters. Baiting the creels with the best bait was risky, because if they didn't manage to haul their creels for a day or more when the weather was bad, they often found that the bait had been taken by uneatable partans—the ones that were soft and white and full of water, unpalatable until October. Sometimes the crabs managed to eat their way out again, or had been small enough in the first place to crawl out the same way as they had come in.

'The Dyker's daft enough to feed a lobster on lemon sole.'

Grandfather shook his head sadly.

'But even horseflesh does a lobster.'

He told me how in George's day one of the St Monans skippers had gone to the Perth sales and brought six strong Clydesdales to pull the herring loads to the station. One horse dropped down dead at the top of the Broad Wynd, and fish and flesh ended up in a dead heap together at the bottom of the brae. Instead of sending it to the knackery at Cupar to give the Fife foxhounds their breakfasts, he sold the carcass to a lobsterman in Crail, and the Crailers baited their creels with great success. But the local farmers disliked it, an inquest followed in Manchester, and horseflesh was proscribed as creel bait.

'In any case,' grandfather argued with the Dyker, 'a lobster is different from a crab. Crabs go into creels on scent, lobsters on sight. You don't even have to use flesh at all for bait—anything will do.'

The Dyker looked away, smiling at the sea.

But to prove his point grandfather set three of the creels aside. He baited one of them with a piece of white rubber from a fisherman's sea-boot, another with a shiny piece of tin, and a third with a broken white plate with a blue border. To the Dyker's despair some of his own creels came in empty, whereas grandfather's three were not only full, but one of them had two lobsters in the same creel.

'There's your answer,' my grandfather said. 'They go in with their eyes and not their snouts, just like I told you.'

I showed this trick to Peem and Gollie.

Peem became a plumber and lost all interest in seawater. But Gollie

151

stole a creel and tied it to a tangle in a rock-ringed puddle just behind the west pier. He caught a lobster with the first tide. Then he stole the blacksmith's long poker, and using it as a cleek, he raked out lobsters from the ring of rocks as if they were magnetized.

Soon he was working with me on the making of our first creel. My own hands were dumb to the language of tools. But Gollie's found a tongue in them and moved mysteriously among the materials grandfather had provided. Gollie was to become a carpenter, making many more creels in his workroom between the cabinets and kitchen tables—till the pull of the tides became too strong for his workman's hands. He left his shop to its sawdust and went out in the small yawls. Years later, when the drifters had disappeared from the coast, he skippered one of the seine-netters, finally graduating to the Antarctic whaling, into a very different set of conditions which had confronted George in his youth.

My boyhood a generation behind me, and on holiday in the East Neuk at the end of a long summer, I heard that my old friend was home from the whales, so I went to his mother's house.

'Let's go for some lobsters,' he said at once.

He was immaculately dressed in a blue double-breasted blazer with silver buttons, grey flannels and a spotted tie.

'How are you going to catch a lobster without a creel?' I asked.

'We won't need a creel,' he said, on the way down to the harbour. 'I'll bet you my old cleek is still where I left it.'

We found the iron rod lying rusted under a ledge on the skelly. The tides of thirty years had come and gone over it. Gollie gripped it firmly, fingering away the cold flakes of rust. His large clean red hands stuck out from his white shirt-cuffs.

We went round all the old holes and crevices, and each time I stood at one end with a stick while Gollie humoured out the lobsters at the other with his cleek. By the time we had fished the skelly we had six beasts in a bucket, and we finished our hunt near the rock-ringed puddle where Gollie had begun his fishing career as a little boy. Lobster-catcher extraordinaire, he never went back to the whales after that, but became a fisherman from one of the Clyde ports. And as a hobby, so I hear, he rakes for lobsters sometimes below Culzean castle.

If there was a heat wave in August, Joe Smith, who bought our lobsters for an agreed price (which was never more than one shilling and sixpence for a whole lobster) would soon produce a blue paper to prove that he had had some lobsters condemned at the Manchester or Billingsgate markets—and down would come the price, sometimes to just one shilling for a whole lobster.

To Joe a whole lobster was one that measured four and a half inches from the end of the snout to the end of the first joint on its back. If the snout was broken it was only half a lobster no matter how big the beast. If it had only one claw it was half again. It was a sad day for Joe when Burgon began buying them by the pound. Then, in what turned out to be a poor season when the beasts were scarce, my grandfather caught a nine and a half pound lobster, the biggest I ever saw, which Burgon bought from him at two shillings and threepence a pound. It was a rare thing for the old man to be able to earn twenty-one shillings from one giant lobster—one throw of the creel.

'A guinea for one of these old grumblers,' he said, 'I just can't believe it.'

His astonishment and his pleasure still register strongly in my seeing of him. Standing on the pier, wrapping up the shilling in the pound note, and dropping it like a pearl into his baggy blue pocket, to lie there with the strands of dark shag and all the broken bits and pieces he carried about with him like a boy.

Once, as I watched grandfather and the Dyker bringing ashore their catches, an old Navy captain who had retired to St Monans, came walking down the pier.

'Have you ever seen a lobster hypnotized?' he asked.

We stared at him.

He took one of the specimens from the bucket, its claws wildly clutching air, and started stroking it all the way from the tip of its snout to the first joint on its back. Under his commanding finger it quietened down, its tail stopped flapping and its claws closed, and he set it down gently on the pier, resting on its snout and its two front claws. Then he bent down close to it. The tail rose vertically like a charmed snake and went taut as a rope under strain. The captain stepped back—and there was the lobster, standing on its head in the centre of a ring of curious old men.

'I wouldn't eat that lobster if you paid me,' one of the old men said.

The Dyker agreed with him by kicking the lobster into the water as though it were a scorpion. He turned to the startled captain.

'Now,' he said, 'have you any more tricks like that on you? For if you have, you can bloody well try them out at the place you came from!'

I heard of a Frenchman who kept a lobster as a pet, taking it for occasional walks on a lead. When asked what he had against dogs, the Frenchman replied that lobsters did not bark—and they knew the secrets of the sea!

The Dyker, however, avoided the things in heaven and earth that were undreamt of in his philosophy. He was concerned with what went on in the sea, and between the sea and the steeples. The worlds under and above the church spires were ones into which he preferred not to inquire.

But these worlds loomed large and lurid now—so close that their unearthly colours were seeping through the simple greens and blues of everyday.

Long before I knew anything of the world and the flesh, Epp had told me all about the Devil, and sometimes even about God. Religion was the rock on which our fishing town was founded, and the varieties of religions it practised, with acrimonious exclusiveness, were the rocks on which true religion foundered.

> *The men who go to work in ships*
> *And on the waters be,*
> *Know well the great deeds of the Lord,*
> *His wonders in the sea.*
>
> *They see the stormy winds that blow,*
> *The waves that rear up high;*
> *How ships sink down into the depths*
> *Or seem to touch the sky.*

All the fishing communities wore the garment of religion, but St Monans above them all was a polemical polyglot of sects, and the many seams in the garment showed through. It was known in the East Neuk as 'The Holy City', its churches as many as the many-tided sea.

There were Roman Catholics and Presbyterians and Congregationalists; there were Open Brethren, Closed Brethren, Fergusson's Brethren and Duff's Brethren—indeed any brethren at all that cared to construct a whole theological alphabet out of one undotted iota; there were the Pilgrims, who brought God under one another's roofs; there were Baptists and Evangelists and Jehovah's Witnesses round the doors—never a Mormon in those days. And there was the Salvation Army, terrible with banners and brass. They hell-fired at you in the streets and summoned you to judgement through your letter-box. They spilled out onto the piers, where the setting suns turned the tranquil harbour to a lake of fire. This was if you did not come to church.

And if you did come to church they leaned over their pulpits and pleaded with you to come forward and be saved until their faces turned purple and the veins burst out on their brows, under the storm-tossed wrath of their raging white hair. They did not offer you their religion like a cup of tea—they shot it through you like a dose of salts.

The Old Kirk stood to the west of the village, a square, squat-steepled crucifix, pointing to the eternity from which the houses tailed away in a curving line to the east. On Sundays the hymns floated backwards like celestial breezes over the red roofs.

> *Holy, holy, holy, Lord God Almighty!*
> *Early in the morning our song shall rise to thee.*

And one by one, in the holy places of the village, they struck up their songs of praise.

From the Braehead Church.

> *Yield not to temptation, for yielding is sin,*
> *Each victory will help you some other to win.*

From the Gospel Hall.

> *This is my story, this is my song,*
> *Praising my Saviour all the day long.*

From the Meeting Place.

> *Blessed assurance, Jesus is mine;*
> *O what a foretaste of glory divine!*

From the Mission.

> *Rise up, O men of God:*
> *Have done with lesser things.*

From a converted fish-shed with a rusted tin roof and a gray accompaniment of drips and draughts.

> *We love the place, O God,*
> *Wherein thine honour dwells.*

Through its chinks and cracks I stared round-eyed at the benched bent breathings and deep holy silences of its congregation. To my astonishment I did not recognise a single soul. Who were they? Where did they live during the week? Perhaps working for a living was also sinful, like the music of the organ which, to the glory of God, never once sounded its trumpet blast against these rotten walls.

From the Pilgrims on the pier.

> *Who would true valour see,*
> *Let him come hither.*

And in the midst of the divine din, the Sally Ally burst from their Hall and swung through the streets to fight the good fight and stand up for Jesus like soldiers of the cross. A brazen batallion, clad in scarlet and black, and wearing the helmets of salvation, the breastplates of righteousness, the shields of faith and the swords of the spirit, they went marching as to war.

God might have looked down in gratitude at the ecclesiastical proliferation of evolution's thrust, but for the fact that they were so divided by their convictions, and finding no room for doubt, found nothing to unite them.

For some it was the music of the organ that was the wind of sin; others could not endure the thorny thought that a man should be salaried for preaching the gospel; others again believed it wrong that one man alone should preach the word of God, while all around him sat His saved servants, whose tongues spat fire in their skulls, flamed by the Church Triumphant, the sparks of the Holy Spirit. The narrowest of them all had been known to wreck the radios of their sinning offspring, throw the works of Shakespeare into the harbour along with the Sunday newspapers, and divide the damned from the saved in their own kitchens, putting up partitions in order to fulfil the biblical injunction not to take meat with sinners. Proclaiming the end of the world and of one another from corner to corner, from pier to pier—the sacred shrapnel flew on Sundays down the long empty streets, as they preached with breaking voices to the screeching gulls and the deaf defences of God's unlikely dwelling places.

> *How lovely are thy dwellings, O Lord of hosts!*

No-one ever stood and listened. No not one.

It all began, naturally, at Sunday school, where we learned to sing to the Lord with cheerful voice; where they suffered the little children to come unto Him—and those who did not come would suffer.

> *Wide, wide as the ocean,*
> *High as the heavens above,*
> *Deep, deep as the deepest sea*
> *Is my Saviour's love.*

But God was no respecter of persons and he was no respecter of years. Even the sins of our tender decades and half decades would be sufficient unto the day of Judgement to ensure that we burned—in the fire that needeth no earthly fuel to keep it aflame.

> *Give me oil in my lamp, keep me burning,*
> *Give me oil in my lamp, I pray,*
> *Give me oil in my lamp, keep me burning,*
> *Keep me burning till the break of day.*

Burning, burning, burning.

> *You will go to hell. You will go to the burning fire.*

Look in the face the fact that you are bad, that you are a cracked vessel leaking sin, that you have done wrong.

> *Oh, you scoundrel, you bad bad boy!*

You do wrong every day of your life, from eye-opening to eye-shutting, you did wrong from the first breath you took, O thou child of weak-willed Adam and foolish Eve. You did wrong to be born at all, thou offspring of original sin.

> *Brought from the Bass by mistake you were.*

Conceived in sin and born in sorrow, you are an error, a living wrong, a perversion of the creation, an affront to Jesus.

> *Jesus loves me, this I know,*
> *For the bible tells me so.*

God sees everything that you do, everything that you think and feel he hears and senses. He knows every lie told, every wicked whisper of the heart. An empty seat in Sunday school, a vacant pew in church is a witness against Christ the Son—and God the Father will not be mocked.

> *Yes Jesus loves me.*

A text unlearned is a failure to love *Him*.

> *Yes Jesus loves me.*

A crude word is a nail hammered into his crucified hands.

> *Yes Jesus loves me.*

And a refusal to believe in Him is the sure and certain road to eternal damnation.

The bible tells me so.

For the bible is God's revelation to man. Kirk and conscience are of no avail in themselves, and a good and caring heart is unheard in heaven if its prayers are not accompanied by scripture. Belief in the bible is the corner stone of faith in God. You must know your bible then, better than you know yourself: every book of it, every chapter of it, every verse of it, every sentence of it, every word of it, every syllable of it is the inspired word of God.

The bible is your sword of salvation. To defend yourself against the Devil and attack the armies of the ungodly, you must first know the length and breadth of your sword. Now, let Satan see that you can wield the whole sword effectively. The books of the bible by heart.

Genesis, Exodus, Leviticus, Numbers, Deuteronomy, Joshua, Judges, Ruth . . .

Right down to *Revelation*.

Now you must know all the vital strokes and how to deliver them with precision and speed. Put your swords under your armpits, and when I say 'Draw your swords' find the following texts.

John Chapter Three Verse Sixteen. Draw your swords!

For God so loved the world that he gave his only begotton Son, that whosoever believeth in him should not perish, but have everlasting life.

The bible tells me so.

Mark Chapter Sixteen Verse Sixteen. Draw your swords!

He that believeth and is baptized shall be saved,
but he that believeth not shall be damned.

The bible tells me so.

First Epistle of John Chapter One Verse Eight. Draw your swords!

If we say that we have no sin we deceive ourselves and the truth is not in us.

The bible tells me so.

Romans Chapter Six Verse Twenty-three. Draw your swords!

The wages of sin is death.

The bible tells me so.

Revelation Chapter Twenty Verse Fifteen. Draw your swords!

And whosoever was not found written in the book of life was cast into the lake of fire.

The bible tells me so.

So with our swords in our hands we were equipped for the fight against principalities and powers of evil. But without faith in our feet we would never even find the way to the war. We were Deuteronomy's children, in whom not even as much as a mustard seed of faith could be found. Our belief was too brittle and our unbelief could not be helped.

Believe on the Lord Jesus Christ and thou shalt be saved.

He that believeth not shall be damned.

The double-edged sword of the bible, wounding the hands of the sinner whose faith is too poor.

Bald-headed white-headed men, who peered over your pulpits, counted my blessings, lamented my fall and demanded my faith— you put a sword in my hands which I was never able to handle. When a red-lipped, blazered and bonneted evangelist asked me after a gospel meeting if I was saved, I shuffled an embarrassed 'no' with my scuffed shoes. The pain was so delicate on her pale forehead, so exquisitely sweet on her sad red lips, that I allowed her to save me. I was converted before I was ten.

Emerging from one of their services was like coming out of the pictures. Those lurid colours of a dreamlike dimension which had tinged the simple blues and greens of fields and sea, were now splashed like blood over earth and sky. The preaching was still going on from end to end of the village, the words whipped up on the four winds to be carried with howls and hosannahs into hell and heaven. The clouds seemed strange and unfamiliar, as though they might fracture at the next fraction of recorded time, to reveal the whole biblical chronology of things from the creation to the last trumpet. And in the huge hole which that would open up in the already darkening day, the village and its people, its works and ways, the safe sanities of its fishing traditions, so seemingly changeless and sure, would disappear in a twinkling down the dark crack of doom.

When the storm did break at last, I was standing outside the Congregational Church, high up on the Braeheads, the last chords of the organ drum-rolling at my back.

'Sky's too blue over by the Bass,' an old man said.

He pointed shakily with his stick.

'There's going to be thunder.'

Down below the firth took on a flat calm appearance, with a quietness in which no wind could be heard. The only sign that the tide was flowing at all was a small uneasy rippling like a whisper on the water. But the purplish grey-blue clouds were massing like anvils low down along the sea-horizons all the way from east to south, showing the direction from which the hammers would come crashing. Higher up, far above the anvils, the whiter clouds were a ghastly contrast, their edges unnaturally bright and dazzling, their faces furious with the blinding wrath of God. The sea melted from mercury into lead and from lead into a black brooding oil. Then the wind sprang up from the south-east, the thunderheads racing in the opposite direction, travelling against the stream of air, and with a flash of lightning across the firth, the storm burst. The Bass roared like a berserk blue bear, its deep growls cracking open the black and battling sky.

But I knew, as I ran screaming for my mother and the smothering blankets, that the storm was not a mad bear at all, because Epp had told me long ago that the thunder was God speaking to the wicked, and that there was no-one more wicked than myself. And though my reasoning brain, which Miss Balsilbie taught to divide, now told me that Epp had been an old haverer, my Sunday teachers knew better, that my unbelief was bad; and the bible told me that what they said was true.

A thousand other sins clamoured against me, raging with the thunder and the hissing rain that fell like fire into the firth. The roses in Miss Balsilbie's bosom. Mrs Guthrie's apples, the half-dressed girl by the doocot and the white shock of her flesh.

Stay me with flagons, comfort me with apples,
for I am sick of love!

The drunken spree on the beach in mockery of Shuggie and Sangster, my bravado with George's harpoon and the oranges offered to the Princess, to Eve in her pagan paradise, as temptations to forbidden flesh.

Thou shalt not . . .

Everything I had done was a sin, smashed down now onto the anvils of the sky to deafen me and drown out the songs of praise from the Holy City. Every cork-tormented snoach, every poisoned whelk, every pinioned pigeon with scandalous messages tied to the leg. The Blind Man with his stick knocked away from him, HoneyBunch spreadeagled and shining on Alec Fergusson's workbench, riding his bicycle into the waves, bells on her toes and the broken bones of combs in her hair. All the crystalised candy stolen from Kate, the filthy bilge herring sold to the widow for her last mite—twelve Judas Iscariots trumpeting my faithlessness, my greed. O ripe and rotting they were, my sins, stinking of mortality—and the anger of God was the corpse of the killer whale, coming at me with skeleton ribs and the face of Tom Tarvit, a half-built boat ready to swallow me like Jonah into the everlasting stench of the bilge.

Do you know what a whale can do?

My great-grandfather's arm was withered and white and too just an arm to save me. It could throw a false prophet down the stairs but it could no more hurt leviathan. Only the Reverend Kinnear's mighty fist could stop that whale with a single blow from his shield-splintering fist. But the Reverend Kinnear looked up at me from the mud in the harbour and shook his purple head. The sky thundered forth his words.

O, thy offence is rank, it smells to heaven!

He let the whale live. I had sinned against Christ. Michael, the archangel, took away his sword, the harpoon fell stupidly in the mud, and the killer closed his jaws. I was inside the belly.

Howling, I tore off the bedclothes and ran out into the yard. Scores of boys were down at the harbour, turning fear into fun by braving the storm on the Blocks.

The Blocks was a gigantic breakwater formation, a zig-zag causeway of colossal concrete slabs serpentining out far into the sea behind the east pier. On either side of this construction, as additional protection, a number of concrete blocks, as big as barns, had been tumbled into the sea. When the heavy south-east seas came crashing landwards, these reinforced monoliths were what took the strain from the harbour walls. Otherwise there were times when the piers would have been demolished.

When the heaviest seas hit the Blocks, the explosions were shattering. Mountains of white flowers rose into unbelievable time, paused, posed, and ran back into the sea in withered waterfalls. To be caught in that suddenness, in one of those monumental growths, was unthinkable.

But every boy eventually had to take the risk, to judge the placing in time of those few seconds of safety that existed before the next sea hit the wall. In that awful span he had to run the naked hundred yards from the pier wall to the far point of the Blocks, where the causeway broadened out sufficiently, with high solid walls of its own, to provide some kind of shelter from the walloping walls of water. Then the boy on trial had to steady his quivering legs, take a pint of air into his lungs, and run all the way back to safety.

Many's the fleeing figure disappeared for agonising seconds at a stretch in sheets of bursting spray Olympus high, only to reappear untouched, still running from point to perilous point, while the white churches of the waves sank to oblivion at his back. Double explosions happened without warning, rising like twin white spires behind him and in front, and he would freeze between them like a listening hare, trembling on his tiptoes. Or multiple blows would hit the wall consecutively all along the breakwater, like machine-gun fire, separated by unassessable fractions, so that the runner's fate seemed certain, unless God were somewhere among those sickening steeples and their white sea-bells.

Miraculously, never a boy fell, or was swept to what would have been a sure and certain death, as the thunder crashed and the lightning flashed, and the worst seas in the world pitched themselves against the town, tons of water splintering among tumbled tons of concrete, salt among sarsens, like white blood at Stonehenge, splashing the ring of watchers. And in the communal shouts and screamings of that deadly game of fun, the fear of God in heaven was dispelled. One safe run to the point of the Blocks and back reminded me of what I had forgotten—my invincible uniqueness, my heroism. And the feeling that God was looking after me for some special purpose.

Breathless and buffeted, I stood on the high harbour walls and saw the beauteous files winging their way homewards to the Bass.

My soul, there is a countrie . . .

Far beyond the stars.
Far beyond the Braehead Church, God was out *there*, with the white pilgrims, winging over the water with which Alec Fergusson had baptized me years ago. I went home soaked and triumphant, reborn of water, my face stinging, and the blood singing in my ears.

AUGUST

The settled silences of summer were over now, berries taking the place of blossoms, seed vessels rattling where flowers waved, green haws where the buds had bobbed in the May winds. But the campion and cow-parsley and dog-rose still brightened the ditches, the convolvolus rang its white straggling bells in the hedges, and the fragile harebells embroidered the braes with blue. The birds took to sitting in rows on the telegraph wires, where instinct strung them out like beads. They were waiting for the end of summer and the autumn mists to rise like a curtain.

Change and decay in all around I see,
O Thou who changest not, abide with me.

But the biggest change in August was in the fields.

Gone were the grateful green congregations of grain, in which the long lines of daisies had stood out like white heads in the pews; poppies spreading everywhere, the bright hats of women. The fields had yielded up their fresh morning scents to the sun—secrets held through the long winter, released at last and forgotten. From the top of Kellie Law I could see the sun weaving into the fields the thick threads of autumn, green turning heavily to gold across the quilted country.

If I closed my eyes, I knew from the varying sounds of the wind in the grasses and the barley that this was August and no longer July. The secret whispers, the long slow susurrations and sighs of satisfaction and fulfilment were giving way to those quick little questionings, the gustier anxieties and aimless surges of another time—the tunes of the turning year playing as the wind winnowed and wove.

Then the whiteness came on the cornfields and they rattled like paper skeletons, pale in the chillier evenings, rustled like papers turned by an anxious hand. And when the restless noises died away at dusk, the setting suns slipped into the grain like drops of blood, frosted by the mists that blurred the barley-banks. The earth hoisted the stars on its shoulder. When I saw the Great Square of Pegasus rising slowly out of the sea, a giant reaper standing over the cornfields, swinging Andromeda to the west like a silver scythe, then I knew for sure that Autumn had come.

SEPTEMBER

Before the start of the Yarmouth fishing in September the nets had to be mended following the huge hauls of the summer draves. This was vital because the few shillings and half-crowns which grandfather sometimes brought home in his spotted handkerchief were a very small part of the heavy sums of money he had to spend on gear. When I was about nine years old he was paying three pounds fifteen shillings for a net, not including its four ropes. There were ninety to a hundred nets at a time in the *Maggie Main*'s fleet. A two-mile messenger warp for these cost him twenty pounds, a box of cutch to bark them was thirty shillings, and a hundredweight was needed to the tub every time they were treated. With the herring sometimes falling to only ten shillings the cran, many hundreds of cran had to be hauled before the men had even covered their costs. Grandfather often used to say that they were fishing for weeks at a time just to keep the boat afloat and the nets in the water. And when the nets were badly damaged the costs soared.

Mending them was the job of the women, usually the old widow women who were paid by the hour and ate with the folks whose nets they were repairing. But my grandfather never minded putting in a needleful when he had nothing else to do. Frequently he whittled away at bone needles which he made as a hobby, preferring them to the wooden ones in his own strange way, and decorating them with tiny carvings of the old sailing drifters, Fifies and Zulus. I helped him by filling up the needles with cotton, and stood and watched him as his hands worked on and his eyes looked back into his head, under his forehead's far away horizon. I could never follow what his hands did.

'Mending nets is just a branch of mathematics,' he said.

Little did Peter and Andrew know that they were pursuing typology on the shores of Lake Galilee when Pythagoras's students were toying with right-angled triangles.

The job itself was certainly an old woman's one though, worsened at this time of year by the swithers—the dried-up jellyfish which made the eyes itch and stream unbearably—and requiring the patience of one who had little to live for but eternity. A drift-net had over half a million meshes, which Leebie called 'masks'. Sometimes she left her sewing machine and came down into the yard on a sunny day to sit with the torn nets till she had teased them back to what they were. She assessed the grades of damage which a net had suffered, using words which are no longer heard in today's young mouths and unhearing ears.

She ignored what she called a 'chip-mask', which was a mesh with only one leg broken. But when grandfather saw them like this on the galluses, he did up the broken leg himself, insisting on a mending that was 'chip-mask whole'. Leebie started her own mending only at the 'crow-foot' masks, where two adjoining meshes had been broken. If the net was peppered with small holes all over, she called it 'picky'; if the breaks were big enough to look as though cannonballs had been shot through the net, she referred to it as 'holed'; if the net had a very large section missing altogether, she patched it with a good part from a discarded net; or new mesh could be bought by the yard. A net requiring this treatment she spoke about as 'a needing netbit'. And if it was too badly torn to be mended at all, then it was a 'lost net', brought home only so that its corks and ropes could be salvaged. When all or nearly all of the boat's nets had been sorely damaged, she described it as a 'destruction', and when the entire fishing fleet had suffered this from rough seas, she proclaimed 'an awful destruction'. Different tones were employed for each phrase, ranging from the dismissive grunt at the sight of a chip-mask to the long keening cry with which she heard that the entire fleet of nets had had to be condemned.

This was the ultimate disaster. It never did happen to my grandfather's boat, but it happened more than once to boats that had gone through huge packs of dogfish. Nets that had been among the dogs made for the worst mending. With their strong jaws these dreaded sea-brutes mutilated the herring as they stuck in the meshes, snapping great half-moon bites out of their backs, shredding the meshes savagely, and often chewing and twisting at the cotton without breaking it, so that every single mask had to be tested to make certain it would hold. A skipper in our street took us into his yard to show us one of his dog-torn nets spread out on the galluses. He stood back from it ten paces, took off his cap, and threw it at the net, telling me to stand on the other side and catch the cap if it came through. Twelve times he threw it at different parts of the net and twelve times it came through. Every net in his fleet was in that condition.

'Do I pay an old wife to sit with them till doomsday?' he said. 'Or do I buy a new fleet? Either way I can't spare the time or the money.'

Mended, boiled and barked, all the nets were then taken back down to the boat, and by the end of the first week in September the fleet had sailed for Yarmouth.

The East Anglian fishing was the highlight of the driftermen's year, and a tremendous excitement was generated during their comings and goings. But Yarmouth was nearly always accompanied in St Monans by loss of life, and we were even allowed out of school to see our folk away, as if in formal recognition of that awful possibility that we might never see them again. I went down to the pier with my mother to see the men off, grandfather, Alec and Billy; and grandmother and old Leebie came slowly down with us, arm in crooked arm. There was a colossal noise going on in the harbour—too much steam on the boats, and they were blowing it off. The wind was a hard south-easter, blowing the smoke from the funnels straight across the town. The crews handed us out some of their hard sea-biscuits and grandfather gave me an apple. Then the ropes were slackened and flung on board, the engines gathered like lions, the stems bristling for the harbour mouth, pennies were thrown on deck for luck as they passed beneath us, their hands waving and their grinning faces looking up from the water, last goodbyes shouted in the grateful confusion, masking our emotion, that sick fear that the sea would take one of ours—and they were gone.

'Aye,' said Leebie, 'and somebody's body will never come home again. That's always the way with Yarmouth.'

Neither my mother nor my grandmother contradicted her as they usually did when she was in these fatalistic moods. We came home quietly, my mother holding my hand hard without speaking. I wanted to eat the apple which grandfather had given me but my stomach was too tight. I went up to the garret and looked out over the bare town. A grey sad silence had settled on it now, emptied yet again of all its men. The days were drawing in. I began looking for something new to fill up my mind.

The bible apart, I had a bookless upbringing. There were no bookshops in the village, no library, and Captain Meldrum's superb collection had gone the way of all paper and of all the eggs in his daughter's shop. Our own family was not a bookish one. I remember only two books in the house—the bible itself, and Milner's *Gallery of Nature*, which was my grandfather's favourite reading. At school it was the letter rather than the spirit of the word which was valued. There was no effort to educate us into the art of literature, and the expulsion of

Miss Balsilbie was the killing of creativity within those graceless walls.

I heard many tales told to me on the tongues of the old folk, but the written word was not so readily available. The first recorded stories I read outside of scripture were in the graveyard of the Old Kirk, which now began to claim my solitariness, my brooding withdrawals from Peem and Gollie and the easy uncomplicated company of the Dyker.

The stories of the stones.

These were what worked first on my creative imagination, producing, in rapt response, an underground gallery of people and plots, fleshing out the bloodless bones which they commemorated.

The kirkyard was an old one—a green wave on whose ample crest a storm-tormented king had first set down a ship of stone to steer lost souls to their promised haven—and the shoals of the dead had been passing through the wave for six hundred years, taking passage on that slow sea which enters eternity. Standing sentinel over their mortal remains was the meshwork of memorials, the earliest ones surviving from the end of the sixteenth century, and the newest additions accompanying the grey tablet to those who gave their lives in the Great War. So human grief, piety, pride and fear had taken its many forms in the slates and stones and marbles into which these and such like emotions had been translated and engraved.

There were the great carved canopies laid out flat on the grass like the lids of sarcophagi, shutting out the unvisited terrors of the tomb. Closed doors they were, huge, heavy, hingeless—no groaning ajar on the green darkness beneath, not the smallest chink of blue sky slipping through till the last trumpet blasted them open like paper prisons. These gave way to the table tombstones of the eighteenth century, on curved Grecian legs, the names and dates of the decreased written out large and long on their sky-facing tops. They were complete with the emblems of mortality—hour-glass and scythe, skull and crossbones, mattock and spade, relentless reminders of those base uses to which we so quickly return; and the Angel of Death spreading jealous wings over all, his sullen scowl a testimony to how dark a door it is that we must all walk through. Then came the upright slabs of the early nineteenth century, their flowering romantic remonstrances ponderous in porcelain, and the hectic proliferations of Victorian times, with their veiled urns and discreetly nightgowned angels casting stone flowers and sorrowing looks into the earth; and all the massive pillars for those stern men with stone faces who had been pillars of the community in their time, and whose funerary expenses proved it. Lastly the memorials of modern times, which were smaller and less ornate, but which still found room on their open pages for footnotes of texts and epitaphs for everyone to read—to warn, console, instruct, advise, and sometimes simply to express regret.

They have remained with me, many of these words on the worn pages—lines of poetry written out on the remembering stone walls of my skull.

Tendir and trewe—A woman clothed with the sun—Today in the Paradise of God—Together with Christ which is far better—And they shall go no more out neither shall they die any more—Awake satisfied with his presence—Alive for evermore—Equal unto the angels—As we have borne the image of the earthly we shall also bear the image of the heavenly—Asleep in Jesus—The morn cometh—Until the day break and the shadows flee away—Not dead but sleeping— Not lost but gone before—I know that my Redeemer liveth—Blest be the tie that binds—Blessed are the dead which die in the Lord.

Years of exposure to the salt-laden suns and the wind-driven rains of the stormy coast had produced subtle alterations in the shapes and substances of the older stones, softening their gaunt contours, cleansing, discolouring, decorating them with the encrustations of nature. When the big tides obeyed the moon-pull and the weather came in wild, they were splashed directly by the sea, and the spray from the breaking waves wetted them every day. Crystals of salt illuminated the letters so that they sparkled in the sun, and lichens blotched the lines like foxing on old brown books. Time had doodled in all sorts of ways in the margins—mosses, mildews and leprosies that had blotted the pages, obscuring the stories.

This only made them all the more fascinating. I hung round them like a revenant, resurrecting the sleepers in my mind, saying their names to the sea air, whispering their years to a wind of weathers. I traced with my finger the lines that grief had graven in stone and that love still spelt through lichen and the stealing sentence of the ivy. I fed deeper and deeper on the shut volumes of their lives. The kirkyard became my other habitation, my city of the dead. The silences of its stone dwellings flowered into song.

> *This quiet dust was gentlemen and ladies,*
> *And lads and girls;*
> *Was laughter and ability and sighing,*
> *And frocks and curls.*
> *This passive place a summer's nimble mansion,*
> *Where bloom and bees*
> *Fulfilled their oriental circuit,*
> *Then ceased, like these.*

169

A TWELVEMONTH AND A DAY

The first monument to which I became an early reader was a large, upright olive-coloured slab, crowned with the Angel of Death. The angel's head and curving wings formed the top of the stone, and just beneath the glowering mouth and sunken chin came the frontal inscription.

1843
Erected by Thomas Brown and Helen Peattie
In Memory of their Daughters
Helen who died 6th March 1839 Aged 17 years
Margaret who died 20th December 1842 Aged 25 years

> Naked as from the earth we came
> And entered life at first,
> Naked we to the earth return
> And mix with kindred dust.
> How still and peaceful is the grave
> Where life's vain tumults past,
> Th'appointed house by Heaven's decree
> Receives us all at last.

On the reverse side of the stone from the holy text, the rustic Muse had inscribed this poem.

> They grew in beauty side by side,
> Each others joy, their parents' pride.
> Soon Helen faded like a flower,
> Her sister watched each restless hour.
> The Spoiler Death stole slowly on
> And Margaret mourned for her when gone,
> And this did choose for her tombstone:
> 'Prepare to meet thy God, thy life's a span.
> 'In unexpected hour the Son of Man
> 'Will truly come, pronounce thy final doom,
> 'And lay thee lifeless in the silent tomb.'
> This said, the subtile poison of disease
> Preyed on her form, whose grace all eyes did lease.
> And here in rest till an eternal day
> They sleep together in their bed of clay.

I could see it in my head with such desperate clarity, as fierce and fresh as if it had been yesterday: the older girl ripe for wedding and womanhood at twenty-one, coming of age at Christmas, only to see her sister's life begin to flicker with the Yuletide fires. In the cold New Year her flame faded and failed and in a bitter spring went out among white ashes. With Helen gone, Margaret's passion for life was never rekindled. In its place there was lit up in her a holy candle which burned for three more winters before it guttered and gasped and left a thin fragrance round a still waxen form. Then nothing. Thomas Brown and Helen Peattie folded up their two children in the same bed for the last time, and left them there together till a long waking would be theirs, and someone else would rouse them on another morning. Two sisters, bone of their bone and flesh of their flesh, dead for the disobedience of Eve, unknown to any Adam, they were bridesmaided by worms—turning to one another in the ground, century by slow century, till the withered roses of their vanished lips met and kissed in clay, and devotion's duty was done. The sadness and sterility of it haunted and harried me. What could it possibly mean?

Some of the stones held me round them for hours at a time, peering into the physical obscurity of their epitaphs, weathered and wind-beaten as they were, half sunken drunkenly into the long grass, and masked by the grey moulds of old mosses, gone dry and dateless over inscriptions which had once been bright fresh tears. From one of these stones I picked off the dead growths in faded flakes like ancient wallpaper, and stood for an afternoon staring at the words—a moth transfixed by a frozen flame.

> Erected by John and Mrs Trotter
> late of the parish of St Monans
> in memorial of their daughter
> Alison Trotter
> who died of a few days illness
> Aged seventeen
> August 25th 1815

And on the other side of the stone was this verse.

> In this green bed sleeps the dear dust
> Of her was once so blooming.
> Stranger, thine earthly form too must
> Lie in a grave consuming.
> Friend for the dead who heavst a sigh
> Know ALLY TROTTER'S yonder
> Where saints in heaven raise the glad cry
> Of gratitude and wonder.
> This is a bounding dashing wave
> On which in life we hover.
> Few days at last this storm's to brave
> And all our griefs are over.

It was like wiping the dust from a faded old photograph and seeing the past in all its bitterness come poignantly to life. The shock of fresh bereavement sprang up round the grave like a scent. A broken couple stood by the graveside, supporting one another like two weepers grief had turned to marble, stone tears on their cheeks. I reached out a hand uncertainly—but I could never touch them. Their eyes were fixed on the brass name-plate as it caught the sun and threw it out of the grave and into their faces and mine. Alison Trotter: 1798–1815. The sun flashed again and again and the flung names bounced back, burning my eyes, blinding me with the sad sweet beauty of human lives. Margaret Peattie, Helen Peattie, Mary McNeil. Princess Titaua Marama.

Elspeth Marr—her name, her years.

But John and Mrs Trotter saw only the name of their only daughter and cynosure of their eyes and age, torn like a rose and thrown back to the earth in pale tatters. So they too, like Thomas Brown and Helen Peattie, put a daughter early to bed. The sexton piled on the clay covers and overspread them with the patchwork quilt of turfs, which the daisies' slow embroidery beautified over the years—long after Napoleon fell at Waterloo and the poppies fell at Flanders, where Ally Trotter had no sons to go to their graves like beds and die for their country. She slept on here, while the world warred with itself, and her story was re-read at last by a reader who would be dust himself in a century from now.

Or would I die much sooner than that?

The graveyard was sprinkled with young lives ended so suddenly.

> Here lyes the corps of Agnes Broun
> Whose breath was snatched by Early
> not untimely Death.
> Hence innocent she fled, just did begin
> Sorrow to know before she knew to sin.
> Death that does Sin and Sorrow thus prevent
> is the next blessing to a life well spent.
>
> She dyed july the 5th 1732
> in the tuelfth year of her Age.

So she had died just before reaching the age of twelve, nearly two centuries before I was born. Yet her death was not untimely, because it denied her the knowledge of that sin and sorrow that lay ahead of her years of innocence. But she was delivered from damnation by the mercies of a mortal disease, which burned out her brain so cruelly that her family were thankful at last to see her die. No death can be untimely which ends the suffering of an innocent child. I was not yet ten years old myself, but I was riddled with sin already—children in the old days seemed to have been so much more pious—and the saving of my soul by the pretty evangelist had been a blasphemous mockery which God must know for sure. The criminal consequences of it burst like a choir of devils' voices round the headstone of the saved girl. Would I be counted little child enough to come unto Him, should I die today—or could death offer me at best a release from the sorrows of my life to come?

A kind of frenzied envy gnawed at me then—envy of that bright shining spawn of the graveyard which had been suffered to come unto Jesus at even earlier ages, ensuring their salvation; gentle Jesus meek and mild demanding that the meek inherit heaven before they had had time to inherit the earth.

Safe in their Alabaster Chambers—
Untouched by Morning
And untouched by Noon—
Sleep the meek members of the Resurrection—
Rafter of Satin
And Roof of Stone.

In their smallness and innocence they would elude the judgement that was reserved for the greater part of mankind, and go straight to God in glory.

There were a great many of them.

Here lie the children of Robert Fowler
Mariner St Monans

Elizabeth died February 22nd 1824 Aged 18 months
Catherine died December 20th 1838 Aged 3 years
James died December 27th 1838 Aged 2 years

GRAVE the guardian of our dust,
GRAVE the treasure of the skies,
Every item of thy trust
Rests in hope again to rise.

And next to this headstone was an even greater heartbreak. It lay at an angle, in a shady section of the kirkyard which seldom saw the sun. A sad gray stone which emanated a scent of resignation and hopelessness.

Erected by Alexander Boyter
In Memory of his loving wife Grace
Who died February 20th 1861 Aged 33
And of their five children
Helen died February 1st 1849 Aged 4 years
Grace died March 17th 1849 Aged 15 months
Robert died August 30th 1852 Aged 4 months
Janet died June 18th 1855 Aged 4 years
Jessie died January 12th 1862 Aged 11 months

Also in Memory of the Children
of Alexander Boyter and Catherine Smith
Catherine died April 21st 1872 Aged 3 months
James died February 2nd 1874 Aged 14 months
Elizabeth died August 27th 1875 Aged 3 years 7 months
Jean died July 6th 1891 Aged 1 year

Alexander Boyter died September 17th 1891 Aged 62 years

Alexander Boyter, married to Catherine and Grace, father of Helen, Grace, Robert, Janet, Jessie, Catherine, James, Elizabeth, Jean, none of whom lived longer than four years. Alexander Boyter, buried a wife and all her children, married again in ten years time, in hopes of relighting the flame of fatherhood to warm his age. The next three children followed the other five. Fifteen years he waited for another child, a daughter who died at one year old. Alexander Boyter, broken and bent, went to the graveyard two months later, to join the laughter and love and sorrow of his loins.

It was a very big stone.

At the bottom they had found room for a couplet.

To have, to hold, and then to part,
Is the greatest sorrow of the human heart.

And on the back of the stone there was another verse.

These lovely buds so young and fair
Called hence by early doom
Just come to show how sweet those flowers
In Paradise would bloom.

And yet there was a comfort of a kind in the way they were clustered together, all sleeping in the one bed. I was struck cold for sorrow at the loneliness of so many of the other sleepers, sleeping out their last sleep with no-one else near them; no brother, no sister, no mother or father laid down in devotion and despair at the beloved's side, to sleep with him, with her, till time had taken survey of the world and come to stop.

In Memory of Isabella Anderson
Died January 15th 1863 Aged 3 months
Short was the little traveller's stay
She came but as a guest
She tasted life then fled away
To everlasting rest.

Bereaved parents had turned to the poets over and over to dramatize their grief in verse and make the stone sing.

The sweetest flower of all the field.

O fairest flower, no sooner blown but blasted!

Riddle of destiny, who can show
What thy short visit meant, or know
What thy errand here below?

Child of a day.

Darkness more clear than noonday holdeth her,
Silence more musical than any song.

And one that moved me most of all.

George Galloway
Died 5th October 1902 Aged 11½ months
Sleep on, beloved, sleep, and take thy rest,
Lay down thy head upon thy Saviour's breast,
We love thee well, but Jesus loves thee best.

And so the two images of Jesus jostled in my jailored brain: the sad-eyed bearded man of the bible bookmarks, laying his hands gently on curly heads; and that pale force from somewhere in the skies that sucked the life out of young limbs to fill up heaven with smiling sunbeams, leaving Alexander Boyter to stare into the grave of all his children, broken for the ninth time to receive the last of all his hopes. And the parents of George Galloway, robbed of the last two weeks which would have given them one unbroken year of their only child, faithfully recorded that pathetic half month at the end of his gravestone, as if to eke out his memory and the fact of his life to the full. Gentle Jesus meek and mild cast a chill into my bones. His name was to be found wherever the leprous stones of the last century testified to the toll of infant mortality, and the tiny white skeletons were scattered like daisies under the grass.

It was a fatal attraction, but I could not stay away. I wandered among the stones for days on end, reading the inscriptions till I knew them by heart. I knew all the characters and dispositions of the dead and the nature of their lives: the corpses of honest and virtuous men, baillies in St Monans, skippers in St Monans, ministers of the parish, and of their steadfast spouses, loyal and true, departed this life one after another, 1597, 1679, 1724—years, months, days and hours had been set aside for them all and they had succumbed. Every mortal minute and hair of their heads had been numbered. And their inscriptions remained to discover death for me in all its dreadful dimensions.

Still they ring like steeple bells in my head.

> On every side lies mortal clay,
> Every date says Come away.

> Why life a moment? infinite desire?
> Our wish eternity? Our home the grave?

> If a man die shall he live agane? All the
> Dayes of Mine Appointed time will I wait till
> My changing shall come.

> Enter ye in
> At the Strait
> Gate for Wide is
> The Gate and Broad
> Is the Way
> That leadeth
> To destrvction.

SEPTEMBER

O how I grieve to leave your side,
my children and my friends.
The Lord of Hosts be your defence
till we do meet again.
And I do hope that when the hivens
shall vanish like a scroll,
I shall you see in parfit shape
in bodie and in soul.

But there was one stone which had more effect on me than all the others put together. Its single line inscription went through my feet like a nail, spiking me to the spot and making my legs quiver. I remember the day when I first saw it, because the name of the deceased had long since faded from the soft sandstone. But the epitaph had outlasted oblivion by virtue of the simple fact that the tomb had teetered and sunk a little, and the straggling grasses had grown up in a green screen round the words that were now level with the surface of the grave. On this particular day the sexton had given the grass its last cut before the winter, and he had gone round all the headstones with a sickle, trimming away the grass round each base. I looked at the stone which I had never known to have anything left on it from the hand of the carver. And there they were in front of me, hitting me in the eyes and screaming in my ears.

O! thou Adam, what hast thou done?

When I first read these seven words, standing on my own in the kirkyard and looking around at the multitude of memorials, I was seized with a shrill horror of the appalling consequences of sin for the whole human race. All this, all *this*—was Adam's work! The dust of this promiscuous boneyard that had once been people—reverend doctors and learned dominies laid down at the feet of infants; servant girls accommodated with their mistresses; seafarers and farmers sweetly berthed; baillies and bricklayers, squires and esquires, drunkards and divines; men of opulence and indigence sharing the same rooms, the winding-sheet and the coffin the utmost bound of all their needs, all class and character died away; even the glutton gone down to a garden of insects that made riot in his flesh. And the worm fed sweetly on them all. All the vivacity and variety of the evolutionary thrust negated and nullified by this dreadful denial— the work of the first great sinner. The bright tide that could have flowed forever, stilled in the dark; a dark green wave, its bone-shoal

picked clean and brittle and bare, hidden a fathom under the sky.
The wages of sin is death.

O! thou Adam, what hast thou done?

I wanted to hate him at first for his legacy of lichen and leprosy and
his bitter bequest of the grave. But in the end his punishment was
greater than I could bear.

Then came the funerals.

They were my first acquaintance with the drama. Raising and
refining human grief to grand tragedy, they were played out on the
coast's rocky colosseum to the amphitheatre of the listening sea—the
great stage of the earth, roofed over by the sky. Penman's terrible bell
bombillated through the town, summoning the audiences, beating
open a black hole in the kirkyard turf, which the sexton covered with
boards until the day of the funeral.

Always a funeral service was held in the house of the departed,
where the corpse was duly laid out, subjected to that last longing
lingering look—a black procession of eyes looking down on the lids
that veiled eternity— and finally kisted and screwed down. A house of
death was always recognisable by its drawn blinds. I often wondered
what it would be like to be on the inside of such a fearful house. The
time came soon enough, when the old ones in our family went the way
of all the earth before I had walked on it for many years. And always
my grandmother would say the same thing. 'And to think we've all to
come to it!' It was as if she had just remembered that cloud over the
sun that puts all earth's folk in the shadow.

The first funeral I remember was at the house of my bereaved aunt
Elspeth, whose husband had been a sailmaker into his old age. We sat
in silence in her kitchen—a heavy black circle of suits and shoes and
dresses, so seldom worn that they creaked and whispered whenever
anyone moved. So no-one moved. We all stared into the fire as if we
were ashamed to look at one another, not speaking, not breathing,
waiting for the minister. The coffin was apart from us in the best
room, old uncle Jimmy lying in solemn state behind polished oak and
brass, alone among the faded family photographs in their cold frames,
alone in the cold and dark of eternity, whose tide we could all hear
now, a hushed roar between the heavy hideous tickings of the
grandfather clock.

Rat-a-tat-tat, bang, bang. The knocking on the door—no timid
fist, that one.

'That'll be the minister now, let him in somebody.'

Mr Kinnear filled up what was left of the room when he came in. Big, black-coated, blowing heavily and smelling of the pews, he rubbed his hands together and nodded to the fire.

'Nice blaze there, yes. Grand to see a fire today. How are you, Mrs Main?'

Silence.

The fire burned. The clock ticked. We adjusted ties, hats, handkerchiefs.

Then Mr Kinnear put his back to the fire and cleared his throat.

'In the midst of life we are in death . . .'

I had never heard the words until that day, not even in church. Now they hit my ears like a great gong, in the same way that, when I was sixteen, the verse of Shakespeare was to ravish me in the nature of a revelation. But at this time I was barely ten, and the triumph of death over my decade, over the rest of my life, was confirmed now by these words that sounded like the bell from the steeple.

In the midst of life we are in death.

It was true. It had always been true. O! thou Adam, what hast thou done? In the midst of life we are in death. The rest came out like all the ills that ever were, from the open box of Epp's coffin, whose lid was left off for me to see, all the days of my life.

We brought nothing into this world and it is certain we can carry nothing out.
We are like grass which groweth up. In the morning it flourisheth and in the evening it is cut down and withereth.
The days of our years are three score years and ten; and if by reason of strength they be four score years, yet is their strength labour and sorrow; for it is soon cut off and we fly away.
Man that is born of woman hath but a short time to live and his days are full of sorrow . . .

And a few words then on uncle Jimmy, who had sat on his low dark-brown bench all the days of his life, with his sailmaker's tools and his heavy drooping moustaches; uncle Jimmy who had always looked so sad because he was born of woman and his days were few and full of sorrow. Uncle Jimmy who was four score years when he died; whose extra-scriptural decade, like my solitary ten, were nought but vanity, whose added strength was labour and vexation. Uncle Jimmy, who was being moved out of the best room now, feet first, and into the waiting hearse, to take his journey to the old kirkyard.

But uncle Jimmy was going to God, said the Reverend Kinnear. For the souls of the righteous are in the hand of God, and there shall no torment touch them. O Death, where is thy sting? O Grave, where is thy victory? Blessed are the dead which die in the Lord. Eternal rest grant them, O Lord. In my father's house are many mansions.

All the men went away then, and I was left alone with the women.

'Well, that's him away then.'

'He had a long haul, old Jimmy.'

'Do you mind how he laughed that day?'

'Aye, they're not long in getting you into the ground.'

> *Rafter of Satin*
> *And Roof of Stone.*

And to think we've all to come to it! O! thou Adam, what hast thou done?

I was not allowed to accompany the hearse to the kirkyard, and no women went in those days. Even a wife was not expected to walk after her husband's coffin, or a mother after her son. They stayed at home among the unbroken shortbread, the unstoppered sherry, waiting for the men to return from that most harrowing of journeys. It was a man's business only. Fumbling with coffin cords, handling the heavy box, watching it swing slowly out of sight into that awful hole in the ground. The grisly practicalities of death.

But on the day of uncle Jimmy's funeral I asked out of the house for a walk, and I stole after the cortège with a wary foot, darting across the fields to watch it from the shelter of a dyke. The hearses and cars wound their way up the steep green mound of the seaside kirkyard, a procession of shining black beetles that gleamed beneath the sun. I moved closer, scaling a rock and scuffing my new shoes, to look down on them. They gathered round the graveside, the small black figures, and the words came floating up to me, resonant with life and death.

> *Since by man came death, by man came also the resurrection of the dead. For as in Adam all die, even so in Christ shall all be made alive.*
> *I am the Resurrection and the Life saith the Lord; he that believeth in me, though he were dead, yet shall he live; and whosoever liveth and believeth in me shall never die.*
> *Forasmuch as it hath pleased Almighty God of his great mercy to take unto himself the soul of our dear brother here departed, we therefore commit his body to the ground, earth to earth, ashes to ashes, dust to dust, in sure and certain hope of the resurrection to eternal life through our Lord Jesus Christ.*

SEPTEMBER

And into that cold hole in the ground, where the worm feedeth sweetly, went uncle Jimmy, Chae Marr, Hodgie Dickson, Miss McNeil, Shuggie, Sangster, and all the whole host of the earth's anonymous. The Reverend Kinnear's voice boomed like a trumpet.

I know that my Redeemer liveth, and that he shall stand at the latter day upon the earth. And though worms destroy this body, yet in my flesh shall I see God.

The men put on their hats and filed away and the first clods came thudding onto the coffin lid. I ran back to the house, my heart thudding for fear, and yet with a wild vibrant thrilling to the triumphant message boomed out from the mound of bones.

The next day I went back to the kirkyard and looked at uncle Jimmy's grave. The sweet green grass had been desecrated by his death—the squares of turf stitched crudely together by the hand of the sexton and battered flat by his spade. But in a year from now I knew the grass would be blowing sweetly over his bones like an invulnerable green sea.

Close to the grave a dandelion clock faded like a white moon into morning—the clock and the tomb, the two things by which our lives were bound, standing side by side in the graveyard; the one quickly blown, the other not to be worn down by a world of winds; time so fragile, eternity so strong.

I wandered away from the new grave towards the older stones which I had come to know so well. What was death? Thousands of bones and skulls separated from me by only a few feet of earth and grass, and over them, standing sentinel until the last terrible day, an army of stone watchers. But Jesus, who raised Lazarus, and Jairus's daughter, said that these vanished peoples were not dead really, but simply asleep. I lay down flat on one of the graves and shut my eyes, my feet to the stone, my head to the west, pointing in the same direction as all the other heads in that green hill; one flicker of life in the whole sleeping shoal, adrift on the dreamless tide.

I opened my eyes again and looked up at the blue sky, trying to see where it began, where it ended, whether it existed at all. Would being dead be much different from this? I should not see the sky, of course; nor should I hear the sea sounding in my ears of clay; or the spray splashing on my stone; or the raindrop ploughing down the carved letters of my name; turning to fire in the sudden sun. But I might just be dimly aware, in my six feet of slumbers, that I was lying in wait for that great and terrible day when Judgement would break open the green covers, cast aside the sheets of clay, and the yellow sounds of trumpets and sunrise interrupt the ground. In the fields behind the kirkyard the farmer's men were busy bringing in the harvest, and the noise of their labours and shouting came to me strangely, mingling with the sounds of scripture that were shaking the earth and the soundless roaring of the dead.

> *Behold, I shew you a mystery: we shall not all sleep, but we shall all be changed, in a moment, in the twinkling of an eye, at the last trump: for the trumpet shall sound, and the dead shall be raised incorruptible, and we shall be changed.*

The darkness exploded into morning and the sky was blinding with the light of the world. The sun was the mouth of a golden trumpet—a dazzling din pouring out fire and fury, filling my eyes and ears, lifting me to my feet with the force of unshunnable law. The marrow moistened my brittle bones, snapped sinews came twisting together, blood ran in red rivers through arteries and veins, and new skin swished over my organs in a pink pulsation, clothing me in living silk for the great occasion. I was alive again.

And all around me I saw the graves had opened to the sound of the trumpeting sun. The time of the harvesting of the world had come at last. The great green bedcover of the graveyard was rumpled and raggled, the stones cracked and capsized. In a thousand broken beds the sleepers stood awake, rubbing their eyes that were dazed with day following the long night—all the phantom figures of those early years, long compounded with clay, now rising up again, new made, to terrify me anew from their graves and fill the world with noise and fury. Kate the Kist threw away her coffin to be fitted for the New Jerusalem. Jean Jeff's ears were opened and she laughed a lifetime's insults to scorn. McCreevie was there, his mad mouth hanging loosely open like the hingeless gates of hell. Peter Cleek held up his hook in a bright new fist and flung it with a whoop into the sea.

> *Good cod roes!*
> *Good God knows!*

They all came at me then—Hodgie Dickson pointing with solemn warning as he advanced; Chae Marr, his black heart beating like a new drum; Tom Tarvit growing terrible teeth and toes and standing straight again; and the Blind Man opening his red eyes for the first time and running at me in his rage. He hurled his stick over the kirkyard wall. It whirled like Excalibur into the waves and he charged with eyes of fire, fists and feet flailing.

SEPTEMBER

Break open your head!
Feed your brains to the fish!

I screamed and fell to my knees, covering my head with my arms.

And the sea gave up the dead which were in it — the drowned bones of my ancestors crawling up the long lifelines of descent, up from the world of weeds and water and coral skulls to answer the call. Mad Maria stood up to her knees in the water and roared and laughed. Bella Bonny Socks ran into the tide that had taken her Tam for forty years and he came reeling off the great line that had wound him into eternity. It was the day of reckoning and Tam would have to pay. HoneyBunch rose then like Aphrodite, came out of the waves shining and singing, stood naked as the day she was born, straddling the grave of Alec Fergusson, demanding to be washed.

They all stopped then in their tracks and lifted up their eyes. And I saw a great white throne and him that sat on it, from whose face the earth and the heaven fled away; and there was found no place for them.

And I saw the dead, small and great, stand before God: and the books were opened: and another book was opened which is the book of life.

Is your name written down in that great big book, my little friend?
Come to the Gospel Hall at seven p.m. tonight and make sure!

For there are a great many souls in the world, and you have to make very very sure that yours will not be a lost one. Supposing, just supposing, that you were so insignificant, or such a borderline case, that the recording angel missed out your name by mistake? Imagine all the saved souls of the world to be written down, and just one little error to exist, a scribal error in heaven, so small not even God would notice — and that error to be the omission of your own name!

But there would be no question of error, for there was surely no doubt where I was going now.

Depart from me, I know ye not!
Go away, you scoundrel!

Epp appeared, dressed in white, her jaw knotted and leering and the poker still in her hand.

There's nothing more for you now!

The firth turned to a sheet of flame in the judgement of the rising sun.

> *You will go to hell now—*
> *You will go to the burning fire!*

O Lamb of God, O Christ my Saviour!

> *You'll get something to cry for there!*

Deliver me, O Lord, from eternal death, in that awful day.

> *And not one drop of water will you get*

Genesis, Exodus, Leviticus, Numbers . . .

> *to cool your burning tongue.*

Burning, burning, burning.

And death and hell were cast into the firth, now a lake of flame.
And whosoever was not found written in the book of life was cast into the lake of fire.

> *Get out of here, you bad wild boy!*
> *Depart from me, ye cursed, into everlasting fire.*

I tried to run out of the kirkyard but Sangster stood at the gates with a flaming sword whirling in her hand and forced me back in my terror downwards and downwards and into my grave.

When I woke up the last of the field had been cut. The workers had gone home and all was bare stubble.

September started with the saturation of summer in the earth and ended with winter pre-echoing emptily in the rising winds, with their early autumnal liking to the north-west. The jam-making had moved through all the crops, strawberries, raspberries, gooseberries and apples, in that order, and finished up with plums and pears—the wasps pirouetting like dying dancers in the midnight purple ballrooms of the half-emptied plums, and the fallen golden-drops lying like honey-coloured eggs in the fresh cool grass. The bees winged their way wearily from flower to fading flower, overtaken by the lighter traffic of airborne seeds; and the failing bluebottles blundered drunkenly into the dew-beaded spider traps that glittered and shivered among rose-hips and brambles.

Daily the harvesting went on in the wide fields, all the efforts of men concentrated on the land, now that the fishermen had gone to Yarmouth, taking with them their new chaff mattresses made from the first cuts of corn. The golden tide withdrew as the reapers cut down wave after wave of the shining grain, harvesting the sea; and soon summer's murmurings were a forgotten dream. Distance was heavy with the lament from the stubble fields, piping farewell to the earth. The sharp still sound of the dead seasons hung in the air like a scent.

But everybody was too busy to pay any attention to that. They stood the sheafs of corn in stooks to face the Bass Rock and dry out in the sun. Peter Hughes set down three huge barrels in the centre of his field. One contained treacle, a second baps, and the third beer. Only the men drank from the beer barrel, but men, women, children and horses clustered round the treacle. I dipped in the floury baps and brought them out again dripping with sweet black molasses. When I could eat no more I staggered off to the burn, drank it down in deep gurgling gulletfuls, and let my head and hands hang in the cold clear water until there was nothing left of existence but the pearled pebbles on the paperweight world of the bottom and silver bubbles singing in my ears.

The month went on, long and lingering, tinging the leaves, peeling the petals from the last of the roses, dropping them in slow cold circles round the ginger-jar's silent mouth. The swallows assembled in their flocks, the cormorants on the skellies, and the robin's autumn song was reddening the wind. The very big swithers and giant bladder-wrack started to come in now on the tide.

'It's getting right back-end like now,' Leebie would say.

The goosy mornings arrived, so-called by the Dyker either because of the coming of the geese, or perhaps because of the pimples raised on our shivering flesh as we stood in the cold light of later dawns, hurrying into our clothes. With the swing of winter already in my legs and lungs, I strode up to Balcaskie to look for conkers. All the field-flowers and feathered grasses that had brushed my knees and wrists were cut down. The roadmen had scythed the verges and cleared the ditches. All that was left was a flowerless aftermath, strewn with daisies and pale pink poppies—and the dandelion clocks were the dead heads of the dominies drifting across the stubble fields, fading bubbles from the backyard boiler, the morning ghosts of the harvest moons dematerialising into day.

In the frosty sunsets the white mists lingered low over the fields, the huge sun sinking like a cannonball bloodily into the milky sea. A stillness like the stillness of spring settled now on the earth. The dew fell heavy from the high clear skies, which had lost the last faintness of the afterglow, and the old friends of winter were reaching towards me once again—Capella glittering in the north-east and Aldebaran well up by midnight. The mellow harvest moons rose slow and large over the bare beds of burnt stubble. We had arrived at the equinox. Light and darkness held one another like two dancers in harmony, poised on a pin-point of perfect rest. But after this moment the music of the dying year would grow stronger, darker, and the fall away of life and light would be like a lament . . .

Towards the end of the month the weather was different in the ears and nostrils and on the tongue. Sharp winds came in from the east, ruffling the water, and soon the gales were girning round the gable-ends of the houses, breaking the stained-glass lattices of the trees. One after another their windows began to fall in and the cold sky came through. The sea resumed its deep autumnal roaring, the shadows clustered thick and dark on the walls, like black roses. The old folk drew in their chairs closer to the fireside, began to mutter about hot toddies and long johns and starting the porridge in the mornings.

It was then that I began looking outside myself with a strange new earnestness—outside the town and the fishing boats and the people, further even than the green hump of the kirkyard. What was it that I was looking for? Something to take me through the dark time of year when we begin to know that childhood is slipping away.

OCTOBER

Archbishop Usher proclaimed that the universe came into existence on the first day of October 4004 B.C. at nine o'clock in the morning, a precisely bookish God setting the pattern not only for the beginning of the academic year, but also for the beginning of the academic day.

Epp handed me my first poetry, Georgina sang me her songs, and the old folk told me countless tales. But other than the scraps of stories written out on the kirkyard slabs, it was the bible which was my first sustained contact with narrative masterpiece in the form of printed literature. There were few pictures in those days to bound imagination in a nutshell, and so imagination curved outwards into the infinite spaces of the brain, where the pictures remained free from the framing limitations imposed by children's illustrators.

Strangely, I never saw the Garden of Eden as beautiful, though it was our first paradise. Darsie and Titaua were the true Adam and Eve, Tahiti was the place of primal bliss, and Johnston Lodge was a little bit of heaven, Paloma's home from home. But the Adam and Eve of the bible—they were creatures of dust and bone. Adam was made from the dreary dust of the ground, and when he slept the Lord God broke open his body, exposing his ribs like a sleeping ship, like the hull of a dying whale, and made a woman out of one of those bloody bits and pieces which I saw in the butcher's shop. God was Geordie Grant with the smell of death on his red hands and white whiskers, slicing and crunching till he had made you what you wanted from the passive carcasses behind the counter—the blade and the board, the chopper and the slab.

Dust and bone with the smell of death on them, they were a grim couple; Sunday School teachers without their clothes, though imagination put never a nipple on Eve. They were shades of people in a shady gray desert where there was no sound or smell of the sea; where a serpent crawled, more subtle than any beast of the field. The serpent was a conger eel, a cold killer without brain or blood, but carrying in its sharp little skull a knowledge of the fascination for the apples of desire. Apples in her bosom as she rested her breasts on the counter, red-cheeked Mrs Guthrie holding out the forbidden fruit. Comfort me with apples, for I am sick of love.

> *And the serpent said unto the woman, Ye shall not surely die:*
> *For God doth know that in the day ye eat thereof, then your eyes shall be*
> *opened, and ye shall be as gods, knowing good and evil.*

Why did the serpent sound so right?

> *Ye shall not surely die.*
> *And ye shall be as gods . . .*

These were no lies, but what I had known all along to be true, that I was different from Peem and Gollie and all the other boys and girls in my class. I *was* a god and I could *never* die. Everyone else had died and gone to the graveyard, but God would never allow that to happen to me as it had happened to George Galloway and Isabella Anderson. I was too special and God knew it. Something would happen to prevent me from experiencing the common fate.

And so there was the temptation.

> *Yield not to temptation,*
> *For yielding is sin.*

But they yielded, and knew at once the sinful nakedness of HoneyBunch walking cool as she liked through Alec Fergusson's cucumbers as he mended his bicycle in the garden, walking bare buff and beautiful into the waves and stark staring mad along the long curving lines of surf-beaten sand.

Then the dreadful disembodied voice of the Lord God was heard walking in the garden in the cool of the day; a walking voice; an awful unseen omnipresence, spying into their sin, telling them that they were found out, that they were the dead.

> *How did you know that HoneyBunch was naked?*

The serpent was punished, the conger eel on the pier writhing and snapping at the Dyker's heels till his heavy boot bruised its head into a crushed and pulpy silence. But Adam would have to eat bread in the sweat of his brow, tilling the green garrisons of the thistled ground to the end of his days, just like the wicked jackdaw which old George had expelled to the wilderness because it ate the morning rolls. And at his life's end Adam would have to go back to the ground from which he was taken, back to the dust of the earth with the old man in Balcormo Den, with the ploughmen I had seen from the top of Kellie Law; the dead burying their dead.

OCTOBER

For dust thou art and unto dust shalt thou return.

And Eve would conceive in sorrow, and in sorrow would bring forth children, and Lisa Leslie would see to the bleak business of birth and death.

So out they went, a flaming sword at the school gates forbidding them any second chance.

I won't tell you twice, you pair, any disobedience and out you go!

They were a dreary desolate couple and they had let us all down. The whole history of the world proclaimed their failure. They spoiled things for the rest of my life. But still I felt sorry for them.

They, hand in hand, with wandering steps and slow,
Through Eden took their solitary way.

Down I went then, into the black well of the bible, into the age-old horrors of life and death.

Cain stood in a field and denied his brother's murder to God's own face.

Am I my brother's keeper?

The callous cry went echoing over the graves of all the folk in the old kirkyard, murdered by sin, and over countless centuries of crimes. Men were murderers all. But even as he denied the knowledge of it, his brother's blood came bubbling up from the ground it had watered—red roses blossoming in the desert, red tongues tolling from the first tomb, crying out to Cain and his God, *What hast thou done? what hast thou done?* And so Cain too was cut off and driven out from kin and community, an exile from happiness to the end of his days, and again the punishment was greater than I could bear.

But Cain knew his wife and she conceived, just as Adam had known Eve and she had conceived and borne Cain. And so men multiplied and daughters were born to them.

And the sons of God saw the daughters of men that they were fair.
And the sons of God came in unto the daughters of men . . .

Strange veils, these words, hung up round the images they never quite created, screening man and woman and what they did with one another; hiding their movement like the long green grasses round the castle walls. For still nobody had told us how we came into the world, what secret recipe started it off; and the facts of life were inferred piece

189

by piece from the hypnotic rhythms of the Old Testament and the whisperings that went on in the grass.

And Adam knew his wife and she conceived.
And the sons of God came in unto the daughters of men ...

What untold knowing was this? What was meant by this *came in unto*? What was the half-dressed girl by the doocot laughing about? And what lay behind the winking grins, the sudden silences in those interrupted adult conversations, taken up again in low voices after I had left the room?

'She didn't, did she? Oh, tell me she didn't!'

'She did, she did, the first time in Balcaskie, and the second time in Peter Hughes's barley—and do you know what happened the third time?'

'What, what ... ?'

Jenny and Georgina crouched so close by the fireside, bare toes touching on the fender, that their breaths met to seal the conclusion with the nearness of a kiss.

'Oh, God sakes, I don't believe it!'

The tinkling broken music of their laughter and low voices, flushed and stirred to pinkness in their long white nightgowns, sending me out of the room.

'Tell me, tell me ... '

'It's not for a wee laddie's ears to hear, away you go now, cockie.'

'Go and read your bible—Geordie's looking for you!'

The secret lay behind the twelve gates, and I was to be in my thirteenth year till I found out the untellable truth.

Other bible stories invaded the last years of my privacy; their characters stalked the streets and skulked on the corners and hung in chains from the harbour walls. They assaulted the last shreds of ordinariness in the everyday.

Joseph haunted me from Egypt, where he lay embalmed in a coffin. And in prison he interpreted the dreams of Pharaoh's butler and baker. The butler had a good dream and was released, but the baker's dream was bad.

I knew all about bad dreams.

Mr Guthrie coming out of the bakery with the baking trays on his head as he always did right up to that last Sunday morning. Three white baskets on the chief baker's head, and in the topmost basket Pharaoh's bakemeats, which the birds of the air came and ate. The three white baskets were three days, and in three days, Joseph told him, Pharaoh would have him hanged, and the birds would eat his flesh. And poor old Hodgie saw the six men coming up the brae, and in six days, poor Hodgie said, he'd be dead.

And so it came to pass.

Mr Guthrie hanged himself from the beams in the bakehouse in the small hours of a Sunday morning dream, locking the door behind him. Nobody knew why. One of the bakehouse men had to break the window to get at him and was sick when he saw what he saw. Mr Guthrie hanging high from a hawser, with his head wrenched to the side and his haddock's mouth bursting a black grape of a tongue. And the seabirds breaking open his skull with their beaks and feeding on his brains.

Break open your head and feed your brains to the fish.

Gouged gobbets of fish-heads falling into the waves.
O horrible!
Thou shalt not desire Mrs Guthrie.
Thou shalt not eat of this apple, keep the change from the messages, steal the strawberries from the gardens, stick corks on the snoaches in the harbour, smoke out Harry Watson from his shed, uncover the nakedness of the girl at the doocot, of HoneyBunch in the wash-house, drink strong wine on the beach from the dead heads of the dominies, speak ill of the dead Miss Sangster, take the name of the Lord thy God in vain...

Saul saw nothing in his dreams, so he went to the witch of Endor to fight the Philistines with the power of forbidden knowledge. But the spirit of Samuel sat at her fireside and told him that he and his sons would be delivered the very next day into the hands of the enemy. So there in the darkness in the middle of the night, Saul suddenly knew that he was going to die, and the knowledge killed him before the battle had even begun. Tomorrow, Samuel said, shalt thou and thy sons be with me.

With Epp and Chae and Hodgie and Miss McNeil, with Alison Trotter and Agnes Broun and Margaret and Helen Peattie, with the Fowlers and the Boyters and little George Galloway and Isabella Anderson, and with old uncle Jimmy; with the whole host of the strengthless dead in the green humped whale of the kirkyard wave, where the bone-shoal waited to come to life. Dry bones rattling like rotten sticks while Ezekiel looked on, Elijah rose triumphant in chariots of fire, and Adam and Jonah waited for judgement in the black belly of the whale, the black belly of the earth.

And so Saul and his sons fell on Mount Gilboa, under the rain of spears, Saul and Jonathan so lovely and pleasant in their lives that in their deaths they were not divided—like the turbot battered to death by the gowking stick. The Philistines smote them so hard that Saul, stuck with darts, fell on his sword and died. Saul and Jonathan, lovely and pleasant in their lives, and in their deaths they were not divided.

They were swifter than eagles, they were stronger than lions.

From the blood of the slain, from the fat of the mighty, the bow of Jonathan turned not back and the sword of Saul returned not empty. Grandfather's arm came down on the beauty of the sea, and George hurled his harpoons at the whales and they sang in the skulls of the slain like the glory of youth in his soul.

And George died in his age at the end of his life. But grandfather fell on Gilboa in the prime of his years, in the heat of the struggle. He never struck me as old, my grandfather, he was always young and beautiful like Jonathan.

I am distressed for thee, my brother Jonathan:
very pleasant hast thou been unto me: thy love to me was wonderful, passing
the love of women.
How are the mighty fallen, and the weapons of war perished!

The stories wove themselves into the fabric of fields and sea and sky, saturating them again with the colours of that other world.

Moses struck the firth with his staff and the whole sea opened up from Fife to Berwick Law and the Bass Rock, where the white pilgrims winged their way to the promised land. The entire East Neuk fleet foundered while Leebie proclaimed an awful destruction. The boats went tumbling to the hard sea-bed, keels naked and barnacled, booted heels kicking at heaven and the crews crashing to the bouldered bottom among the broken wheels and spears of Pharaoh's charioteers; the splintered masts sticking like swords in the sides of the dying horses, the ice-cream man's horse among them that fell dead one summer's day at the top of the wynd; and the lobsters crawling out of their holes to feed on the carcasses, sails covering them all like torn and bloodied shrouds. Then the sea rushed back—a green forest with white flowering tops, and grandfather was revealed walking on the water, coming from the other side on the backs of the invisible silver shoals.

But the ice-cream man's horse died a thousand deaths that year, dead again at the top of the brae, a river of honey flowing like milk down the hill and pouring from its side into the harbour; till Star

Jeems lifted the dead horse with his enormous strength and put it across his shoulders and carried it through the town and threw it into the sea.

And the stars in their courses fought against Sisera. Jael smote him as he lay asleep in his tent, broke open his temples with a nail and a hammer, struck him till his brains ebbed out from his head.

Break open your head . . .

And David watched HoneyBunch washing herself in the waves and sent Alec Fergusson into the front line of battle to face the shells from the German ships, and the Reverend Kinnear looked at him from the pulpit with his purple face and shook his shield-splintering fist. *Thou shalt not.*

And Chae Marr stalked his elms like black-hearted Ahab in Naboth's vineyard and Elijah pointed his finger at him. Hast thou found me, O mine enemy? *Thou shalt not.*

And the dogs ate Jezebel by the wall of Jezreel. And Nebuchadnezzar went on all fours like Tom Tarvit, red-eyed and raving. And Hodgie Dickson saw the writing on the wall for all eternity, and pointed at the terrible truth. *Thy days are numbered.*

And my grandmother took the tongs to pick up the fallen embers from the fire. She placed them on Isaiah's mouth, and with burning coals on his lips the prophet flew out from the fireside and along the midnight streets, shouting *Watchman, watchman, what of the night?* 'It's long since we've heard from Yarmouth now.' And Penman rang his bell. *Babylon the great is fallen, is fallen.* All flesh is grass, Isaiah sang to Lisa Leslie, and she took the wet dripping bundles of new-born babies and dropped them into the green waving sea of the old kirkyard, and the Ancient of Days bent down and shrouded them with his long white hair that was raging like the sea.

They were larger than life itself, these characters, inseparable from those of the town. They dwarfed the figures of the New Testament, dimmed its grace and glory. The crosses on Calvary were consumed in a sky that burned like Jamieson's forge, and rising over Golgotha in blood-red clouds came all the inescapable horrors.

> *Then shall he say,*
> *Depart from me, ye cursed, into everlasting fire,*
> *Depart from me, I know ye not.*
>
> *And the wicked shall go into everlasting torment,*
> *but the righteous into life eternal.*

Absolute extremities of grace and law, sharp as a two-edged sword.

Who is it who remains, who comes up out of the New Testament wilderness, terrible with truth?

Lazarus.

Lazarus the Snailer.

Lazarus full of sores, lying at the gates of the rich man as he fared sumptuously every day, McCreevie the clown, clothed in purple and fine linen, establishing his idiot authority over the meek and helpless of the earth, the crumbs spilling from his leering jaws into the mouths of the dogs that came and licked the poor man's sores. Lazarus the Snailer, who became indeed a beggar at the end of his life, eating the snails from the gardens, exhibiting his sores.

A good drink of snail slime and they'll be fine.

Lazarus died and went to heaven and the rich man died too and was buried, and in hell. From there he cried out to Abraham, so bitter his torments that his voice carried across what unimaginable gulfs of space and time separate those two dimensions hell and heaven, and his voice was heard by Abraham. Send Lazarus, for mercy's sake, just to dip the tip of his finger in some water to cool my burning tongue, for I am sore tormented by the flames.

A good drink of snail slime and you'll be fine.

Send Lazarus, send Lazarus, for pity's sake!

But Abraham reminded him that he had had his share of good things.

You've had all there is, you wicked, wicked boy!

And Lazarus had had his share of pain, and now the scales were reversed, and the rich man would have to burn.

And not one drop of water will you get!

Blind pink mouths mewing for mercy.

The great gulf was unbridgeable, deeper than four hundred fathoms, deeper than a great line could reach, deeper than the bottom of the world. It was all too terrible. If only Lazarus could be sent to warn the rich man's brothers that hell would be theirs. If only someone were to rise from the dead, maybe they would listen. Ah, but someone *has* risen from the dead, and how many listen? They have ears and hear not. Are you going to hell like Lazarus in spite of that supreme sacrifice? Come and hear more of the wonderful story. Now is the hour of salvation.

And the other Lazarus did rise from the dead, even though he had been gone for three whole days. Everybody was affronted at the thought. *He stinketh*. But Christ went to the mouth of the cave that was a tomb and shouted down into the tunnel that led to eternity.

Lazarus, come forth!

Shouted into the coal-cellar blackness, into the awful black hole of the lum, where the Devil sat sniggering, the crumbs of kittens spilling from his jaws.

And to my horror, Lazarus came forth, bandaged and blind as a mummy, like a white caterpillar cocooned, like Epp with the napkin over her eyes, asleep in her chair, stiff and stern in her coffin now with the napkin knotting her jaw. Waiting for the call. Come forth, come forth! Lazarus heard it and came out into the sun and everybody shouted a miracle.

But nobody thought of asking the most obvious question of all. Nobody asked what a child would have asked.

'Lazarus, what was it like being dead?'

So the great question stayed unanswered.

In the end it is the Book of Job I remember best. It was never taught to me in Sunday School, and I never read it through till I was in my teens. But George broke it open for me in his own mouth many times. He never read it from the page. He told the story instead in his rough distinctive way, which I can recall with no difficulty, almost word for word.

This is how he told it.

Job, you see, was a real toff, because he was a very well off man, but he was also a man of God, and he had a heart of gold.

One day, when God was holding forth, Satan turned up.

'And what have you been up to?' God asked.

'Wandering round the compass,' Satan answered. 'North, south, east, west, on land and sea. You know how I like to travel.'

'Have you heard tell of my servant, Job?' God asked. 'Did you see any sign of him? Now there's a man of faith for you! He's what you call a pillar of the kirk.'

'Och, him!' scoffed Satan. 'Aye, I came across him all right, but he's nothing special. He's got every cause to be religious. Just look at how you've feathered his nest all these years. Cupboard love, that's his religion.'

God took that a bit hard.

'Right,' he said. 'Do just what you like with his gear, but no harm to the man himself, mind.'

Satan went away rubbing his hands.

Next thing you know, Job was tucking in as usual, when one after another the messages started coming in.

Bandits have raided your cattle and murdered your men—I'm the only survivor!

Lightning has struck your sheep and their shepherds—I'm the only survivor!

Fierce tribesmen have carted off your camels and done their drivers to death—I'm the only survivor!

A whirlwind from the wilderness has smashed your son's house to smithereens, and all the young folk have lost their lives in the ruin—I'm the only survivor!"

These were some punches.

But Job took them like a man, right on the jaw.

This is what he said.

> *Naked came I out of my mother's womb, and naked shall I return thither: the Lord gave and the Lord hath taken away: blessed be the name of the Lord.*

And he never said a word against God.

Next time God was holding forth at the bench Satan turned up to put in his needleful.

'So,' said God, 'where have you been stravaiging to this time?'

'Oh, the usual,' said Satan. 'Boxing the compass, round and about. North, south, east, west. You know how I like to travel.'

'And what have you to say about Job now? He's still the godfearing body he always was. Even though you made me wreck him, he didn't crack, did he?'

'Skin for skin, as they say,' Satan answered. 'Hit him in the flesh itself, right into the very bone, and he'll soon squeal.'

'All right,' said God, grim-faced. 'He's all yours, but don't make it fatal.'

Satan took a meads on the earth and went for Job like a gannet. He struck him with saltwater boils, blistering him from the soles of his feet to the crown of his head, and he sat in agony in the ash-hole, itching uncontrollably and scraping himself with shards of shattered earthenware.

'What about your precious God now?' asked his wife. 'Curse him and die.'

'You're havering like an old fishwife,' said Job. 'You've got to take in torn nets some time or other. It's God's will that matters.'

But then his three cronies came and made things worse by trying to comfort him. They sat down and wept salt scalding tears, and that just made him see how bad a state he was in. So he opened his mouth and cursed the day he was born.

I wish I'd died in my mother's belly and never sucked at her breasts. I'd rather be lying right now, a still born bairn in the old kirkyard, with kings and counsellors of the earth, dead in their tombs and their crumbled castles, dumb as the gold and silver they piled up for nothing, for other folk to spend.

There the wicked cease from troubling; and there the weary be at rest.

Why are folk born at all to be burdened and bitter souls, their only comfort to yearn for a death that never comes, their only treasure the tomb, their only gladness the grave?

You try to live a good life and you see what you get for your trouble.

Man that is born of woman is of few days and full of trouble.
He cometh forth like a flower and is cut down: he fleeth also as a shadow and
continueth not.

But God answered Job out of the storm-wind.

Who's this darkening my door with debate, blethering like a daftie?

Get a grip on yourself, man.

You don't know who you're talking to, you worm!

Where were you when I sank the foonds of the earth and threw it up in six days?

When I poured out the sea and tethered the tides and all the morning stars struck up a song?

Ever tried telling the sun to rise?

Go on, have a go, make the morning come if you can, take hold of the horizon and shake down the stars, keep the pole-star pointing to the north and tell the Plough not to rust. See if they listen to you.

Ever seen what lies on the sea-bed, have you? or behind the gates of death? or gone into a snowflake or a hailstorm? Are you the father of frost and rain and ice and dew? Could you freeze the seas to stone, do

197

you think? Could you tie up the Pleiades or loose Orion's belt, tame the Bear or dim Arcturus?

Job was quiet through all this, but he never agreed.
Then God tried one last shot.
You know how to fish, I suppose? You use a hook and line.
Now try it with a whale.
Can you get a hook through his snout or bore through that jawbone with a thorn?
How do you think you'd get on?
I'll tell you.
You can hurt him with harpoons, stick him full of spears, butcher him with barbed irons—all that's straw and stubble to him. You'll piss your breeks in the process!
His teeth are like marlin spikes, his eyes like harbour lamps, his nostrils like funnels, belching smoke and fire.
His heart's like a millstone, his sides like a battleship, his brow like a boulder. His spout's a tornado, his tail a typhoon. A whale is made of whinstone, my man—and I made him what he is!

After that Job saw the point.
'I don't know what came over me,' he said. 'I'm just a bag of wind, a pier-head blether. I can see how small I am—worse than nothing. From now on I'll keep my hatches battened.'
And God gave everything back to Job—as a matter of fact he doubled his fortune.
Keep your mouth shut then, and let God do the talking.
And none of your backchat.
It's just not worth your while.

In his most scripturalist phase, before he failed, old George loved to sermonize. He taught me the bible in this direct and vivid manner of his, only occasionally referring to the big book itself.
But he had one other method of teaching, which combined both scriptural and nautical instruction in an age when both were soon to be out of joint with the time.
Besides the painting by Lorimer in his room, there was one other ornament. It was a print, a coloured print of a Gospel Ship, never seen now in the houses of today, even in the fisher houses. The ship was not a full-rigged vessel—it had twenty-four sails—but on every sail and key part of the ship there was a key quotation from the bible. George

used to make me learn the names of the sails and parts of the ship time and again, and with my eyes shut I had to tell him the quotations, chapter and verse, on every part, and on any single part that he might pick out at random. This went on every Sunday. I have never seen a Gospel Ship for nearly thirty years, but I can see old George's yet in my head, and all its biblical texts.

The ship was guided by the Morning Star, shown blazing in the sky, with Revelation 2.28 printed underneath. *And I will give him the morning star.* At its stern a lighthouse revealed the rocks it had come safely through, and round the tower was written Psalm 119.105, *Thy word is a lamp unto my feet and a light unto my path.* A flock of seabirds followed the ship, carrying a message from Ecclesiastes 10.20, *A bird of the air shall carry the voice.*

Every sail had its text.

On the Outer Jib: *'Tis better on before.* 1 Corinthians 2.9.

On the Inner Jib: INSURANCE: *They shall never perish.* John 10.28.

On the Foresail: *Land ahead.* 1 John 3.1.

On the Forecourse: ROYAL CHARTER: *God so loved the world that He gave His only begotten Son, that whosoever believeth in Him should not perish, but have everlasting life.* John 3.16.

On the Lower Fore Topsail: BERTHS SECURE: *Him that cometh unto ME I will in no wise cast out.* John 6.37.

On the Upper Fore Topsail: VICTUALS: *My God shall supply all your need. He careth for you.* Philippians 4.19.

On the Lower Fore Topgallant: CREW: *Striving together for the Faith of the Gospel.* Philippians 1.27.

On the Upper Fore Topgallant: ETERNITY: *One that inhabiteth eternity.* Isaiah 57.15.

The Fore Royal was furled and bore no text.

On the Main Topmast Staysail: MAINSTAY: *Without shedding of blood is no remission.* Hebrews 9.22.

On the Mainsail: ACCOMMODATION: *And yet there is Room.* Luke 14.22.

On the Lower Main Topsail: TIME OF SAILING: *Behold Now is the accepted time.* 2 Corinthians 6.2.

On the Upper Main Topsail: FARE: *Without Money and Without Price.* Isaiah 55.1.

On the Lower Main Topgallant: PASSENGERS: *Christ Jesus came into the world to save sinners.* 1 Timothy 1.15.

199

On the Upper Main Topgallant: CAPTAIN: *Lord Jesus Christ, Captain of their Salvation.* Hebrews 2.10.

On the Main Royal: *Be not carried about with divers and strange doctrines.* Hebrews 13.9.

On the Mizzen Topmast Staysail: CAPTAIN'S CRY: *Where art thou?* Genesis 3.9.

On the Mizzen Sail: BEWARE: *Beware lest he take thee away with his stroke.* Job 36.18.

On the Lower Mizzen Topsail: WARNING: *He that being often reproved hardeneth his neck shall suddenly be destroyed, and that without remedy.* Proverbs 29.1.

On the Upper Mizzen Topsail: INVITATION: *The Spirit and the Bride say Come. Whosoever.* Revelation 22.17.

On the Lower Mizzen Topgallant: EMIGRANTS WANTED: *Come unto Me, all ye that labour and are heavy laden, and I will give you rest.* Matthew 11.28.

On the Upper Mizzen Topgallant: *Jesus only.* Matthew 17.8.

On the Spanker: COME: *Come Thou.* Numbers 10.29. *Come Now.* 2 Corinthians 6.2.

Each of the masts had a reference which I had to look up and learn.

On the foremast 1 Peter 1.25: *The word of the Lord endureth forever.*

On the mainmast 2 *Timothy* 3.16: *All scripture is given by inspiration of God.*

On the mizzenmast John 8.32: *And ye shall know the truth, and the truth shall make you free.*

There were other references without the texts, which again I had to find and learn.

On the bowsprit Ephesians 2.4: *God is rich in MERCY.*

On the figurehead, which was a winged lion, Psalm 139.14: *I am fearfully and wonderfully made.*

On the gunwale, after the words GOSPEL SHIP, Romans 1.16: *I am not ashamed of the gospel of Christ.*

On the anchor 1 Peter 5.9: *Steadfast in the faith.*

On the rudder James 3.5: *The tongue is a small member and boasteth great things.*

On the log, which trailed in the water from the stern, there were two references:

Romans 13.11: *Now is salvation nearer than when we believed.*

OCTOBER

Psalm 39.4: *Lord, make me to know mine end and the measure of my days, that I may know how frail I am.*
On the ship's lifeboat John 11.25: *I am the Resurrection and the Life.*
On the compass John 14.6: *I am the Way, the Truth and the Life.*

All the ship's flags had their texts and references.
On the flag showing the port of destination, Colossians 3.4: *To Glory.* And beneath the reference the words LENGTH OF PASSAGE: *Time to Eternity.*
On the House Flag there was the crest of the Great Company, a bright red cross of Christ, with two references:
Colossians 1.20: *Peace through the blood of his Cross.*
Galatians 6.14: *God forbid that I should glory save in the cross of our Lord Jesus Christ, by whom the world is crucified unto me, and I unto the world.*
And on the flag at the top of the mizzenmast, showing the port the ship had left, there was the reference Joel 2.2, and the words, *From Land of Gloom.*
The ensign, showing the ship's nationality, was scarlet.
It had one reference, 1 Peter 1.19: *Precious Blood.* And at the bottom of the flag came the words, *Heaven only is my home.*

The ship's helm was the *Spirit of Truth*, John 16.13; its ballast was *Grace and Truth*, John 1.17; in its wake came *They which be of faith*, Galatians 3.9; and it sailed in the *Sea of Time*, Revelation 10.6.
Tossing in the water alongside the Gospel Ship were the broken masts and spars of a foundered vessel. They too bore inscriptions:
Hebrews 2.3 : *How shall we escape if we neglect so great salvation?*
Isaiah 53.6: *All we like sheep have gone astray.*
Matthew 22.14: *Many are called but few are chosen.*

Along the hull of the ship were written the words, *Though billows encompass my way, yet shall I fear not.*
And at the very bottom of the picture was a little couplet:

> *Jesus, Saviour, pilot me,*
> *Over life's tempestuous sea.*

I was given plenty of time to contemplate the age-old connections between religion and the sea during the long period of the Yarmouth fishing, when grandfather and his crew shot their nets in the name of the Lord, following the god-sent shoals of herring. There was something mystical about this wonderful fish, which multiplied so miraculously and fed so many thousands. The old Germanic word for a host or an army was an apt name for the colossal columns, miles long and miles wide, which came for their spawning to the seabed of the British Isles, and swam through our history till we ceased to respect them such a short time ago.

My grandfather believed, with all the old men of his time, that the herring swam down from the Arctic and put a ring round the British Islands once in the course of a year; and that for every ring that it made round Britain, time made a ring on every one of its scales. By counting the number of rings you could tell the age of the fish, just as he taught me once, in the boatshed, to tell the age of a tree that was destined to become a keel; just as he counted the ring of candles on my twelfth birthday before his own last candle was snuffed out, and the smoke hung in the air ever after in a kind of fragrance.

Modern science has discredited the notion that the herring completes a mystical circle. But what mattered was that grandfather believed in that circle, all the way to the end of his own abrupt lifeline. He sat me down on the pier and pointed out the features of the fish which made it so unique. He showed me the rings on the scales, the streamlined shape and forked tail which helped it to swim fast and far; the silvery-white belly and blue-green back, the one merging with the sky and the other with the sea, giving it a two-way protection from predators of feather and fin. He held a female in his hand once and showed it to me.

'Thirty thousand eggs a year come out of that one little belly,' he said. 'If I didn't catch them the seas would be solid with herring from coast to coast. Can you imagine that?'

I imagined it and saw grandfather again walking on the water.

He laughed at my expression.

'As long as they keep coming I'll have to keep on catching them, I suppose.'

'Won't they ever stop coming?' I asked.

'Not till I stop catching them,' he said. 'When I stop, they'll stop. We're inseparable, just you wait and see.'

Then he was off to Yarmouth leaving me with his words for the rest of my life.

Always in the full and rising moons I see him, hunting the herring that came to the surface by moonlight to feed on the plankton—and always waiting for the right kind of wind.

'Northerlies bring you nothing,' he used to say. 'Give me a good steady south-west breeze and I'll bring you a hundred cran of herring with every shot.'

As so often happens, marine science confirms now in theory what our grandfathers knew anyway from practical observation. Always the fish swam into the wind in the unseen currents between the surface and the sea-bed, and a compensating flow in this stream took them in the opposite direction to the wind, and at a faster rate of drift, and so the herring made their way. A north wind held up the southward movement of the shoals and an east wind lured them further from the coast, scattering the pieces of silver. But a south-west breeze brought them down and close to shore, where the nets were waiting.

When the tide and the time and the wind were right, the fishermen looked for the other clues that nature provided—the hungry gulls and the blowing porpoises, and the colour of the water—a thick milky tinge like ginger beer in winter, and a reddish-brown dye in summer. They used their ears too—suspending a lump of lead on the end of a wire in the water and listening for the tell-tale ping when the fish hit the line beneath the waves. And the old men stood on deck with their nostrils flared, waiting for that rich oily smell coming out of the sea that was often evidence enough.

'I don't have to sniff for herring,' grandfather once said to me. 'If they're there I can taste them in the air.'

So the crews cast their curtains over the starboard side, fifty feet deep and two miles long, steaming on their way till the long meshed wall was unfurled in the water. And it hung there while the boat drifted quietly with the tide, coming back on board like a sheet of shining silver, mad in the moon. They steamed furiously for the harbour then with their highly perishable cargo, and their sweat would not grow cold on their faces before they were back to the herring grounds and fishing in the same old way, all through the long months of September and October and November. And they did all this on beef puddings and rhubarb duffs and suet duffs for food, and for their medicines Friar's Balsam and Sloane's Liniment, Gregory's Powder and Carlton's Dutch Drops; and red flannel bandages made from their women's petticoats, soaked in paraffin for the stings of the jellyfish and the saltwater boils.

Leebie used to say that if there were no frost by October the frost would be late in the year and would last long and hard. But the goosy mornings often came early—a dark blue sky glaring white at the horizon, with a still shiver in the air. Later in the day, sure enough, came the first geese, winging their way over firth and fields. The frost was on its way. I could hear it in the sea, a sonorous echo as the full tide splashed among the smaller stones of the beach, crackling like tinfoil—a sound that I had not heard since the last winter. The crabs became sluggish and indifferent to the touch of my toe.

'She's got her head on a north-west pillow tonight,' the old men would say about the October winds, as they heard the north-westerlies falling away at sunset, ghostly over the fields.

And in the morning came the frost.

The first white fingertips of winter, parting the curtains of the year. The frost set fire to the trees and they burned like braziers in the milky mists; yellows and reds, oranges, blacks and golds; torches of rowan and ash sending up flares through the falling leaves, signalling the death of the year, the months of desolation and decay. A single poppy sticks in my mind, drooping in a ditch beside the stubble, its shrunken petals drained of blood and grey with the frost—the lost heart of summer cold in winter's clutch.

Early October mornings were a golden gate, a pale wash over streets and sky. I awoke to the farmers breaking up their fields again, the ploughs pulling behind them the long fluttering streamers of seabirds, waving a furrow's length behind the horses, vivid wings hovering over the rich brown earth. The sun's white fist was punching holes in the clouds that went charging along the tops of the low dykes, the wild rains blowing by, the last shows of light sweeping the fields in broken golden arcs.

But the strong cold winds were whipping up the bay, where the gulls rode at anchor. Further out in the firth the white roses were bursting and blossoming, seabirds swirling like lumps of spray on the wing, tattered handkerchiefs blowing about the sky; and at my feet the wind over the sea-bone on the beach, splinters of sun like broken bottles in the cart-tracks behind me, withered wisps of straw in the lumps of dung. I turned away from the waters, levelling themselves in shining thunder on the wet sands, and curtains of spray ghosting inland.

There was the town etched sharply against the black and silver sea, the chimney-smoke from the houses scrollworked across the clouds, a million mute and more beneath the bare earth, and worse weather yet wintering on the low horizon.

Afraid of the vast unstoppable nature of change, I ran up

frantically into the country, where the fingertips and hands and arms of the trees were showing through as the winds stripped them of their leaves. They took them and made out of them a coloured paper pantomime of snowflakes. The rose-hips were like new constellations in the alien universe of the altered autumnal landscape, but on the shining black coffins of the last brambleberries, the flies laid themselves down and died.

What was that song Georgina used to sing?

> *Not a flower, not a flower sweet,*
> *On my black coffin let there be strown;*
> *Not a friend, not a friend greet*
> *My poor corpse, where my bones shall be thrown:*
> *A thousand thousand sighs to save,*
> *Lay me, O where*
> *Sad true lover never find my grave,*
> *To weep there!*

Love lay like a cold bird's egg, cold and unnoticed like a stone all the year long, till the loss was seen at last in the bare hedgerow, and death cracked its shell.

I came back heavily at sunset and sat in the garret, thinking of Georgina in Yarmouth now with the men, and remembering her songs. The moon rose like a drowned skull out of the sea, and the clouds shrouded it hastily. The voices from George's bible came creeping under his door and stood on the stairs and listened, their gray whisperings putting an end to the songs of love.

> *Vanity of vanities, saith the Preacher, vanity of vanities; all is vanity.*
> *One generation passeth away, and another generation cometh:*
> *but the earth abideth forever.*
> *All go unto one place; all are of the dust, and all turn to*
> *dust again.*
> *There is no new thing under the sun.*

I tried to sleep.

But October was blasting the walls and windows, blowing through the stars that would never feel a wisp of decay in my own short leaf of a lifetime, and yet were burning to waste. October winds—and the sea shattering itself uselessly on the cold sands down there night after night, and the foghorns baying wildly in the dimension of the dark like voices out of hell; and me lying awake again and asking myself for the first time who I really was, while the night turned over and over without sleep.

But nobody wanted to sleep on Hallowe'en, the last night of the month.

I dressed myself up in my father's old Navy clothes, brought out of the mothballs in the bottom drawer—only the clothes were left now, and I never thought to ask any more about the man who had worn them. And bell-bottomed and striped and navy-blue, I went out into the chill darkness to meet my friends.

Gollie was a caped lady in yellowed pearls and ancient crinolines; lipsticky, powdered and rouged, and bestoled with foxfurs slipped stealthily out of his mother's best wardrobe. Peem was a Red Indian; Big Chief Sitting Bull with seagull feathers dyed scarlet and green, and the hatchet from the woodshed in his hand for a tomahawk; whooping all to himself by his back door.

We went over the turnip fields to make our witches' heads, and as we crouched in the damp earth-smells of the dreels with claspknives and candles, we saw the scattered lights of other guisers bobbing through the dark. The glowing skulls came closer, encompassing us; orange eyes and jagged teeth grinning from the hideous heads of the turnip lanterns, swinging near ground level; and though we grinned back at them uncertainly, we were trying to see beyond and above them, into the false faces of our friends, to find out who they were. Boys and girls in long trailing skirts, baggy trousers, feathered hats and strings of beads, soot and satisfaction all over their faces.

'Who is it? who is it?'

'No, don't you come near till you tell me who you are.'

'You tell me first.'

And when recognitions were made, we pointed and screeched with desperate laughter, and joined up in a band with our communal tin, to knock on all the doors and beg a few coppers to help the guisers.

> *Give us our cakes or fall into sin,*
> *Our feet's cold and our shoes thin.*

Some doors were never opened, year after year. But most folk let us in, and we stood in a weird wet huddle in halls and vestibules and the yellow pools of warm kitchens, sweating and self-conscious even under our disguises. Then they asked us to sing for our supper.

'Come on now, do your turns. You first, Lady Muck. Now what about you, Buffalo Bill?'

And all of us sang or recited something one by one or together. 'Old Meg she was a gypsy', 'Oh I do like to be beside the seaside', 'O wha will shoe my bonny foot?'

'You with the sailor's clothes on, whose are you?' an old crone cawed at me from the ingle-nook.

I gave my name.

'But you're Christina Marr's laddie, aren't you?'

I shook my head. I had never heard of Christina Marr.

My mother's name was Christina, but not Marr. Her maiden name was Scott, my grandmother's maiden name was Gay, and my grandmother's mother's maiden name was indeed Marr, though I never knew that at the time. Old wifies who wanted to determine the answer to the usual question, 'Whose are you?', would blithely miss out the males of four generations and ignore your father. It was a matriarchal society.

'Well, give us a sailor's song anyway, wee man. Your dad was a sailor, and so was Captain Marr.'

And I astonished them all by singing 'Drake's Drum'.

> *Drake he's in his hammock an' a thousand mile away,*
> *(Capten, art tha sleepin' there below?)*
> *Slung atween the round shot in Nombre Dios Bay,*
> *An' dreamin' arl the time o' Plymouth Hoe.*
> *Yarnder lumes the Island, yarnder lie the ships,*
> *Wi' sailor lads a-dancin' heel-an'-toe,*
> *An' the shore-lights flashin', an' the night-tide dashin',*
> *He sees et arl so plainly as he saw et long ago.*

'What kind of an English song is that now for you to be singing?'

'Is that one of Georgina's daft-like songs?'

'His father was an Englishman, wasn't he?'

'Wheesht! We all sail the same sea.'

And at the house of the old retired schoolmaster I sang the whole of the song about love and death, which I had unearthed from Georgina's piano-stool.

> *Come away, come away, death,*
> *And in sad cypress let me be laid;*
> *Fly away, fly away breath;*
> *I am slain by a fair cruel maid.*
> *My shroud of white, stuck all with yew,*
> *O prepare it!*
> *My part of death, no-one so true*
> *Did share it.*

And the old man listened gravely, standing with both hands on the knobbly head of his black stick. He stared into the worn carpet while

207

his little wisp of a wife sat by the fire with her faded head to the side, nodding and smiling faintly. Then he tottered towards me.

'That is a most unusual piece for a young man,' he said. 'And it's by a very great writer.'

He opened my hand and pressed into it the chinking coins, warm from his own hand.

We went outside into the wind.

'What did he give you, what did he give you? Let's see.'

Two half-crowns.

Two silver moons shining in the night, and old Epp on her bony knees on the bare flagstones outside our door. Old Epp lying up in the kirkyard now, cold and lonely, away from our singing.

After that the group made me sing Georgina's songs at every door. But they never made an impression on anyone else.

Then it was home to dooking for apples and eating treacle scones and counting our winnings. We sat by the fireside in our creased and dirtied disguises, our faces streaked with treacle and the faded remains of our make-up, and the dowsed turnip-lanterns stinking in the grate. And Leebie told us stories of ghosts and ghouls, and of witches and warlocks flying about the cobwebbed and spidered sky.

'Those born tonight,' she croaked, 'will have the *taish*.'

'What's that?' we gaped.

'The *taish* is the second sight—you see something happening long before it happens.'

And she told us the story of Captain Meldrum.

His grandmother had the second sight, and on the day he was born, the old woman pointed at him in the bed where he lay in his mother's arms, and this is what she said.

'Many's the green wave will he go over—but many's the green wave will go over him.'

And that's how it turned out. Agnes married him much against her mother's wishes, for the old woman was herself a seer, and he died in the China seas, drowned forever.

I shivered at the thought of knowing the future, like Saul who knew in the middle of the night that he was going to die. I was tired and cold, and it was after midnight now.

We were into November—the gloomiest month of the year.

NOVEMBER

It was the wind month.

Not the clear winds from the north-west and the north with the quiet frosty weather, but the heavy easterlies and south winds of winter that ferried the Flanders frosts to the coasts, and the coldest conditions of the year. The wild winds and fierce groundswells ran for such a long time that mountain ranges of weeds were thrown up all along the sands—not the slack heads now but whole masses of oarweed and tangle, torn up by groundswell and gale from the seabed and dragged inshore. They stretched for miles, seven or eight feet deep in places; and the farmers, who had finished their ploughing and laid up their implements for the spring, came down and collected them by the cartful. This was when they took the old 'waur-paths', the expression referring to the tracks along which the sea-waur or tangle was transported to the fields for manure. There, where the sheep were nibbling narrowly at the sliced turnips, they wasted through the long slow winter.

Nothing was slower than November.

These heavy swells and the gales ceaselessly blowing in the North Sea and the Atlantic kept the big white waves pounding the shore, perpetually in our feet and ears. The divided labours of the sun and moon conspired with them to prevent the waters from ebbing effectively, and so the sea never went to sleep. It went on with its worrying and its wakefulness all through the month, when wind and water, the oldest sounds in the world, were all that ever were. Change and decay would have been welcome visitants to the scene: the effect instead was one of boredom and barbarism. When the tides did go back a little the coast was strewn with bare rock pools in which nothing winked or waved except the bitter ruffling of the water all day long. Standing disconsolately in one of these pools, I lost sight of my rubber-booted feet at once in just three or four inches of muddy water. The clarity would not return to it now until the spring.

The wind visited all places, quickening the hands of the harpist rain. There was uproar in Balcaskie, where the limes and ash trees were already ruined choirs and cathedrals latticing the sky, and the elms and beeches and oaks were losing their turrets and spires. The wind came up from the water and the gray roaring in the woods was an answering sea, the trees battling like the masts of men-o'-war, the burns clattering angrily in spate. Leaves whirled in wet windy flurries, hurrying from the woods like homeless hordes over alien tracts of land. They flew through the broken window-panes of derelict sheds, ran rustling in rills and drifts along the dykes and wynds and byroads; tattered black scraps of those lush green hours that summer had stolen for us out of time.

Coming down from Balcaskie I bent my head beneath the low glooms of the sky, eyes fixed on my feet. Sodden flowers and their dead seed vessels beaten into earth, black death-smells oozing out of the ground. I sheltered in a deserted byre, where Sunday afternoon was an eternal puddle on the floor, the cloudburst finding the rusted hole in the roof; and the rain hammering on the corrugated iron was the rattle of rotten tongues, coffin nails deadening the tunes of eternity.

It was November, when minutes were stacked like bars of lead; the dismal trough of the year, choked with leaves, and black branches wetly streaming. It was November—and all was rawness and rotting and rain; the bleak blasting month when the earth's empty stage was swept by thin curtains of fogs and the old men of the woods went storming to their graves. Drizzling dawns and drearily drifting skies and long unlovely days; voices in the wind tormented spirits howling round the graveyard of the world. The clouds were always on the march, restless armies trailing fitful rags of sky—brief banners catching a lurid sun on the other side of existence.

In this hard weather, when I thought things could only get better, they grew worse instead. The rains fell harder; the line of hills and the sea-horizons disappeared; the gales gathered in strength; the trees tightened their toes in the earth, clutching at stones and bones.

And yet it was at this time, when it seemed nothing could live, that the winter migrants were coming back to the coast—flocks of fieldfares, the swallows of winter, clinging to the softer ground of the shore, where they scratched for their bare existence. Tough as they were, these birds, I sometimes found one of them after a few days hard frost, or a redwing perhaps, huddled in behind a banking or a dyke, dead where it had lain for shelter. Snow swaddled it in the Christmas month, and when spring came there would just be a few feathers in a tiny cage of bones, and amid the burgeonings of the new season the deserted nests of the previous year, and cold cracked eggs like fruitless blue moons.

NOVEMBER

The curlews too were active on the land, along with the lapwings and crows. The sky darkened with the wintry whistlings of the geese— spears flung from the north. And just offshore great flocks of mallards came in on the smooth water made by the north wind. All day they bobbed silently in the bay, as if they had come for no special purpose. Then at sunset they rose with one accord and flew in over the bare fields to pick up the stray potatoes before the onslaughts of frost and rain turned them to purple stones or a black mush. Often as I stood on the landward side of our house I could hear their quack-quacking coming from the moonlit fields where they continued to feed well into the quiet nights—if the nights were ever quiet.

Mostly the nights were wild and eerie.

As the weather worsened, the heartbeat of the hearth grew stronger, redder, and we felt the simple things more keenly— steaming mugs of tea at ten; a stone hot water bottle like a volcanic island in the arctic drift of the bed; the music of a tale to take our minds away from the monotonous monochrome dribbling at the windows, the howling of the roof in the winds and rains. Old urges surfaced, instincts deepened, and closer kinship with all earth's vanished folks, who crept into the room and joined us round the fire.

The Druidic New Year began on the first day of November with the festival of Samhain, the feast of the dead, and Orion's wintry belt rising at nine o'clock between the castle and the kirk. Our Hallowe'en antics were the faint impulses from that not quite forgotten rhythm of life, just as the old church sanctified it with the sedater landmarks of the liturgical year—Hallowmas, All Saints and All Souls. Like matter, the old customs changed their form but were not destroyed. The white-robed files were no longer to be seen wending their weird ways to the summits of Kellie Law, Largo Law and Dunino, after every spark of life had been allowed to die out in crannog and cave before midnight. But still we burned the whins on the braes, as if in recognition of a truth that darkness and blight were now about to triumph, and the Beltane celebration of life and light half a year dead already, pervaded by present conviction of desolation and decay.

There were no charnel-houses to be thrown open as in the old days, when they were stained with torchlight and hung with flowers; while crowds of villagers thronged through the vaults to visit the bodies of their friends and relatives, saluting shrouded skeletons with inquiries after their welfare in eternity. But even into November, if there was a decent enough day at the start of the month, one or two shawled old wifies could be seen sitting up there in the kirkyard, pursuing their knitting among the graves. And if any young folk said anything to them about this custom, they would shrug and say, 'Och well, we're among our own folk.' And if no-one actually believed that unhappy spirits returned to their old firesides, Leebie still kept the kitchen warm overnight on All Souls and left food and drink on the table before she went to bed, when nothing was ever left the following month for Santa Claus. It was the time for remembering the dead, she said, and for nothing of a festive nature.

> *If you wed in bleak November*
> *Naught but woe will you remember.*

And the weather seemed to confirm everything she said.

> *November's sky is chill and drear,*
> *November's leaf is red and sere.*

So we worshipped the red rose in the grate and turned our backs to the shadows. Leebie became the dark deity of the hearth, filling my head with the wild old wine of her tales and ballads. At this fireside season of the year she was particularly fond of chanting the old Scots folk poetry, much of which she knew by heart.

> *There lived a wife at Usher's Well*
> *And a wealthy wife was she;*
> *She had three stout and stalwart sons*
> *And she sent them owre the sea.*
>
> *They hadna been a week from her,*
> *A week but barely ane,*
> *When word came to the carlin wife*
> *That her three sons were gane.*
>
> *They hadna been a week from her,*
> *A week but barely three,*
> *When word came to the carlin wife*
> *That her sons she'd never see.*
>
> *I wish the wind may never cease,*
> *Nor fashes in the flood,*
> *Till my three sons come hame to me*
> *In earthly flesh and blood.*
>
> *It fell about the Martinmas,*
> *When nights are lang and mirk,*
> *The carlin wife's three sons came hame—*
> *And their hats were o' the birk.*

NOVEMBER

And so that is how it came about, in the dark and dismal days of mid-November, just like we're in now; when the year was deep into its autumnal gloom and country folks were slaughtering their cattle and salting them down for the winter—the old wifie's sons came back from the dead. And she was so taken up with this that she failed to spy the birch leaves in their hats that would have warned her what they really were—no creatures of flesh and blood as she had wished for that sat down at her fireside dripping wet and asking to be fed, but beings from another world, from behind the gates of death. So she puts them to bed and grows sleepy by their side. Her chin falls into her neck, the candle splutters out, and darkness and silence commune. Nothing moves in that room all night long.

Then the east starts to bleed—a slow wound.

> *The cock doth craw, the day doth daw,*
> *The channerin worm doth chide,*
> *Gin we be missed out of our place*
> *A sair pain we maun byde.*

'But if the birch leaves were from Paradise why do they have to be eaten by worms? And I thought they were drowned men . . . are they ghosts?'

Ah, it's a blessing we know nothing of life beyond the grave!

But just imagine what she said when she woke up to the blue light of morning and a torrent of tousled sheets fallen from the bed. They had been restless sleepers . . .

> *Fare ye weel, my mother dear,*
> *Fareweel to barn and byre,*
> *And fare ye weel, the bonny lass*
> *That kindles my mother's fire.*

What an awful thing it is to have to say your last goodbye to this earth. But it comes to us all sooner or later, when we'll envy the very servant lass her dirty start to the day in cleaning out the fire, because a morning has come when the world will go about its business without us. Well, that's the way of life, even for you bold boys, with your beer and bright coins and girls and full gullets at first. Before you know where you are it's just work and worry for the best of your years. Then a dry stick between your legs, veins on your wrists, and an ounce of baccy to sweeten your musty old mouth. What's left? A head in a pair of hands with a candle in the window. The broken bowl at the fountain and the silver cord untied. You'll not know it, but somebody will be hammering nails into a box and throwing dirt over your face one day soon enough, and the play's over. The last act's always the same and you're never there to see it. What's it all for, eh?

The ballads elevated Leebie to her inspired role of priestess of pessimism, and she in turn embodied their fatalism and impersonality. 'Lord Randal', 'Clerk Saunders', 'The Unquiet Grave', 'The Bonny Earl of Moray'—she crooned them to me out of the sunken core of her quavering Adam's apple, and the illustrations were the blood-red pictures in the fire.

Her favourite was undoubtedly 'Sir Patrick Spens', the story of the East Neuk seadog caught up in the corrupt currents of the court and driven into the web of fate.

> *The king sits in Dunfermline town,*
> *Drinking the blude-red wine.*
> *'O whaur will I get a skeely skipper*
> *To sail this new ship o' mine?'*

Who else but Sir Patrick Spens? the skipper who loved the sea so much that he couldn't bear to be away from it when he wasn't afloat. So when the royal command reached him he was daundering up and down on the beach, his hands in his pockets, whistling to himself—just like your grandfather.

'Which beach?'

Oh, hereabouts, I wouldn't wonder, or at Fifeness maybe, or Kingsbarns, or Crail—there were seafaring Spenses in Crail seven hundred years back, in the time of King Alexander the Third, I know that much.

It was a bad time of year to be out on the sea.

But the winter gales don't blow down the corridors of power where the braid letters are composed. Bad breath is all you get there, blowing on hot wax, with the flunkeys fixing the seal to a man's fate. So against his will Sir Patrick was appointed to sail to Norway, to bring the Maid to Scotland.

The voyage went ahead. On the day they were due to sail back, one of the sailors told his captain that he'd seen a bad omen in the sky.

> *I saw the new moon late yestreen*
> *Wi' the auld moon in her arm,*
> *And if we gang to sea, master,*
> *I fear we'll come to harm.*

'Why did they go to sea then?'

What's before you will not go past you. If a thing has to be then it has to be. And sometimes a man has to be a loyal subject first and a good sailor second. Anyway, they weighed anchor and the storm struck.

It was some storm.

Think of a night just like this—one that's near hand bringing your chimneys down and lifting away the roof. The yawls in the harbour break from their moorings like wild horses and they're waltzing higher than the kirk on the waves. It's a night when no fisherman would want to be within a mile of the sea, and Peter Hughes is the only man in the world who wouldn't put his poor sheep into fold and his beasts in the byre. That's the kind of night it was when they were hit.

> *The ankers brak and the topmast lap,*
> *It was sic a deadly storm,*
> *And the waves came owre the broken ship*
> *Till a' her sides were torn.*

Can you picture it?

The anchor chains splintering like glass; the sails dripping a ton weight of sea, but ripped to shreds and carried on the wind like a boy's broken kite; the seamen scuttering round the hold with fear in their bowels and wading up to their armpits in water, hauling up bales of silk and coils of rope to bind round her hull and bung the breaches in her sides. Their finger-ends are frantic, frozen blind, their hearts are jumping off the stalk. They do everything humanly possible.

But that cold blue sea just keeps on pouring in.

> *O laith, laith were our gude Scots lords*
> *To weet their cork-heel'd shoon,*
> *But lang or a' the play was played,*
> *They wat their hats aboon.*
>
> *And mony was the feather bed*
> *That flatter'd on the faem,*
> *And mony was the gude lord's son*
> *That never mair came hame.*

Leebie closed her eyes.

In the white amphitheatre of her skull sailor-lads and lords were levelled by the neutral sea, where they foundered together with all their fancy gear and frenzy for life. And she held in her cupped hands the howls of women inside castle-walls and girls tearing gold combs from their hair.

At the final verse, with its picture of the common sea-grave, she would stretch out her arm, part blessing, part malediction, the landlubber dandies doing obeisance in death to the great sailor in whose veins the salt sea now ran forever.

Half-owre, half-owre to Aberdour,
'Tis fifty fathom deep,
And there lies gude Sir Patrick Spens
Wi' the Scots lords at his feet.

The ballad of 'Sir Patrick Spens' plunged Leebie into her direst depths of misgiving. She put her head into her hands, rocked herself for grief by the fire, and wept without tears for the Yarmouth fleet. Her keening was sharper than the wind. I was afraid her anxieties and agonizings would tempt providence the wrong way, that her prescience and pessimism would be a kind of curse.

A crowd of shadows sat with us in the room, listening.

She paused in her rocking, poked at the log, sent a new flame licking round it. Sparks thronged the grate like bright bees and for a minute she was a drunken dancer going daft on the wall. Then the flame died and she was a statue again; a shawled skull in the red shadows; a kirkyard thing. A memorial. For all that she did then was to sit and remember. She was a remembering mouth for an old November night.

She remembered story after story of disaster by drowning, and she connected them convincingly with fetches and foreknowing and intimations of eternity.

There was the story of Fergus Hughes, who appeared to his old mother, Alice, at the moment of his death. He left for the sea one wicked night on the *Harvest Reaper* with the rest of the boat's crew. It was their last chance to save their anchored nets off Kingsbarns. Fergus was on duty at the halyards when the tackle snapped and he was pitched into the sea.

Less than half an hour after he'd left the house, as his mother sat with her knitting by the kitchen fire, she saw him suddenly appear in front of her. One arm was leaning on the mantlepiece and he seemed to be warming himself or something in front of the coals. He had his back towards her. But to her horror she saw that he was still wearing his oilskin dauper, and she knew that meant only one thing. He was a dead man. Or he was in mortal danger. Sure enough, he just turned his head then and looked at her. His white lips moved without the sound of words and she saw the water streaming down his face before he disappeared into the fire like steam sucked up the chimney by the wind.

'I've never seen a ghost.'

Ah, but that wasn't a ghost she saw, old Alice Hughes. No, no, that was his spirit double—what the old folks used to call a fetch.

The old folks. I tried to imagine folks older than Leebie, with her white walnut head and her close kinship with distant deaths. How could she live with the familiarity, the certainty, of such knowledge? Was she really a witch?

'But how, but how . . .?'

How can you be here if you're somewhere else?

Picture yourself drowning.

It's a dark night and you're tossed into the water with your oilskins and boots and all your heavy gear. You kick your arms and legs and try to gather the sea to yourself like a basket of bread, like a stook of corn. But the harvest is too big. Soon your arms are full of the sea and your legs are tired. You stop your threshing and let the sea do the harvesting. The firth is filling your boots. You go down like a stone. You think you can hear your shipmates crying to you far above the waves and you vaguely wonder how they are going to get you out on a night like this when every man is fighting for his own life. But it's only the roaring in your ears that you hear—the roaring of the darkness telling you that you are a drowning man.

At such a moment where would you most wish to be, do you think? 'At home.'

Aye, at home, with your mother and your own folk, and drying off at your own fireside. That's where the drowning Fergus Hughes most wanted to be in his dying seconds, and that's where the force of his longing projected that last image of himself, causing it to materialise before the eyes of his mother. It was her son's last wish that she saw, and not his ghost.

The same thing happened to Euphemia Christie.

She was just a young thing, poor lass, her man at Yarmouth for three whole months, and a month old bairn that he'd never seen, lying sleeping in the crib on the floor. She was making a bairn's clothes with her lonely hands and her foot was rocking the cradle as she worked. Andrew Christie was caught in the chest by a swinging boom and went straight into a heavy sea. He was never seen again— except by Euphemia. She looked up from her work. Her foot and fingers froze. He was coming across the kitchen floor in his oilskins, so real that she spoke out loud to him.

'Mercy me, Andrew Christie, what's this that you're home from Yarmouth without a breath of warning?'

He answered her never a word.

He bent down and looked hard and long into the cradle, his sea-swept eyes taking their fill of the bairn he'd never seen. Then he faded from human sight. The telegram came the next morning to say that he'd been lost, but she hardly needed that. She was already wearing black when she answered the door to the boy from the post office, and he read it through to her without her ever so much as turning a hair. She had shawled the bairn in black as well. A message like that was nothing to the one she'd had the night before, when her husband came for the first and last look at the son he'd never see in the flesh.

That was just exactly the same situation, you see—the man appeared in his mortal struggle just where he yearned to be.

'I wonder where Captain Carnbie yearned to be . . . I wonder if he ever appeared to anybody?'

Ah, Captain Carnbie, that poor man.

Leebie lifted the log with the poker, turned it gently. A whisper went through the fire. In the lapping flames I saw again the low tide at the point of the pier, and the two men in the yawl fishing with boathooks in the water, disturbing the clear mirror in which we saw our own faces, the small crowd bunched at the edge. Another face was at the bottom of that mirror—not a shadow like ours, but a white face, dark with mud.

'Who can it be?'

'Who is it, do you think?'

'Can't tell that yet. We've got him, though—haul away, Jock!'

The body rose slowly, approaching the surface. The mirror quivered violently, noisily, burst into fragments—a crowd of white stars. We lost sight of our own faces as the drowned face came up closer, into the air it no longer needed, up to the world of men.

'Who is it? who is it?'

The stilled eyes looked through us, fixed on the sky at our backs. The white hair was slicked down over the forehead. Somebody started to wipe away the oil and mud from the front of the face.

'Oh, my God, it's Captain Carnbie!'

Blind Captain Carnbie.

'This is your music teacher, this is Captain Carnbie. He'll teach you to play the piano in no time.'

Which he did for five years.

218

NOVEMBER

Black braided blazer with the gold buttons, bolt upright at his grand piano, straight as a poker, sitting in his high windows overlooking the harbour. Captain Carnbie, always breaking off the lessons to sing and play his songs of the sea, always yearning for something that lay beyond the sea . . .

'Right, we've had enough of scales for the day, they're as dead as fish-scales the way you play them. What about a song?'

> *In the harbour, in the island, in the Spanish Seas,*
> *Are the tiny white houses and the orange-trees,*
> *And day-long, night-long, the cool and pleasant breeze*
> *Of the steady Trade Winds blowing.*
>
> *There is the red wine, the nutty Spanish ale,*
> *The shuffle of the dancers, the old salt's tale,*
> *The squeaking fiddle and the soughing in the sail*
> *Of the steady Trade Winds blowing.*

'Ah, those were the days, son, when I had the Trade Winds up my nose and Spanish waters in my ears!'

'Off you go, now!'

Going off now by the harbour, coming back again along Shore Street, wishing for the rest of my life that I had never forgotten my sheet music, left there on the piano with Spanish waters ringing in my ears. And stopping in my tracks at the top of the stairs, chilled by the sound of the hard voice through the open music-room door, murderous accompaniment to the lilting piano.

Lady Carnbie standing at his side, her head thrown back in a savage aria, teeth bared like the skull of a wild animal as she hissed and mocked and spat.

'Captain Carnbie! God save us, you bloody old fool, your whole life's been a fake!'

The Captain's brow was furrowed and the line of his lips was tight. But his fingers responded with infinite gentleness to the sound of the taunts.

> *Spanish waters, Spanish waters, you are ringing in my ears,*
> *Like a slow sweet piece of music from the grey forgotten years.*

'So now it's sea shanties for little boys—the nearest you'll ever come to the sea, you blind old dreamer! God help us, when are you going to earn us a decent living before you die, that's what I'd like to know?'

> *Telling tales and beating tunes, and bringing weary thoughts to me,*
> *Of the sandy beach at Muertos, where I would that I could be.*

219

The playing went on as if the whole world of his music was invulnerable, inviolate, beyond the reach of the wounding, hateful words.

> *It's not the way to end it all, I'm old and nearly blind,*
> *And an old man's past's a strange thing, for it never leaves his mind.*
> *And I see in dreams, awhiles, the beach, the sun's disc dipping red,*
> *And the tall ships, under topsails, swaying in past Nigger Head.*

'And that bloody old bitch down in the schoolroom, do you think I never knew about *her* all these years?'

What did it mean?

The melody faltered but went round the thrown stone like a stream. Though his eyes could not see Lady Carnbie, he turned his head away from her and towards the window, to the blue glintings of the sea.

> *I'd be glad to step ashore there, glad to take a pick and go*
> *To the lone blazed cocopalm tree in the place no others know,*
> *And lift the gold and silver that has mouldered there for years*
> *By the loud surf of Los Muertos which is beating in my ears.*

'But you *will* listen to me!'

The shrieking drowned the music. The wizened old witch reached out with both hands, slammed down the lid hard and fast on the old man's seeing sensitive fingers. He cried out in pain as she stood and screamed uncontrollably. The blind eyes blurred, the hard horizon of the lips trembled and broke, and the head finally bowed. I fled down the stairs in my terror.

Spanish waters and tormented howls of triumph ringing in my ears.

'Did he fall in, do you think?'

'God alone knows—but he had a dog's life, I can tell you that much.'

'And there's a woman not very far away from where we're standing now could tell you why.'

'Dear, dear.'

Dear Captain Carnbie, his eyes wet and his head bent and the water streaming down his face. But as he lay in the harbour all through that night, arpeggios of sea gusted gently over his drowned corpse, plucked by the wind's fingers from glimmering strings of salt. And the singing in his ears never went away.

> *And o' nights there's fire-flies and the yellow moon,*
> *And in the ghostly palm-trees the sleepy tune*
> *Of the quiet voice calling me, the long low croon*
> *Of the steady Trade Winds blowing.*

NOVEMBER

The November winds blew louder down the lum, raising sparks from the log in the grate. Leebie sat like the witch of Endor, conjuring up the spirits of all those that had taken their own lives in her lifetime and her father's. There seemed a great many. She brought them before me into the room, one by one, to terrify me with her winter's tale.

Yes, Captain Carnbie, a strange business, some folk said. Though there's nothing strange, in my opinion, to be tired of living when you have a wife like that one, and no eyes to get away from her.

But a very strange case, and the strangest one of all, in my recollection, was that of Mary Prett.

She had seventy years on her back, and she'd had a good life and still had a good man to help her while away the hours between them and the kirkyard. They went to the Whist Drives in Anstruther every Saturday night. That's where they'd come from on the night she took her life, home on the last bus, happy with a couple of drams inside them, and her talking nineteen to the dozen as usual all the road home.

Well, it was three in the morning maybe, by John Prett's reckoning, when she rose, and pitch dark it was too, and the worst night of the year for gales and rain that folk could remember. He thought she'd gone down to the water closet when he heard the back door bang, and so, with the bed empty he dug down deeper into the blankets for warmth and went back to sleep. When he woke it was as light as it could ever be on such a terrible morning. But there was no Mary to be found inside the house or anywhere round about. They searched the town from east to west without finding a hair of her. Fearing the worst by then, they combed the shore and looked over the end of every pier, probing the tangles round the point of the Blocks.

'Wasn't she drowned?'

Oh, she was drowned all right, no doubt about that, but the manner of it was strange. It was late forenoon when the bobby came up to John's door and told him that she'd been found—at Kilconquhar. They're late risers there—too many retired and retarded folk round thereabouts. Anyway, they got up out of their beds to discover the body of an unknown woman floating face downwards in the loch, a white nightgowned thing among the reeds and flag rushes, and nothing on her feet.

Why on earth had she done it?

That's the first mystery, why she was driven to go through that particular gate in the first place. But then to consider all the other circumstances. A woman perfectly all right in the head all her days gets up in the dead of night and decides to drown herself. She has less than fifty yards to walk to the harbour. But instead of that, she goes two miles in her bare feet, and nothing on but a nightgown, along a road she never travels. She makes her way through solid sheets of rain, ripped and shredded by the winds. Some folk say the night was so bad that if she'd just turned at the loch and walked all the way back again to St Monans she'd have been dead by the time she reached her door. But she threw herself into that dark and freezing place, far from her own fireside, and left other folk to work out the whys and the wherefores.

'Maybe she was . . . made to, somehow.'

Cold covers to look for in the middle of the night, that's for sure. They closed over her all the same, and she went back to sleep. Nobody knows what kind of mind she had that night, or what went through her head on her journey.

'Why do you think she went there?'

It's an unsain place, Kilconquhar Loch. Maybe she was called there by something. Some spirit of the water. In the old days they soomed the witches up there.

> *They took her to Kilconquhar loch*
> *And threw the lummer in,*
> *And a' the swans took to the hills,*
> *Scared wi' the unhaly din.*

'Were there witches in Fife?'

There were witches everywhere. They cursed our corn, blighted our bellies and caused fishes to forsake the firth. Lighthouse lamps went black and barns became beacons, luring ships to the foaming reef. A fall from a horse, a lost footing on a slippery deck, curdled milk, sour beer, a dead infant. Ah yes, the witches were busy in Fife like all places else on the earth, where the Devil roams to and fro, and up and down, seeking whom he may devour, like a slavering tiger. They were his servants, and they sowed skulls in kirkyard and sea.

In St Monans here they burned them between the kirk and the castle. The beadle scattered the ashes to the four winds and the charred bits of bone were lodged in the kirk loft just under the steeple, and there they stay to this day. A funny thing for those in the Sunday pews, a vault of black bones over their pious heads, behind the whitewash. A rotten roof for kirk folk, but fine enough for whited sepulchres.

At other places along the coast they tied the witches to a stake at low water and condemned them to suffer the washing of two tides.

NOVEMBER

'I'd rather be drowned than burned.'

Would you?

Drowned at the stake. How would you feel watching the tide coming in that day, I wonder? Would you think of apple-blossom, seeing the lines of surf advance? First it tickles your toes and washes your feet—that's all right. Then it's slapping at your legs and thighs, you're wearing wet gloves, and chilly fingers are clutching your groin—not so nice. Think of it up to your chest, with the noise of the waves like thunder in your ears. You take your first mouthful of cold salt water—it tastes bitter. You don't want too much of that. But it's filling your nostrils now, sucked up in hard hurting lumps into your lungs. You struggle with the combined powers of wind and tide for two paltry minutes. Then all your struggles cease. Your eyes are sightless as water, the waves are combing your hair—tossing like tangles without a wish in the world. Your head is filled with foam—it lolls and lollops with the turning tide. Now all's still. A drowned statue stands at the stake, underneath the sea. The crabs and conger eels advance.

Wouldn't you rather suffer the red tide of the other stake? Spreading from your toes to the top of your head again, a million times more agonizing, but faster, I suppose, than a six-hour flood. Would you live to hear your own skull burst like a bomb in the blaze and your heart crack as though it were a roasted black chestnut, a shrivelled up stink? I wouldn't think it likely. But what terrible ways to have to die. Burning or drowning: cinders or salt on your tongue; ashes or silt behind your eyes; your skull a hot white shard, or a cold coral stone.

The winds shivered in the chimney again. Large gobbets of rain crackled and spat on the red-hot coals, broke up and bounced along the fender like drops of blood. Veins bursting, eyeballs popping, and the lobsters scrabbling again at the lid as the pot began to boil.

Old Leebie was coming into her season.

She who feared so loudly for the safety of our men at sea— nonetheless she drowned them nightly in the very clamour of her concern. They foundered in her foreknowing, in her retrospection. Her white head was a graveyard of memories that came to grisly life at this fireside time of year when she appeared to revel in the ranks of death from where she groaned out her reminiscences. Her father had been a sexton. She remembered all his tales and passed them on to me, a disquieting bequest of unquiet graves. All she ever gave me.

His fingers were among articles of death; his whole life long he lived among the dead. He rang bells in the earth—his spade bright on the tongueless skulls and stones. Oh yes, he knew of many a queer death, did my father. But then I've known them myself. Not so very long ago now, just after you were born . . .

The two brothers, James and Thomas Morris, who lived above their sweet shop in the Back Gate. James turned not so well, and his brother shut the shop to look after his needs on the top floor. The bairns looked in at the melting toffees and tablet in the window down below.

It was hot summer.

'Thomas, open up, we want our Lucky Bags!'

'I'll open up again when Jimmy's better—away with you, now!'

They went off with sad faces.

The sunflower sun burst in the sky every day for a fortnight, bigger and hotter every day. Not a drop of rain to give the tatties and barley a drink. The chocolate drops in the window ran wild and ended as brown sludge in the corner.

'Thomas, Thomas, we're fair needing some lemonade!'

Shouted up from the street.

'Aye, aye, he'll be better soon, just wait a wee while!'

From behind sealed shutters in a burning blue sky.

'They must be suffocating in there. All that lack of air cannot be good for a well man, never mind a sick one.'

'How's your brother now, Thomas?'

'Oh, he's fine, he's fine, it'll not be long now.'

A faint voice from somewhere inside.

Three weeks passed.

Everything else was wilting, but the sunflower in the sky throve. If only it could be sprayed with something!

'Can you give me something for the heat rash, Dr Gray? It's right in at the unmentionable places.'

'Rub this in twice a day. Get your wife to do it if she wants to see you squeal a bit. How's things in St Monans?'

'James Morris is taking the devil's own time to get over his 'flu, doctor.'

'James Morris! What are you blethering about, man? He's dead and buried three weeks since.'

'He may be dead, doctor, but I don't think he's buried.'

They had to break the door down in the end, the doctor and the policeman, and two men from the boatyard. They wrenched it off its hinges like a scab off a wound.

NOVEMBER

It hit them like a sea. A hot stench from a black broken belly. They had to stand in the street and be sick before they could go back inside.

James was propped up on the pillows, a putrefying corpse, and he was smothered in hot water bottles. The pans and kettles of water were singing away on the stove and at the side of the grate as if it were the middle of winter. The fire roaring like a furnace too, and the town blistering in a heat-wave. Thomas had been doing nothing else since the day the doctor had called and pronounced his brother dead.

'Oh no, don't move him, please let him alone, he doesn't need you. He'll be fine yet if you just let me keep him warm.'

He wept when they took him away.

They tried to burn the mattress down in the mud but the fishermen would not allow it. That was an unnatural death-bed, you see, and it had to be taken a long way out of the town to be destroyed.

Betsy Crieff's was another bad burial.

I never saw that myself but my father did, being the sexton. She was twenty-five stones when she died on a Monday morning, and the undertaker made her box a big one. But when he tried to install her at the kisting that night, she wouldn't go in, no matter which way they tried to work it.

'Nothing for it, Davit,' her widower said to the maker of coffins, 'you'll have to bring a bigger box and take better measurements this time.'

Davit Wood swore he'd never skimped a body for room in its dead-kist. It wouldn't have been in his interest, would it? Six hours later, back he came with a new box. Would you believe it? She still refused to be accommodated!

'She's got bigger!' he roared, furious that his workmanship appeared to have failed again.

But he was right. She was expanding, the gases in her building up faster than he could build her box. So she was hurried off with him to his workshop where he could ply his trade with her right under his nose. And a quick coffin she got this time.

They lost no time in hauling her up to the kirkyard, I can tell you. But just as the minister had said the bit about rising again, there was a crack like the crack of judgement. The coffin lid flew off, the sides splintered, and Betsy Crieff sat up in the clay with her eyes wide open. She was bloated to twice her life-size, sitting in her grave and spouting like a gargoyle. They were horrified.

'What'll we do?' stuttered the minister.

'Hap her up, hap her up, for the love of God!' her man shouted to my old father.

And he shovelled in the soil with her still sitting there, and didn't stop to take a breath till he'd covered up the staring eyes. She has a green roof over her head now, like everyone else, but she's nearer the rafters. For although she's just a rickle of bones by now, she's still buried there sitting up and waiting for doomsday.

'Tell me about the buried giant.'

It was in the stormy season.

Once the sea-facing kirkyard wall caved in during the night of a heavy south-east gale, and bony feet began to peep through where the brae was eroded. When the sun came up my father swore you could almost have seen their toes wiggle. It's a long sleep beneath these blankets before you scent the morning air.

They were busy repairing the wall when another storm got up, worse than the night before. All their work came tumbling down like the walls of Jericho. They sought the arms of the strongest man in the town, Big Jamieson—that was Jamieson's great-grandfather. A monstrous man he was, and he stood on the brae and tried to shore up the wall, with the white sparks of the sea flying all about his head, and him so used to labouring among the red sparks of his own forge. It's a mercy there wasn't loss of life there, because he was washed off the wall twice, and came back to the task with masonry crashing all around his grimy skull.

Then my father shouted to him, 'Look out behind you, man, there's a sea bearing down on you like the Pyrenées!'

There was no time for him to come off the wall.

'Hang on! hang on!' they bellowed, running for their lives.

'Right!' he roared back at them, as they turned to look. 'I've a holdfast here!'

And then the sea hit him.

There must have been a ton of water went over him, my father said. It broke on his big back and went so high it near hand knocked the steeple flying off the kirk above him. They didn't think to see him come out of it with his head still on or air in his lungs. That man had a head like a boulder and lungs like his own bellows. Next thing they knew, the sea was falling back again and dragging Jamieson with it, still clinging hard to his holdfast.

And do you know what it was? He'd found the handle of a coffin sticking out the side of the kirkyard brae—a great solid leaden coffin it was. When the sea hit Jamieson it took out half the brae, and blacksmith and lead box and all came away with it, not to mention a generation of bones.

Jamieson stood up among the rocks a hundred feet away.

'Give a hand here!' he shouted.

But as they dived into the sea he was already dragging it upshore by the strength of his own enormous hands.

They pulled the box out of the reach of the pounding seas. And then they just stood there, dumb as boulders, staring at it.

It was the coffin of a nine-foot giant if it contained a human being at all. But they couldn't believe it did. They imagined they were rich for life. Jamieson ran to the forge and fetched along his tools. A weird hammering that was, on the anvil of the rocks, while the wind blew up the firth and the white flames licked their faces.

And when they had done with their groaning, and the lid came clattering onto the boulders of the beach, they looked at their treasure. What had once been a crusading knight of long ago—white bones now beneath heraldries that still shone bright; a red shield and a snarling lion emblazoning a vanished breast; and armour empty as a crab's cast shell.

They removed the helmet and the jawbone dropped off. Jamieson picked it up out of curiosity and put the white thing to his own sooty jaw. And do you know, it fitted right round his! Yes, he could get his entire chin right inside that man of war's. What a size he must have been when muscles moved those bones! Jamieson was so taken with this he went running through the town, holding the jawbone to his own, and crying to one and all to come and see the sight of a man that was three feet bigger than himself.

All and sundry flocked to the old kirkyard. The whole town was there, standing up among the stones to look down on an armoured knight that was lapped in lead and nine feet long, but reduced by mortal rage to a bundle of bones and teeth and nothing more. All the rich proud cost of his outworn buried age had not prevented his decay, or a village blacksmith's comic capers with his stern jaw. And the sea came crashing in and wetted his armour that itself had not a spark of rust.

'And did they bury him again?'

Eventually everything was repaired, including the coffin and the kirkyard wall. These days they would have put him in a glass case to be gawped at, I expect. But at that time the minister's word was law.

He said the kirkyard was not going to be robbed of its biggest and noblest tenant, and nor was the tenant going to be deprived of his rightful place in the ground. Jamieson wanted to keep the jawbone to hang on the smiddy door beside the horse's shoe, but the minister wasn't having that either.

'He should have been in a tomb.'

There was only one vaulted tomb in the kirkyard.

It belonged to the ancient family of the Anstruthers of Balcaskie. There were four chapel walls without a roof, a stone floor, and in the centre of the floor a great slab with an iron ring at each corner. It took four men to raise it, and the steps beneath led down to the vault.

A young woman of the family was buried alive once in that vault. Her unkisted corpse—or what they took to be a corpse—was laid to rest in that place of shrouds and skulls. A place of shadows and dust where wishes had ceased and even the worm could not thrive. The mourners came up the steps, four men replaced the slab, bowed to the four winds, and everybody went home then to grieve and forget.

They weren't to forget her so soon.

The minister was in his nightgown and pouring himself a drink to take to bed, when he heard the thud at the door and the single scream. He ran out—and saw the shrouded figure of the woman he'd buried that afternoon, lying dead on his doorstep. A corpse this time for certain.

It's hard to put yourself there—and yet not hard. Waking up freezing cold, bandaged in blackness, wondering where you are. You put out your hand to try and find something familiar, to calm your rising fear. God knows what exactly your fingers touch, but they tell you in a white flash of light what has happened. When you have screamed your throat raw, you start to grope about among those hideous inhabitants of the tomb, whose smiles seem to mock you. Till you have found the steps. Then you are struggling with a hundred-weight of stone. Sheer terror moves it for you, nothing more, and you see the stars glittering like coffin nails in the black roof of the world.

Was it the effort that killed her—or the effect of fear on her frail heart? All that is certain is that she expired on the steps of the manse after rising from the tomb.

After that they replaced the slab with an iron grill. Autumn leaves drifted down and swept the floors in gusty tapestries. Dirt and dust and seeds collected in restless corners. The frost crept and crackled in the vault. Its blade-hard fingers slid into the sleepers, cracking their bones. It laid its white nightcap on each exposed pate—a helmet harder, colder even than the death's-head itself. An upturned eye-socket framed a winking star and a thought from the past shivered in an empty skull. Spring came. The grass and nettles grew up round the bones. Dandelion suns blazed in a pair of eyes—and went out like morning moons.

A number of years went by before there was another death in the Anstruther estate. When they trooped down again to the vaults to bury their dead they were appalled at the state their noble ancestors were now being seen dead in. It all had to be cleaned out, they said.

My father was about this work when he accidentally struck the wall with the handle of his broom. Plaster came away in lumps, revealing a sealed niche, which contained a small coffin, its lid heavy with metal. He looked at it carefully. There were no signs of screws or nails, and sure enough, when he tried it, off it came very slowly—a snug fit. To his amazement he found himself looking down on the perfectly preserved features of an infant boy of maybe two hundred years before his time. He was white but hardly blemished. The old man ran for the big house. But he soon got out of puff and had to walk the most of the mile. By the time the Anstruthers had come down in carriages to see the ancestral infant, the face had gone out like a light. Sudden exposure to the air had made the child's body crumble to dust within half an hour. Brown dust where a white rose had been. And so dust was all there was to see.

On the nineteenth day of November 1875, five sailing boats were lost with all hands on their way back from Yarmouth.

It was a black day for the East Neuk.

The ships were the *Vigilant*, the *Janet Anderson*, the *Excelsior*, the *Rising Moon* and the *Agnes*. Thirty-five men lost their lives and one hundred and thirty children on several miles of Fife coastline lost their fathers. Some of these children never even saw their fathers, being born after the disaster.

One St Monans skipper always made sure of being home before that day because his father had been drowned in the storm. But most of the fishermen stayed on till the end of the month, or even longer if the fishing was good, and I rarely saw grandfather before December.

So on the night of the nineteenth, with our folk still at sea, and our hearts in our mouths if the gales raged hard outside, we gathered round the fire and sang the mariner's hymn.

Eternal Father, strong to save,
Whose arm hath bound the restless wave,
Who bidd'st the mighty ocean deep
Its own appointed limits keep:
O hear us when we cry to thee
For those in peril on the sea.

But all the time our men were away, the word kept on coming through by telegram, letting us know precisely what the various boats were catching. This news was in fact known simply as The Word.

As my mother sat at the switchboard taking the messages as they came in, I was often sent round with The Word to take to the skippers' wives, and at some houses I came to count on anything between tuppence and sixpence for my trouble, depending on the strength of the shot. Unlawfully, I prayed for huge hauls.

A typical message would read like this.

The *May*—150 cran; the *Twinkling Star*—140 cran; the *Boy Peter*—120 cran; the *Plough*—100 cran; the *Acorn*—80 cran; the *Good Intent*—75 cran; the *Rejoice*—50 cran. And the *Unity*—30; and the *Violet*—25; and the *Daisy*—20; and the *Harvest Moon*–15.

Smaller shots of under fifty cran were preceded in this way by the word 'and'. It was usually the smaller pre-war steam drifters which collected the smaller shots and the powerful steel boats that came away with the lion's share. Thus my mother came to christen these smaller wooden drifters the 'Ands'.

By the end of the month they were all coming home with the changing weather—the hardening moons and the first touches of white and sprinklings of snow. If there had been the heavy rains early in the month, with the swollen streams running high, then a period of dry, quiet weather, followed by hard and rapid frost, the waterdrops clinging to the overhanging grasses quickly froze, and the weeds hung like wintry chandeliers across the ballroom floors of the burns, whorled and patterned as if by ghostly dancers during the night.

But the main part of the month was always a dark time, a dead time. That first whiteness was the sign of the last month of the year, when winter would blow through our bones and the weather would always be so much more bracing in deep December with its warm robin redbreast heart.

DECEMBER

Every day grew colder.

A ghostly hand was gripping the earth. There was no wind with it, just this huge hand, cold and hard as iron, with fierce inflexible fingers, creeping out of the north and the north-west. Everything was in its clutch—breathing became a conscious exhiliration, my frail chest crushed in the frost's unremitting fist; tighter during the soundless nights where silver cities of stars winked distantly in the naked trees like the leaves of an unearthly season.

With a strange new consciousness growing in me, I took to creeping out of the house when everyone else was abed. I walked along the Braeheads to the kirkyard, startled by the sound of my own footsteps echoing in the unpeopled, star-crowded night; the planets popping in the blackness of space; the sea snapping like swords at the shore. And I stood on those tingling nights when the frost lit a fir-tree in my lungs—white-hot needles blazing up to the brain—and listened and listened to the windless wintering of the hours. Yes, I knew that the time would come when I would be nothing more than white bones frozen beneath an impenetrable armour of ice that would be the cold coffin of the world; when even the folk who had forgotten those other folk who never ever knew me, would themselves be nothing more than a breath exhaled on a lonely shore. Not even that. And my gravestone would be fiery with rime—then rime itself.

But something told me that this was nothing compared with the sheer splendour of the suffering world and the extremes it touched: height and depth, silence and dark, and the unutterable iciness of the stars—cold sparklers that were really hotter than Jamieson's biggest fires, yet so far away that they were no more than a lacework of spray flung from a wintry wave onto the very edge of existence.

Tighter and whiter went the fingers in the clenched fist, whiter and tighter every day. In the crackling mornings Geordie Baines's milk horse stood in the meal-white streets, clothed with its own breath, stamping and snorting and steaming as though it were a horse of brass taking shape in the fiery clouds of the forge. Geordie himself stood slamming his arms crosswise round his chest, beating the ends of his frozen fingers and laughing and cursing loudly.

'Right brass monkeys weather, this, bugger me!' he roared. 'Hurry along there, you young fry, watch your tits don't drop off out here! The milk's solid!'

I ran out behind Jenny with the pitcher, holding it beneath Geordie's urn to catch the rich waterfalls that he sloshed carelessly off the back end of his cart and into the jug. Chunks of frozen milk splashing and clashing together like icebergs in a white sea that was a welter of bubbles and froth.

'All the road from the North Pole this morning, my lad!'

Once he handed me a frozen white cylinder, shaken manfully out of his largest urn.

'There you are now, cockie, stick it in the hottest place you can find!'

And he bent down from his cart and whispered something into Jenny's tingling ear. She screamed and let fly at him with her own jug across the side of his big bull's head while he laughed hugely; and I hugged the pillar of milk and ran gasping with it into the house, crashing it into the sink among the startled women; then stood back and slapped my burning fingers round my body just as foul-mouthed old Geordie had done, hopping and howling as if the ghost of Shuggie had risen and given me six of the best.

'Right brass monkeys weather, this, bugger me!' I roared at them. 'Watch your tits don't drop off into the milk!'

And a multitude of hands descended on my head in shocked retribution for my first public admission that I had mastered the art of swearing, with a vengeance.

I ran out whooping into the white tight world.

Then came the day when the great hand relaxed its grip a fraction, releasing the first few flakes of snow. They drifted down from the sky like the early gannets seen round the Bass sometimes in mid-December. But the sky darkened and the flakes thickened—fell in soft flurries into the fields and streets; a fast shroud woven about the bare dead bodies of the trees; a furious whirling; a mad dance without melody or meaning. The sky was a ghostly shoal of silent flecks, bound for nowhere on an endless tide—a soundless drifting. Night closed in quickly and the snow fell and fell. And in the morning the earth was a white bride, bearing in her driven bosom the yellow bouquet of the winter jasmine, the only flame in our garden. The hand opened right out now, and the bridal bouquet faded. The old familiar lines of life were blotted out. A deathly purity reigned supreme.

But dark December's bareness was softened and brightened by these sudden white blossomings of snow. The misty rains of the previous month melted away in the briefly returning skies. The sun stood like a pitcher of frozen golden wine placed high on a wide blue shelf, blinding our eyes that had become so used to the November glooms. Rime glittered on the trees and powdered the black fields. From the roadsides to the far hills the ice-shields flashed, puddles signalling to ponds like sentries to legions of soldiers, like armies talking of war. Even the small sea-pools froze on the rocks and sand, where the marram-grasses stuck their frosty swords in the sun.

It was a bracing month, sharpening the blunted senses and penetrating the fogs of forgetfulness.

It had its hardnesses too: the starved fieldfares huddled in the needle-thin traceries of hedges, their foraging instincts crushed by the cold, while the insects and grubs slept out the winter unmolested in their rotten old walls and stumps of trees; the gulls standing sentinel day-long, night-long on steeple and shore, till they were turned to stone and their hearts cracked in the cold like the sculptured birds on the kirkyard tombs that split asunder with the ferocity of the frost; the blood of the rabbit and hare—tiny red footprints wounding the snow, fading out over the fields where the animals kept solitary vigil over their own dumb agonies; the stiff brave breast of the robin, his cold fires upturned like rusty ashes to the sky; and those freezing draughts of air drunk down in dark dawns when our numb thumbs were fiddling blindly with buttons and strings and we stood and shivered uncontrollably. And sprays of kirkyard coughs passed round like wreaths in the pews.

But there were mixtures of syrup and honey and rum for the coughs; there were crazy careerings of sledges and tea-trays slithering down the wynds, and daredevilling on studded feet down lumpy rivers of glass that made glaciers out of the braes; snowballs and snowmen and snowbroth boiled on our tinny fires on the beach when we took a break from arduous discoveries of North Poles yet unknown with the Bass Rock a giant white polar bear asleep on the skyline, liable to be wakened by the first gannets that had perched on his back since October. Glued leaves crackled like rifle-fire underfoot and we fell heavily in the snow to the invisible cannonade each time somebody fired. But we rose again, weary with immortality, to fight the retreat from Moscow with Russian guerillas picking us off all the way from Balcaskie to the Blocks, where we finally turned our backs to the sea and resolved on one last stand. Cut off from further possibility of retreat, we charged the gauntlet, the white cannonballs of our enemies' fire bursting on our ears and the grapeshot of waves spraying our legs. Epp would have been proud of us, I thought, and her two sons, as we rode boldly and well into the jaws of death that waited for us on the east pier. Up the ladders then, beneath the terrible white rain which our heads and shoulders took as though we were men of iron, and with murderous cries we were through the lines and running red-faced for the west end, where we yelled fit to wake up the dead in the white frozen wave of the kirkyard.

Our blood was up.

It was chap-door-run, for we were men of the snows and the Muscovite campaigns and no-one could face us in our accustomed element. We made for the homes of the aristocrats, Mr Pagan-Grace the lawyer and Mr Brock the banker. Side by side, their gardens were always immaculate—not a crumb of bread disturbed the spotless white tablecloths spread out from windows to garden walls. Conquest by division was our strategy. We split into two forces, crawled on our elbows and knees through the squeaking new snow, rumpling the tablecloths, and stood up breathlessly in front of their imposing facades. Doorknockers that burned our fingers yearly with flickering white fire, even through our woolly gloves. But we gripped them hard and hammered horribly and long at the iron heads of lions and Greeks, running for the pavement, where we stood and waited, allied armies, our snowballs in our hands. An opened door, an astonished red face, and our missiles already committing murder in their marbled vestibules, knocking pictures off the wall.

'I know all your names, I know every one of you, just you wait!'

But already we had run the length of the echoing street, triumphant with howls of derision. The banker's west Highland terrier had sunk deep in the drifts in its over impetuous attack on seasoned soldiers. Mr Brock came wading through the street like a big St Bernard, red-cheeked with brandy, making for the stuck sounds of the stupid yapping coming from the white hole in the ground. Before he could complete his mission of mercy we turned and pelted him with snowballs. He spluttered and sang out in his claret-coloured quilted smoking-jacket, so powdered with snow that the streaks of crimson showed through like blood.

'You'll pay for this, you'll pay for it, you'll pay for it!'

We ran on and on into the eternal world of the snow, our chests heaving like Jamieson's bellows and our hearts like his forge, each one a red pulsation in the mighty whiteness of the dead bewintered world.

Word came through then that the fleet had left.

Thirty hours later, in the smallness of the morning, we were gathered at the harbour, a huddle of families waiting to see the lights coming over the firth and our folk tie up the ends of another year on the safety of the pier. As they came closer, the almost forgotten sounds of life returned to our quiet harbour, which had known only the eerie creaking of the condemned old sailing vessels on the windy November nights. Now the sea was shouting again, bringing Christmas presents on the tide—nuts and fruits and Yarmouth rock, dolls and pistols, glasses, plates and china. The wedding-flags were run up with cheers on the bridegrooms' ships, and the brides-to-be brought out their house-fillings from below the bed: the vases and pictures, the linen, the crystal and crockery which they had been saving bit by bit since they left the school, and which their fathers and grandfathers had been bringing back to them year after year from the great fishing season of the south; piece by precious piece. For now was the time of marrying, and at last old Leebie relaxed her gloomy rule concerning the wisdom of human nuptials celebrated in the brazen face of time.

When December snows fall fast
Marry and true love will last.

Each man also brought back with him a barrel of salt herring for himself and his family. Grandfather's was a half barrel and Alec and Billy brought a quarter barrel each. Throughout the year we had existed largely on herring, but the first salt herring from Yarmouth, rinsed and then roasted on the brander till their dripping had dowsed the fire—that was a high point of the return. They were served with heapings of potatoes, rifled from the pits in the fields, and cauldrons of kail and boiled beef. And as Christmas drew closer Guthrie's window filled up with rounds of shortbread, each one bearing the design of a different drifter and its name and number.

Work was over now for the driftermen till the second day of January. Only the fireman spent a laborious week inside the boat's boiler, chipping away at three months of encrusted salt. But grandfather was hardly home a day before his restless legs were west the coast again, gathering seacoal from the shore, which sparked and spat all night long. For coal was often scarce and our fire was never allowed to die.

In my last winter at school the wrath of the sea provided us with a bounty of timber to fuel our fire through the chilly season. A boat called the *Martin Luther* was driven onto the Lady's Rock, where King David was wrecked and he and his queen came safely to shore. They knelt on the nearest dry spot where the waves reached out and wetted their hair, and with the wind streaming through their clasped fingers they prayed their thanks to God and built a church.

The *Martin Luther* had been overloaded with pit props bound for the west of Fife coal mines. We were sitting with a new headmaster when we heard the stirring cry, 'Ship ashore!' The shout came from the bottom of the single corridor that was our school. We looked at Mr Campbell, our mouths wide.

'Well, what are you waiting for?' he demanded, with fierce jollity.

We rushed to the classroom door. The policeman was pedalling sedately up the corridor, booming it in at every one of the seven rooms. 'Ship ashore! Ship ashore at the Lady's Rock!'

We were a hundred pairs of legs.

The sea was breaking her up when we arrived. The hull was a broken hive and the white bees were fizzing round the hole, the dark wound in her side into which the salt was pouring. I fought hard to resist within me that tiny golden core of joy, sweet as honey, that glowed and grew, as I witnessed for the first time the brute magnificence of the sea destroy in minutes what the men in the boatyard had laboured so slowly to bring to life.

But there was no time for groaning or guilt. The ship came apart like thunder, and her contents, the thousands of spars of timber, came spilling out into the sea as easily as matches from a broken box. Men, women, children, waded into the pounding surf on the lee side of the rock, everyone anxious to reach the timber before it was swept out of reach.

It was a dangerous game as the heavy spars jostled and swung among us. They came surging shorewards with the speed of battering-rams, and we dived on them, riding them onto the beach like human torpedos. Then the cargo drifted onto the Black Rocks, where there was a dancing sea, and the timbers were picked up by the waves and flung high into the air, so that the men cursed and swore at us, hauling us out of the waves by the scruffs of our necks, yelling at us to get back to the safety of the beach. We paid no attention, running back into the water with the madness of lemmings upon us, though one of these lumps of wood coming down on a thumping sea would have cracked a skull like a nut.

All day we slaved at dragging what we could of the cargo clear of the waves and onto the foreshore. Horses and ropes were brought down the following day and the timber was carted back to town. It was stacked on the field opposite the school, where the nets were dried in summer, and split up among all the households in the town, each widow receiving a double share to warm her in her age. For this was the usual way with salvage.

DECEMBER

That winter the village fires burned brightly and the busy chimneys were sooty black against skies that were filled with snow.

The following summer I was looking for lobsters on the west rocks when I came across the rudder of the *Martin Luther*. It was bolted together with three yellow bolts. I drove them out with a lump of hard blue whinstone and took them to grandfather. He gave them to Jamieson, who made them into marlin spikes—a cold memoir now in my kitchen, among the gear of another time, a foreign culture.

Just for a moment the sun was a cinder, a white shard, a pale candle guttering at the point of extinction. But the moment was a pin-point in the year, on which the universe danced. It passed—and the fires of life were blowing again.

And then it was Christmas Eve.

After dark I went out with grandfather and we took the deserted country road to Balcaskie, white and winking in the moon. We were off for our Christmas tree. Grandfather walked slightly ahead of me, the end of his cigarette glowing redly in his cupped palm as he shaded it from the wind. We sang together as we walked.

> *Brightly shone the moon that night,*
> *Though the frost was cruel,*
> *When a poor man came in sight,*
> *Gathering winter fuel.*

When we neared the wood we stopped the singing and went in whispers. Then we walked in silence through the trees, the snow starting to fall again in the world outside. Grandfather still led the way, his cigarette-end bobbing like a red lamp through the dark. He stopped and knelt down, taking a saw blade from underneath his jacket. Quietly, gently, his cigarette in his mouth all the time, he took down a small fir, the property of the rich man in his mansion. And on the way out he picked us a sizeable log for the fire, a special one, and we lifted up our voices again when we were well clear of the estate.

> *Page and monarch, forth they went,*
> *Forth they went together;*
> *Through the rude wind's wild lament*
> *And the bitter weather.*

It was a small tree, but I worshipped it like a totem that held the secrets of the wood. Around its bole we laid a clutch of gifts, offerings to the spirit of the leaves. I lay flat on the floor and looked at it through half closed eyes. It rose straight and tall into its own green firmament that glittered with tinsel stardust and snow. It spread its sacred influence round the room.

Applewood and birch spat in the grate and the candles spluttered on the mantlepiece, their crimson wax dripping down the tiles like blood to congeal on the fender; holly and ivy made a grove of the walls; the berries were bright droplets on the evergreen spears of life; bowls of oranges burned like suns, the gorgeous constellations of grapes green and purple among the redskinned planets of war; walnuts, hazelnuts and butterscotch, bottles of beer and whisky and rum, and presentation packets of cigarettes, all stacked and scattered on tables and dressers. It was as though Old Yule had stood on our roof, kicked the Devil off for Christmas, and blown his horn of plenty down our lum. His merry red breath blew up the fire on the way, the flames flickering from yellows and greens to reds and stormy blues, making our hearth a forest scene. Birdsong whistled from the wet wood, and grandfather's screwtops hissed and sang as the mulling-poker was thrust into the dark ale like a sizzling white-hot sword.

Georgina sang us a carol.

> *A Spotless Rose is blowing,*
> *Sprung from a tender root,*
> *Of ancient seers' foreshowing,*
> *Of Jesse promised fruit;*
> *Its fairest blood unfolds to light*
> *Amid the cold, cold winter*
> *And in the dark midnight.*
>
> *The Rose which I am singing,*
> *Whereof Isaiah said,*
> *Is from its sweet root springing*
> *In Mary, purest maid;*
> *For through our God's great love and might,*
> *The Blessed Babe she bare us*
> *In a cold, cold winter's night.*

Grandfather took the Yule-log which he had chosen from the crackling candleflames of Balcaskie's spruces and pines. He burnt half of it away, pulling out the other half to light up the new log on the following Christmas. He ran out with it on the shovel, into the yard, where he threw it spitting and snarling into the snow, dying among clouds of smoke and steam and popping sparks. Out here was so different from the warm heart of the kitchen. The trees' skeletons stood vigil over the shrouded corpse of the world, white in its snow-linens. Our chimney-smoke drifted to the stars, oakwood into Orion. Down below us, over the rooftops of the town, the black sea was battering the rocks, the breakers foaming like mad white teeth, grinding the shore.

I went up to bed, where I used to lie and wait for Santa Claus to swing into our tiny port, tie up on the pier, and perform his secret ministry. But grandfather was really Santa Claus, and the unseen presents from Yarmouth were waiting downstairs.

Still I could not sleep. The winds were searching the chimney in my room, putting a tongue into every wordless skull that lay in the old kirkyard tonight with the whole history of the world behind it and the whole earth below, and the snow falling steadily down. Midnight was striking. I lay wide awake, listening to those wild white chimes of winter flung from the black belfry of the year. And as I lay and listened in the cold drift of the bed, the other bells answered from along the coast—all the kirkbells, it seemed, jostling and calling one to another across the bombillating seas. And the cold carols of the dead were sung once more in the twelve winter towers of my years.

On Christmas morning I woke early, the sky still loaded with stars—an iron morning, and the white unruffled swansdown of the overnight snows calm and pure at daybreak as the swan's last song. The lights came on early in all the other houses in the town where there were young folk, the windows turning to orange and yellow and red like fires of autumn leaves burning briefly in the black forest of the dawn.

Then after the presents we were swept along to the kirk to be given some good Christmas advice from the elders.

> *Amidst the freezing sleet and snow*
> *The timid robin comes.*
> *In pity drive him not away,*
> *But scatter out your crumbs.*
>
> *And leave your door upon the latch*
> *For whosoever comes;*
> *The poorer they, more welcome give,*
> *And scatter out your crumbs.*
>
> *Soon winter falls upon your life,*
> *The day of reckoning comes.*
> *Against your sins, by high decree,*
> *Are weighed those scattered crumbs.*

And outside it snowed and it snowed.

I came out onto the new unbroken bread of the morning. The kirk was a white-caped monk, considering the precise white manuscripts of the fields. The sea was foaming frostily on the shore, the surf piling up on the sands in snow-drifts that sang and roared. The graveyard was incorruptible now, and the marble maidens, unravished even by death, stood in their stone petticoats, penitential among the monuments, over their ankles in snow, unspeaking in that white wilderness. Only one rose bloomed there, at the feet of a weeper. A stone head, snow-shawled, contemplated its crystal crimson centre—Our Lady of the Snows staring into the stopped heart of summer.

Leaving these stillest of all stones, I closed behind me the heavy iron gates, black purgatorial rails imprisoning the sculptured dead. Light was draining through a keyhole in the clouds. Nothing moved. I stood and watched the light fade, alone with my marble memories of things. A gull drifted by like a life that might have been led—and vanished out of all reasonable speculation. I realised over again, with fiercely renewed anxiety, that time was endlessly slipping and streaming away through that keyhole in the clouds, that every hour was like the one before—a precious drain for the lifeblood of all the days that ever were. Time was sliding away and there was nothing I could do to stop it.

The whiteness faded into grey—a slow frown. Still nothing moved. The day went out and was gone. I went home to a fire where the log was whispering something to the grate which I was not allowed to know, and the fender winked conspiratorially. Only the clock knew the language of the silent room and took part in the conversation. For the first time I felt banished from the fireside. I went to the window and felt the age-old bleakness of winter.

> In the bleak mid-winter
> Frosty wind made moan,
> Earth stood hard as iron,
> Water like a stone;
> Snow had fallen, snow on snow,
> Snow on snow,
> In the bleak mid-winter,
> Long ago.

But in the week between Christmas and the New Year, the windless golden mists hung in the air over woods and sea like the fragrance from Spanish white wine; a mellow memory lingering out of the past. The smoke from the chimneys stood unwavering like painted plumes;

like poplars spearing the sky; white quills feathering the sooty inkpots along the roofs—and the Bass was statuesque on the horizon. It was now that the folk began to come round in the evenings for their fireside chatter, and our kitchen held at nights a crowd of men, fishermen mostly, all of them sitting round the fire talking about the year gone by and the Yarmouth fishing, and singing their songs and telling their stories.

It was all talk and tall tales by the fire at that time of year. Tall tales, and the tall tongues of flame licking the lum; and the sparks flying outwards to the stars like the golden syllables that went out forever with that time, as they gave their fears and fantasies a voice; passed on their reminiscences, their stories and their lore.

The stories were mostly of sea and sail, and I heard them along with the hearty uncles and the fey and flighty aunts and the sad-moustached great-uncles and the ancient frail great-aunts, and all the other numberless scions of our family that came together as a tree for Christmas, to listen to grandfather's friends and George's remaining cronies exchanging their talk in the last few nights of the year. Bent and drooping they were, like flowers heavy with age, their withered heads lolling on the slender stalks of their dry faded bodies.

I remember these stories of yesteryear as easily as I forget the best-sellers of today. The story of tinker Johnny, whom the men of St Monans buried alive for fear of typhoid. He knocked and knocked from inside his coffin (they had taken him for dead at first) but they put him to his grave all the same, and let the earth that they heaped around him soak up his cries. A story so terrible that in later life there was only one way to exorcise its spirit from my haunted brain—and that was to write it down, to give it literary form and substance. It is the only way I have ever known.

Leebie presided over these last day ceilidhs from her creepie-stool at the side of the fire, threading her own snippets of old rhyme into the warp and woof of the stories and songs.

> *Four and twenty mermaids who left the port of Leith*
> *To tempt the fine auld hermit who dwelt upon Inchkeith;*
> *No boat nor waft, nor creer nor craft had they, nor oars nor sails;*
> *Their lily hands were oars enough, their tillers were their tails.*

She may not have believed in mermaids herself, though she talked of them, but she was a strong believer in the kelpies, whose cry had often struck terror into the hearts of the oldest fishermen who sat round our fire.

The blackening wave is edged with white,
To inch and rock the sea-mews fly,
The fishers have heard the water-sprite
Whose screams forebode that wreck is nigh.

'Yes, I've heard that weighty melody coming off the sea many's the time before today,' she said, 'and it has filled me with dread and foreboding—for I know just the sound it makes when fisherfolk are about to die.'

'There's no denying it,' an old man says here. 'I've heard the sea's dead groan myself more than once in my lifetime, which has foretold the drowning of some poor souls out on the deep.'

The weighty melody, the dead groan of the deep. Phrases that struck sparks from my imagination as we sat round the fire. Words never spoken now—but the talk of only yesterday, when men believed there was more to life than brain and bone and muscle and blood.

They spoke too of the sea's firing, of phosphorescence round the mast in calm weather, foretelling the death of a crewman or of one of the crew's kin. Or of St Elmo's fire, which protected them from danger during a storm.

These superstitions, which were so often brought out of the dark rag-bag of the old December nights, arose out of the perilous business of their working lives. Their eyes and ears were always on the alert for bad weather or calamity, and so grew haunted. Even grandfather, who was not by nature a superstitious man, passed on his lore religiously to my uncles, though in his case it was observation which confirmed traditional belief, and not a matter of credulous acceptance.

When you hear the burl cry
Let you the boatie lie;
Two ebbs and a flood,
Let the weather be never so good.

Thus, even in a period of steady good weather in June or July, the old men noticed that the gull would suddenly put its head between its legs, bring it up slowly, and then emit a long shuddering wail. A few hours later would come howling gales, thunderstorms, and torrents of rain. Many's the fisherman on his way to sea heard that cry and followed the advice of the old rhyme, letting the boat lie for nineteen or twenty hours before setting out to sea again. And many's the man ignored the warning wail of the gull, so the old folk said, only to go down where seagulls never come.

Even when he was not at sea, which was seldom, grandfather's eyes were always on the sky, searching for the signs of bad weather and contrary winds.

When the wind backs into the sun
Trust it not, for back it will run.

He often said that as he directed my eyes to what he called the sun in his glorious array and the moon in her magnificent nightgown, warning me to beware of their beguiling splendours: a dazzlingly white sun, for example, suggestive of unsettled weather; a 'sundog'— a bright patch on the horizon very close to the sun; a 'packman'—a rainbow segment either above or to the side of the sun, denoting fragmented weather; the 'moonbroch', the cock's eye round the moon, or a broken ring, the gap showing the direction of the wind to come; a bright crisp moon heralding frost, which would set up the wind at the shore side, and bring in the kind of nights when the older sailing boats used to hug the coasts. Long goat's hair clouds in strands were a sure sign of strong hard winds, grandfather always told me with pointing finger. The heavy dark clouds with silvery tops he called Iceland clouds, telling me that I could be looking for strong northerlies in a very short time. And he was never done pointing in the sky to what he termed 'headings'—points where the long lines of cloud converged like arrows on a target, showing him where the wind would be springing from in the morning.

He knew the tides too, of course, so intimately that he could predict the winds and breezes associated with them almost to the second. When the tide was halfway either way, ebb or flood, he knew that a wind would invariably come in off the sea, even in the stillest weather, and when the tide was on the turn the wind would come up regularly, as if at his command. In the periods of good weather, with their quiet, warm fine forenoons, the sharp breezes would come in at mid-day or around one o'clock from the south-east off the sea. Sometimes they fell away almost at once. But frequently they blew all day then died off, and there would be a flat calm on the sea by sunset. All through the night the calm would remain until, in the morning, grandfather would say, 'Up sun, up wind.'

And it would happen as he said.

Childhood was a dream. With both eyes now open and the cold light of understanding flooding in, I can see again how much of this was pure and simple observation, with now and then a little calculation. For grandfather had no time for the superficial sorts of superstitions with which the town was riddled.

Bad omens abounded in those days in people's minds, to an extent which irked him beyond patience. Knots in laces or pieces of rope were believed to cause bad weather. Whistling could stir up winds—and though he scoffed at this, grandmother would never blow on the bannocks or oatcakes she was baking when her man was at sea, though she did so often enough at other times with her hard drawn breath. Mooing cows reminded the morbid folk of foghorns and wrecks, and were soundly cursed along with other beasts of the field, such as hares, rabbits, foxes, and above all, pigs. These were never actually named as such, but referred to obliquely as grunters or grumphies, just as salmon were redfish, kirks were bellhouses (the bells muffled during the herring seasons in case they scared away the fish), the minister was the man in black or the queer fellow—and salt was simply never mentioned at all, though it was in and out of their lives every day in one form or another.

Certain rituals also had to be adhered to.

Nothing had to go against the sun. If you walked in the kirkyard, visiting graves, you had to move in a clockwise direction, and if you dared go widdershins three times round the holy edifice, you would meet the devil at the close of the third circle.

Turning the boat in the harbour was governed by the same law.

'Put her head west about!' they used to shout.

When baiting lines inside the house they locked the door in case an unlucky person should enter and step over the lines with his evil foot. A woman was never allowed to step over them, though in some houses she spent much of her life baiting them.

A fisherman on his way to the boat was not to be asked where he was going. If it was a Monday he had not to be asked for anything at all, even the time of day.

'The devil tear your tongue out!' he would reply.

Friday on the other hand was a good day for laying down a keel, for shipwrights too had their superstitions. They believed that certain boats were unlucky because they contained an unlucky 'spehl' or 'skelb', which was a small splinter of wood. By examining the way a skelb came off they foretold a boat's fortune, for good or ill, as if they were casting bones. Some shipwrights even claimed to know the boat's fate or fortune by the feel of the axe when striking the first blow to the keel.

And that was how they lived, most of them—watching and listening all the time, their eyes and ears in the wind; above all on the dark autumnal nights and the closings of the year, for howling dogs, screeching owls, breadknives falling, pictures coming off the wall, or, worst of all, the eerie sound of the 'canny ca' ', or, as Leebie sometimes called it, the 'deid-chap'—the dismal sound of knocking on walls and windows, betokening a coming death.

But it was death and danger at sea that the talk usually turned to once the men were home for Christmas, as if it were a relief to speak freely and in safety of the ghosts that dogged their heels on deck all the round of their precarious year. Leebie contained within that white skull of hers an encyclopaedic list of all the wrecks and drownings of the East Neuk, not only in her own time, but in the transmitted memories of her mother and grandmother.

Her appalling death record began at 1795. She could tell us—and she did so every winter—the names of the boats and their crews, the weather conditions in which they perished, and the dates on which the disasters occurred, even to the very days of the week. In addition she knew exactly the numbers of widows and orphans that each particular wave had created. She cited them relentlessly like a tragic sybil till the room rang with the sound of the raging sea and the drowned corpses floated round the walls.

The terrible toll began at Monday 23 September 1795, with the loss of the *Good Shepherd* on the Beacon Rock and the deaths of seven men, leaving five widows and seventeen children orphaned.

It went on from there, her tongue beating like a bell.

On Wednesday 3 February 1800 the *Good Hope* was caught in a south-east gale when coming home with herring bait, and was driven onto Skellie Point. Lost were Philip Anderson, Leslie Brown, William Muir, James Fowler, Thomas Smith, Thomas Christie and Andrew Robertson. There were thirty-three bairns orphaned by that wreck. The only survivor was William Watson, who left the boat and swam to Craw Skellie. He walked along the skellie as the waves crashed over it, and so appeared to the watchers on the shore to be walking on the water. He was always called Water Willie after that, and lived for another half a century and more, dying on 2 February 1858.

None of this was written down. It was all in her head, and had to be released each winter, as though some such force as moved the Ancient Mariner worked upon her that same compulsion.

And so she continued on and up the years, and as she talked, I saw again, swimming in front of me, the inscriptions in the old kirkyard.

A TWELVEMONTH AND A DAY

On Monday 24 June 1805 the *Nancy* was lost off Crail in a black squall and all of her crew perished.

> *But thou! my friend and brother,*
> *Thou'rt speeding to the shore,*
> *Where the solemn knell of parting words*
> *Is heard again no more.*

On Saturday 31 December 1814 the *Halcyon* sank one mile east of Inchkeith in a westerly gale. Thomas Smith of St Monans was the only survivor.

> *A watery grave we do not dread,*
> *The sea shall render back its dead,*
> *And restore each scattered bone,*
> *And end each widow's, orphan's moan,*
> *And land us safe on Canaan's shore*
> *Where wind and wave divide no more*
> *Our souls from those at home.*

On Wednesday 16 May 1844 the *William* was lost near the Bell Rock in a midnight gale with all eight of her crew. Twenty-one children lost their fathers and five wives their men.

> *O Christ whose voice the waters heard,*
> *And hushed their raging at thy word,*
> *Who walkedst on the foaming deep*
> *And calm amid the storm did sleep:*
> *O hear us when we cry to thee*
> *For those in peril on the sea.*

On Tuesday 23 April 1846 the *Boy Peter* was lost in a hurricane fifteen miles outside the May Island. James Allan of Anstruther came ashore twelve hours later on a bundle of corks. He was the only survivor and no bodies were ever recovered from that disaster.

> *O Holy Spirit who didst brood*
> *Upon the waters dark and rude,*
> *And bid their angry tumult cease,*
> *And give, for wild confusion, peace:*
> *O hear us when we cry to thee*
> *For those in peril on the sea.*

DECEMBER

On Wednesday 10 May 1865 the *Helen* was overtaken by an east-north-east gale in the North Sea. All eight of her crew were seen to perish by the *Lord Melbourne*, which could not reach them in time to save a single soul.

The list of ships and men went on: the *John and Mary*, the *Heroine*, the *Anna*, the *Southern Cross*, the *Victory*, the *Olive*, the *Magdalene*. On into the twentieth century and up to yesterday, with all those sailors drowned anew in Leebie's precisely recollecting mind, and all their children orphaned again, and all those women's tears.

And as Leebie spoke into the fire I saw them over and over, my ancestors, rising and falling like the sea, rolling in drowned generations through my head. Pale upturned faces that no-one else saw—sank slowly through the water, dreaming their last bitter dreams of kirk and kin. A quiet cradle and a pair of milky breasts. The waves close like curtains over the sea-dreams, salt water has filled up every corner of the skull, the last particle of the dream falls out like a silver coin from a turned-out pocket, and the dreamless head bumps gently on the bottom of the sea and rests there for the tiny fish to take the place of darting thought.

I saw hands coming out of the sea and clutching madly at the sky, their wrists laced with foam, their fingers scattering silver rings.

I saw bones bloodless as shells. They smelled not of the earth, like those that lay beneath rose-dust and bluebells and bees, but of crabs and castaways and broken lobsters' legs.

I saw constellations cold as limpets and lonely stars like starfish dried on the shore.

I heard deep bells that rang in skulls deep down, that even the foam-loving mermaids never heard.

And shawled heads in the pews and the cradles filled with crying, as the sea took salt from the eating place and love from the sleeping place and hardened the long narrow lip of the cold horizon.

Snow shrouded the stars.

And snow fell on snow.

The seacoal sang in the grate, the driftwood whistled and sparked. The old men's eyes brightened as they came out now with their strangest stories for Christmas.

I distinguish no faces, no people now—I only see eyes that glitter in the firelight, I only hear voices in the darkness of the room. Old shadows and tongues, and the clear salty smell of their stories remaining.

I was a great swimmer then, you see, and I did a lot of diving. I can tell you a story about that.

There was a ship had gone down near Southampton, and about a month after it had sunk I was sent down to investigate the situation for salvage. The weather had been so bad for weeks it was the first chance I had, but the water was still thick and muddy that way, and I could hardly see a thing.

I didn't have to go down too far. The boat was lying in ten fathoms of water and she was only slightly tilted. I managed to get to the galleys and the cabins through one of the doors in the superstructure of the hull. I had a little lamp in front to guide me, otherwise I'd never have seen a thing down there. I swam through the galley accommodation and reached this cabin door, poking my light into the dim darkness. And that's when I saw what I still keep seeing in my sleep, old as I am now.

Six corpses.

Drowned things that had once been men—entombed in the ship when she went down, and floating about now in the thick mistiness that my light produced in there. It gave me a bad turn. I started back with as much quickness as I could muster with sixty feet of sea on top of me and my heavy diving suit on and lead-weighted boots. And as I turned my lamp away, the corpses withdrew, it seemed, into the murkiness and silence where anything might have lurked—that's how frightened I felt at the time.

Just when I reached the cabin door I felt something like a nudge. I swung round my lamp as fast as I could—and there was what remained of a face, a face made of decay, grinning at me through the vizor of my helmet. My legs went just like the element I was walking in. My heart came right off the stalk. I never felt like it—ever. How do you turn and run ten fathoms below in bulky diving gear and an iron hulk all round you? I did my best to imitate the process, I can tell you.

There was worse to come. When I looked over my shoulder I saw that the eddies and the suction currents were drawing in the corpses through the door, and as I waltzed like mad along the galley they came after me—a procession of dead men sailing along behind in a slow saraband, and me their leader, the living leading the dead in single file. Do you think you wouldn't sweat underwater? Let me tell you the sweat was pouring from me like water underneath my suit. It seemed a long time till I got to the end of the galley, to the door. Then I turned and I tried to shut it on these six ghastly companions I had acquired.

I wasn't quick enough. Just as the door was shutting one of the corpses flitted through and escaped. Its grey grin passed just inches from my face, a current of water seemed to catch it like a hand and it jerked quickly out of the space and jigged and bobbed and nodded away into the dark distance, dancing a kind of daft dance of freedom and escape. When I looked back at the door I saw the next corpse coming at me in the same way. I closed the door tight—and I swear, as God's my judge, the look on its face changed. It would have turned your blood to ice in your veins, it was so awful. It was just as if that ghastly grin had changed to a look of sorrow and despair when I confined it again to its tomb of iron and salt water.

I'm glad to say I'm too old now to come to grief at sea. I'd rather lie in the earth than go about the inside of a boat like that for a coffin, though I've spent my whole life in boats, mind you, and sometimes it felt like I was more in the water than on it.

Aye, there are some strange dead men going about the bottom of the ocean. We lost nets in the North Sea, I remember, and when we hauled them up with the grading irons a body came on board. That was our only catch of the day, and one we could have done without. But that was only the start of it. He hadn't been too long dead—he was that pale green colour. Anyway, we couldn't have a thing like that on board and us a week at sea, so the skipper said we'd better sink him for good and all this time.

I was sent below to fetch a firebar. We made it fast to his feet and dropped him over the side. Somebody said a verse from a psalm and we thought that was it. I remember his pale face disappearing—and just like the corpse in that other story it seemed to me as if his features were changing as he sank, as though he too wanted out of the water.

Well, we were just getting back to our work when one of the crew shouted.

'Look, he's coming up again!'

My God, it was true! His pale and pallid features broke the waves for the second time, the weather desperately calm all of a sudden, and this ambassador from the sea returning for what unfinished business nobody knew, nor wanted to. Further and further out of the water it came, and nearer the boat, its open eyes that had been shut before fixed now on us all.

I heard a hoarse cry from somebody.

'Good God, it's coming aboard!'

We stood like the statues of sailors along the starboard side. Not a foot answered the helm. And that thing was making for the boat, true enough, and with what awful consequences to our souls we could only imagine. It was a thing that the devil himself had brought up out of the deep, to terrify us.

Then, as we watched petrified, it started to circumnavigate the ship. Round it went, disappearing below the bows. There was a sickening silence on board, and round the whole horizon you could have cut the air with a knife. And it was in silence that we rushed to the port side then, for it was moving against the sun. It passed right under the stern and came opposite the wheelhouse one more time. Horror of horrors then—it stood right up in the water and gave a huge despairing howl that travelled right round the circle of the skyline, and the echo went on forever.

And then it sank.

But as it did so, it stretched out both its arms, just as though it were asking for help, and I watched its pale and hopeless face disappearing into the gradual darkness of the sea. That was the last we saw of it—that desperate sinking face and these outstretched arms. And ever since then I've seen that face sinking away from me as I fall backwards and backwards myself in dreams, and I can't seem to stop myself falling. And I wake up sweating.

You should have woken up, Jock, before you dreamed up that one!

As God's my witness, I'll hear you say now. But let me tell you one that is true, and one that I know to be true, for it was told to me by my father, and he neither touched a drop nor told a lie in the whole of his born days.

It was around 1860 this took place, when my father was berthed on an emigrant ship bound for Boston Massachusetts. There was a young boy on that ship who might have been about ten years old as I recall my father saying now. He was as bright as a button, this lad, and he had a really good voice. His mother, who doted on him, had taught him a great many songs, and so he charmed and delighted crew and passengers alike.

Anyway, they were only a few days out at sea when the sinister shadow of a dark fin was seen lingering in the ship's wake, day in day out, and catching the moon by night. The sailors didn't like that, because if a man went overboard or there was any kind of accident, that shark was always there. But that wasn't all, no, it wasn't the worst of it, because the older seamen believed that when a shark followed a ship as doggedly as that, it was a sure sign that there was going to be a death.

DECEMBER

Well, after another few days the wee boy fell ill, and the shark's fin never left them, appearing now on one quarter and now on another, with sometimes the ripple of its back just breaking the surface. One night, not long after that, the boy died. His mother was distraught enough, as you can imagine, over his death. But even worse than that was the thought of her son's shrouded corpse going down straight into the gullet of a shark—that was more than her flesh and blood could bear to think about. So she begged the ship's carpenter to make him a little coffin.

He made it by the next morning, and punched a few holes in it so as to let it sink and settle to rest. A service was held and the coffin was lowered over the side. Well, maybe they should have thrown it in with a splash to let it fill up at once. The fact is they didn't—they lowered it very gently into the water, for the mother's sake, and it was while it was still bobbing about on the surface of the waves that the terrible dark form rushed from underneath the ship without warning and hurled itself hard against the box. There was a splintering of wood in those rows of white razors, a huge jerk of the black bullet head, and the small shrouded figure was thrown up into the air and caught. The hysterical mother rushed to throw herself overboard and had to be restrained. But the last she saw of her son was him being swallowed down by this shark—its gullet was his grave—and the water turning red all round them.

Yes, I can believe that story, that I can, for I'll believe anything of sharks.

My grandfather—and that's going back a long way now—told me about a slave trader coming up in the 1830s from the coast of Dead Ned and crossing to Jamaica. But they just couldn't get a wind—contrary winds the whole time—and so they just had to come north and north and north and north and north all the way, to keep trying for that wind.

The poor old niggers had to be aired each day for a couple of hours, just to keep the poor devils fresh and alive. And one always jumped overboard if he could get half a chance, because he thought his spirit would sail right the way back to the homeland. So the captain declared he would cure them of this by making an example of one of them and giving one of them a taste of what it was like to be in the water.

Now by this time they had come so far off course that they were nearing Northern Ireland. Anyway, on the captain's orders they

251

looped a rope from the yardarm round the armpits of a woman who'd made a run for the side, and they proceeded to lower her into the water. Maybe they were going to keel-haul her, the poor wretch. My God, they had only dunked her the once and pulled her up when she came up screaming a kind of scream that they'd never heard before. The sailors were all horrified, hardened brutes though most of them were, to see the water churning red with sharks and only the top part of the woman dangling from the rope. She'd been bitten in half, bitten from the waist down, and she was still alive and screaming when they threw her back in to let the sharks make a quick finish of her for mercy's sake. They had come from Dead Ned, these sharks, all the way from the Bight of Benin to Belfast, breakfasting on those who threw themselves down deep, never wanting to see the light of the sky again.

We brought a shark on board once.

We slit it open and discovered inside it the decomposing remains of a man, still with bits of boots and clothes on what was left of him. We didn't feel like looking too closely, I can tell you, but we felt obliged to bury him. We were sewing him up, with a good drink in us, when I noticed an oilskin packet inside the tatters of his coat. It contained his papers—and blow me down if I didn't know the man! It was six months since I'd seen him when we were deckhands together on another vessel. It's strange what comes up out of the sea, which is so big that you'd think a thing like that just couldn't happen. But it did.

The sea soon shrinks a bit when you've sailed on it some years.

I remember once when we were hauling in the Aberdeen fishing grounds, I saw a whale—about thirty feet it was—with a clean-cut hole in the dead centre of its dorsal fin, and I saw that very same whale for five summers running.

Oh, the whales were all right though. They just swam below and blew the herring out the nets and took what came out. But they never once damaged our nets—not like those bloody dogfish, and the sharks with their stupid greed. Even the big sixty-footer whales were gentle enough, though their blowholes sounded like somebody beating a drum in a tunnel, or a train going through the kirk hall. The worst sight I ever saw was when the herring whales were being attacked by sharks, packs and packs of them, and the poor whales were leaping right out of the water trying to escape.

But they were massacred.

I tried to harpoon a whale once.

Of course it was nothing like what old George there would have used in his day.

It was like this, you see. The tunnyfish sometimes came about the boat in summer. I tried baiting a line with herring but the tunny wouldn't take it. They took the loose ones I threw over the side, but never the ones on the hook. So I got Jamieson's father to make me a three-foot harpoon for spearing the tunny, with an opening at the end for a boathook. Well, I was once feeding a whale with herring off Fraserburgh when one of the crew said to me, 'Why don't you have a go with your harpoon?'

I wasn't keen to do it, but they pressed me, and I made fast a tracking line and shot. The whale just leaped once and dived back into the sea. I doubt I didn't kill it, but it took away with it that lovely little harpoon of mine that had been made for a tunnyfish and not a thirty-foot whale.

I saw a whale killed once, but it was not with a harpoon, and it was a cruel brute of a man that did it.

I was feeding a herring whale with mackerel when the mate just came up at my side and crashed a great big ballast stone right down onto the poor creature's head. It had just been coming up to blow. I think he killed it instantly. I can still see it sinking down into the clear sea, its beautiful mouth with the long narrow white stripes, so tender and so delicate. Yes, God made the sea and all that in it is, just like the world. The sharks are brainless and greedy and have no soul, like some folk I know. But just the creation of that whale's mouth was a wonder in itself.

I don't know about that. I reckon the giant skates were the boys to hold the top of the league for the wonders of the world. I've seen four men work for an hour trying to bring a big one on board, and if they didn't get the clips on its head quick enough, it would be away. Have you ever tackled one of these barn-door skates, or the thorn-backs? Boy, they don't come in like a cod, I'll be bound.

The last boat I was on had a hold like a dance-hall, and the last skate we caught on board that boat was bigger than the floor of the hold when we spread it out.

It took some killing.

We caught a big one like that years ago.

When I bent down to start on it, its tail came up and slammed me right in the crutch. I was sent right over the side and into the sea. It was lucky for me it was calm weather. They had me out in less than a minute, but I can tell you I was in some pain. I didn't even wait to dry off. I made straight for that skate and I tore into it and threw its guts to the birds.

You shouldn't have done that, not so fast. I've gutted a big skate in a hurry and ended up with a gartlin hook in my hand that the fish had swallowed in a tussle with another boat's lines. It took my hand right open. I took skate guts out with some care after that, I can assure you.

I think we had the biggest skate in the sea on one of our lines, but we lost it, and it was all because of a drunk man.

It was bad weather, mind you, I mean really bad. We should just have been lying dodging seas instead of shooting lines. Anyway, fishing is what we were doing, and we had this monster on one of our lines. Then I saw a sea bearing down on us the size of Largo Law. I shouted back to the man at the helm to watch out. It was Johnny Cook, and he'd been at the bottle all the night before, the drunken beast. He didn't feel too great that morning but the skipper said he was going to do his turn at the early watch. We'd no more mind of him until at that moment I remembered we were all in the hands of a known drunkard. God help us, when I looked up there was no sign of him. I think he'd fallen asleep on the wheelhouse floor, though he said that he'd hit his head and passed out.

Then the sea came down on the boat.

Just about everything went and we lost every one of our lines. But we worked hard with the irons to get them off the bottom and we recovered nearly them all. You ought to have seen the things we lost though. Even the radio went—washed right out the boat. We spent fifteen days at sea fishing after that, without a bloody clue in the world as to where we were. It didn't matter. We had great catches and we were in business again by the time we came into Aberdeen. But all the money had to go to replace the lost gear.

And the skate?
Ah, the skate. Aye, we never saw the skate again, all because of that bloody drunkard.

There's some men might never have seen each other again if they'd kept him on at the fishing.
They didn't have to. He came to a hell of an end.
He was supposed to help the fireman to chip the boiler before Christmas. That was on the *Quiet Waters*. He never did his share, and the fireman said he was going to leave it for him to finish. The skipper told him he'd do it or he wouldn't have a berth to come back to in the January. Well, he never showed face the night before, and so another man was given his berth. It was too late to finish the boiler into the bargain, but they just clapped on the bolts and got under way.
God Almighty, it was three months later they opened up that boiler, and though it wasn't like anything human they found inside, the bits and pieces of boiled bone told the tale right enough. He must have crawled inside on New Year's night, full's a puggie, more steam coming out of his head than there'd be from the boat. Even in his stupor he must have realised it was his last chance to finish the job and keep his berth. It cost him his life. He must have fallen asleep in there dead drunk and when there was no sign of him the next morning they just fastened everything up and set sail.
What a way to die, eh?

What must he have felt like when he woke up to the water coming in and starting to warm up?
He must have screamed.

But nobody heard him.

Boiled in his own soup, just like a lobster.
Like a partan in a pot.

Some terrible things happen at the sea, sure enough. Ah, but the sea's the life, the sea's the life.
The only one—now let's have a song.

255

A TWELVEMONTH AND A DAY

And they sang the moon down the sky before the year was out.

Oh blithely shines the bonnie sun upon the Isle o' May,
And blithely rolls the morning tide into St Andrews bay;
When haddocks leave the Firth of Forth and mussels leave the shore,
When oysters climb up Berwick Law, we'll go to sea no more—
No more—we'll go to sea no more.

With their songs and stories ringing in my head I crept up to my bed and fell asleep.

The winter sun drifted down the sky on its last day of the year, a yellow-faced invalid, put out briefly for the brandy of one more day and a whiff of sea-air. Little was left now in this soundless tottering towards extinction's brink, the season's terminal, the fields' last constitutional. It turned its face to the skyline's blank wall. Straw glistened in pale stray wisps in autumn's dung. The solitary crow sat on the fencepost like a priest.

Soon the star from the Christmas tree would be sunk with the sea-gear in the loft. On Twelfth Night the tree would be lopped, the model snowstorm of cards dismantled, the lights put out, the greenery burnt. Tinsel would be harvested from walls and floor, cake crumbs and pie crusts gleaned from the baking trays and thrown out to the gulls, and the jolly red moonface of Christmas fade whiter and whiter into the blind bandaged snowcloud of January. Trinkets trimly tidied away in the kist with that forgotten segment of time that was already in my mind the year before.

I came home desolate.

Even now the house had a forlorn look to it. The holly leaves were brittle and its berries shrivelled and dry. It was a wineless day. I heard no sound of carols from the sun, saw no pictures in the fire. I put on the last of the logs I ever sawed with grandfather, a beech log cut from a green hour in Balcaskie one old summer when we had made the creels. It crumbled now to a white ghost in the grate, dead quiet in the last ashes of our Yuletide fires. It was past midnight.

Regulus would rise on the first day of January at nine o'clock—a starseed of spring sown in darkest winter. And grandfather would be off to the winter herring on the second day of the year. It was all over, and I knew that something had been lost which could never be recovered. Not this time.

256

DECEMBER

But a new January and February were waiting for me now, twin monkish months, whispering their secrets one to another, quietly contained in their bare heads and hardly overheard by the rest of the year.

Spring songs singing in a pair of winter skulls.

AND A DAY

And so the day fell when it all finally came to an end.

Not the cycle of the seasons and the life of the shore—these go on forever, though the boy who watches them intently so often becomes a city exile, where fifty miles might well be fifty million, and the years that intervene between childhood and today be fifty million light years. Or more.

The experiences I have described are now on the other side of the universe.

A day came when it no longer made any difference to me whether it was summer or winter, whether leaves were on or off the trees, the tides ebbing or flowing, the winds from the south-east or the north-west; whether there was dewfall or rain or thunder or frost. Or whether there were herring in the firth. I now pursue an occupation where what mattered most to me in my first twelve years and more is no longer of any account. In this I am hardly alone—it is a fate shared by millions. And most of us grow old and move off from the places of our birth, and all of us die. So of that no more need be said.

But the deaths of whole communities and cultures is a tragedy worthy of notice, where the fates of individual folk fade into oblivion. Fishermen like my grandfather are no longer to be found in the East Neuk of Fife, where a revolution has taken place in fifty years.

The disappearance of the herring fishing has been the main factor in that revolution—chased out of existence by the thoughtless greed of the laissez-faire system, in which quick money was the only goal. Just before the second war all the talk in Fife was of how the ring-net fishermen from the west coast were going to sweep the firth clean of herring.

'I think I'll take a broom and give them a hand in their sweeping up,' said my uncle Billy. 'I'm going to take what's going.'

His comment crystallised the attitude that prevailed among the men of his time, and still does today. They saw the writing on the wall and adopted the devil-take-the-hindmost mentality which was the line of destruction and despair. There is now no fishing in the firth. All

259

of the boats have to go much further afield to be sure of their catches, and the Icelanders are almost unique in forbidding the catching of herring except by drift-net, to preserve their stocks.

The herring had the misfortune of being the only marketable fish that laid its eggs on the bottom of the sea, and so it was destroyed at birth or shortly afterwards by the seine-nets that dragged along the sea-bed looking for cod, the few herring that survived being easily swept up by the purse-seine. The government of the day should never have allowed these nets into the nursery grounds. But to expect any government to think fifty years ahead is to expect precisely ten times too much. And so it has gone on, with newer boats and more efficient engines, boats no bigger than the drifters but with a horse-power ten or twenty times what they were, and all dragging gear along the bottom of the sea. So between them the ring-net men and the seine-netters fished out the firth while the politicians looked on, and what was left was a graveyard without memorials.

There are some people who believe in a time when King Arthur of Celtic legend will return to Britain and revitalise his ancient haunts. For myself I have a dream that one day the shoals will return to the firth and I will wake up to a cry that cracks open the morning.

'There's herring in the Haikes! there's herring in the Haikes!'

Only a dream.

As for the men, they work in a comfort that my grandfather would not have thought possible, or necessary—though it can hardly be a cause for regret that a man on watch at the helm can now be relieved without danger. Up the ladder from the cabin to the wheelhouse these days without once having to step on deck. Too many lives were lost in the past by naked exposure to wind and wave as the boat rolled easily in the swell, lightened by the discharge of all her nets. Yet I never heard of a single drifter lost through stress of storm. With their high heads and long heels and the draught of water they commanded, they were splendid fisher kings and nobly took the strain. The super-structured monstrosities of today are scorned by the older fishermen still alive.

'The sea needs something to hit,' they say, 'something good and solid, and not that aluminium rubbish—like a top-heavy dustbin!'

The truth is that many of the young fishermen of today can scarcely be categorized as fishermen at all. They are employed now mainly as labourers, as the owner of the boat provides all the gear, to which those who handle it experience no particular attachment. The young make no attempt, for example, to learn how to mend the nets, nor have they any great ambition to be their own skippers. Torn nets are put ashore where old men in sheds are specially employed to mend them, and perhaps remember the days when they mended their own. Yes, and cared for them. Yesterday was it? Or the day before . . .

The role played by the women in the life of the fishing community has diminished to the point where it is negligible. That has not been altogether a bad thing. My grandmother was left on her own for long periods, and there was nothing romantic about baiting hooks or sitting by the fire in January mending wet nets that were impossible to dry outside. When it did dry out, the alum used to preserve the nets produced a whitish dust which settled throughout the kitchen and covered the bedclothes. Fisherhouses were difficult to keep clean at any time and in winter grandmother's life was a hopeless trial.

Nowadays the fishing does not even come through the front door of the house and the women no longer enjoy such close involvement with their men's work and the fortunes of the boat. Fishing has become more of an industry, a service—a wage-packet that used to be a way of life.

The creel fishing has not changed so much, except in the numbers of pots that are now shot. Whereas the Dyker used to shoot only fifty or sixty creels a time, a modern team can easily put three hundred creels over the side. We could never have collected the bait for anything like that number when I was a boy. I can remember lugging a basket of fifty cods' heads for more than a mile, my trousers soaked and stinking with slime and blood. But each lobster boat now has its own van, of course, and they collect their bait from Pittenweem, where the local boats are allowed to land just as much rubbish as they want—small fish that would die anyway, to be used for creel bait. So the creel men can have as much bait as they wish without having to go to the bother of working for it. And the Dyker went to such lengths to procure good bait!

But there was too much poverty between the wars.

At the end of a black winter herring season some fishermen were known to string themselves up from the rafters out of sheer penury and despair. Most of the time, undoubtedly, it was the company which kept them going. Families were large and closely knit and folk were never really lonely, though the men were away so often. I suppose the greatest single image I have of my own childhood is the impression of being surrounded by relatives. They still encompass me like a great cloud of witnesses.

261

That glory too has departed.

The family has fallen foul of the forces of contemporary society. The eccentrics and cracked old characters, born of poverty and isolation no doubt, have disappeared into dull conformity and uniformity. The fishermen no longer gather at the pierhead as they used to do, or talk in the shelter of the dykes on the windy days. Only a few very old men can be seen doing that now, while the young watch the shadows of the modern world on their television screens, and exchange cliché for cliché where they can be bothered to talk at all.

Nearly everything that I have described, in fact, has gone.

Balcaskie and the Bishop's Walk, which I Lord-Byroned my way along in my early teens—these are no more. Somebody wanted a view of the sea, somebody said—and a wood stood in his way. A worker told me that when they were tearing up trees by the roots, strange shoals of skulls were fished up in the great fibrous nets. If so they must have been screaming ones! The conservational damage done to woods by the Fife lairds and farmers is incalculable, and so often it is done in the name of the almighty pound. It is said that when James IV was building the Scottish Navy he had all the woods in Fife cut down just to build one mighty vessel. That was a high price to pay, even to make possible ships like the *Great Michael* and sea-captains like the legendary Sir Andrew Wood of Largo. Still, the defence of Scotland was a noble end. Nowadays they tear up trees and place caravans on the desolation. Primitive peoples used to worship trees because of the spirits which they believed resided in them. If their beliefs have any foundation in truth I know some Fife farmers who must go haunted to their graves. Their greed for gold has caused one possible derivation of the name of Fife (a Danish word meaning 'the wooded country') to become less appropriate in our own time. Some folk can see beauty in nothing but a pound note.

St Monans I return to now with more than a tinge of reasonable regret. It has been quaintly taken over, like many such, by functionless foreigners. The old shops of the butcher, the barber, the chemist, the cobbler—once the essential people in a community— have gone, and their seaside homes have been prettified by the National Trust, shot right up outside the price-range of any local buyer, inhabited briefly by effete antique dealers and fifth-rate television personalities, and put up for sale.

I regret too the death of language and landscape.

The first is inevitable. Just as the forest leaves fail and fall, so words have their day, wither, and are heard no more. I have made no attempt to let the sounds of the East Neuk's rich old dialects into these pages. They would not be understood, even by the young Fifers of today, who call a gull a gull, and not a 'clow' or a 'coorie' or a 'cuttie' or a 'maw'. Nor can they point to Jarsteen or Craw Skellie, or tell you much about the sea that daily washes the doorsteps of their lives. On the other hand they know all about punk rock and Dallas and all the other fantasies and lies which the television both fabricates and purveys.

I go back, I smell tar and tangle, I try to catch these old ghosts of the fishing that flutter in the meshes of the new nylon nets and linger in the smartly coloured lobster creels, where rubber and plastic piping take the place of the boughs my grandfather cut so carefully. The Common Market lives, the cod-end of the net bursts like an obscene sausage on the deck of the trawler, now a floating factory, and the life of the sea spills out brutally and without discrimination. The old fishing ways and the men who followed them are pale shadows of the past.

It has all been broken up—their community, their art of the story, their feeling for the sea. The faces in the firelight have faded into the garish light of the TV screen and of what is sometimes called progress. The folk culture is now embalmed in the Anstruther Fisheries Museum, the saddest place in the East Neuk. The fishing is going the way of the herring it spoliated, the boatyards are strangely silent that once made the towns redolent and ringing of sawdust and salt. Above all, the religion brought to the East Neuk by St Monan nearly twelve centuries ago is a frailer thing by far than the power which once drove saints to take to the sea, and, like angelicised Vikings, to sail their ships to bless rather than to plunder the benighted peoples of Fife. People will argue that the long night of ecclesiasticism was worse than the darknesses of barbarism or of boredom. The religion given to me by St Monan and by St Monans filled me with exquisite fear, and I have recorded this, perhaps rather ruthlessly. Maybe it has even made me neurotic. But in spite of everything I would rather have my neurosis, my fear, if that is what my religion is, than have nothing at all. I heard a retired lobsterman say that in the old days there were crews of religious men and crews of drunks.

'Now,' he said, 'there are just crews of drunks.'

The strains on my own Christianity are very real. Still, the pull of the old is strong, and the strains of the rock of ages still abide with me, drifting in from the sea of faith, no longer at the full, over the harbour walls of memory, into the haven of the years.

They are all gone then—the days and the people, and their

language and their ways, and the stories they told me. Unforgettable stories and folk and ways of the sea. I could never have dreamed then that the herring were so soon to disappear from the firth, that there would be no more shoals to be caught from St Monans or Cellardyke, that my grandfather would be dead so quickly, and anchor no more nets near Kilrenny Mill Bay, and shoot no more gartlins off the May, and that the great fishing grounds of the firth would be fished no more: from Fifeness to Elie Ness, from the Carr Rock to the Bass Rock, from Berwick Law to the Fidra and beyond.

All finished now.

The end came with astonishing swiftness.

It was finishing even as I shed the last years of my innocence—though the last steam drifter to leave the East Neuk for Yarmouth sailed out of Anstruther as late as 1956.

I knew well before then, of course, that my father would never be coming home again from the Navy, from the War.

Maybe the departure from Eden began on the day I saw the Princess for the first and only time. I saw a fat sad lady in heavy Edwardian velvet sitting in her garden one summer afternoon, drinking tea, watched by a servant. She had been brought out to die. I had just left Primary School. She might have been one of my old teachers. I stood looking at her, and stared and stared.

Grandmother died at fifty-nine, her heart weakened by the constant assaults of asthma on her frail form. Leebie lived on longer, but at last she lay like a fallen white candle, its top end guttered and gone out.

Alec went off to Australia and the East Neuk knew him no more. Uncle Billy stayed at the fishing, and still fishes today—but out of southern harbours now. The Firth of Forth is a cemetery to which he never returns.

Jenny married as happily as people can and moved to Glasgow. Georgina married unhappily. Her husband became an alcoholic and she was unable to have any family. She worked for years as a dreary divorcee in a shoeshop. There was an unplayed piano in her house, with stained brown keys, out of tune.

The Dyker died of cancer.

Old George took a stroke the following year. It took five more strokes over two years finally to kill him. He died in a coma.

AND A DAY

Grandfather was drowned one night at the winter herring.

I had just turned thirteen. No-one saw him go over the side, or understood what had happened. It was on a calm sea off Crail, a flood tide was running, and the body was recovered at Anstruther the following forenoon.

He was sixty-five years old.